Key Film Texts

Graham Roberts
Senior Lecturer in Communications Arts, University of Leeds

and

Heather Wallis
Lecturer in Film Studies, Leeds College of Art and Design

ARNOLD

A member of the Hodder Headline Group
LONDON
Co-published in the United States of America by
Oxford University Pr

First published in Great Britain in 2002 by
Arnold, a member of the Hodder Headline Group,
338 Euston Road, London NW1 3BH

http://www.arnoldpublishers.com

Co-published in the United States of America by
Oxford University Press Inc.,
198 Madison Avenue, New York, NY10016

British Library Cataloguing in Publication Data
A catalogue record for this book is available from the British Library

Library of Congress Cataloging-in-Publication Data
A catalog record for this book is available from the Library of Congress

ISBN 0 340 80767 9 (hb)
ISBN 0 340 76227 6 (pb)

1 2 3 4 5 6 7 8 9 10

Production Editor: Wendy Rooke
Production Controller: Martin Kerans
Cover Design: Terry Griffiths

Typeset in 11/13pt Palatino by Cambrian Typesetters, Frimley, Surrey
Printed and bound in Great Britain by MPG Books

What do you think about this book? Or any other Arnold title?
Please send your comments to feedback.arnold@hodder.co.uk

This book is dedicated to
Brian Wallis
(and the memory of Jane Russell)

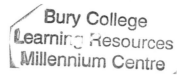

CONTENTS

ACKNOWLEDGEMENTS

The authors would like to thank:

Lesley Riddle for support and understanding beyond the call of duty; numerous colleagues and students at the University of Leeds and Leeds College of Art and Design for fuelling our enthusiasm and/or curbing our more ridiculous flights of fancy.

Many thanks also to the colleagues who supplied copy for the following entries:

Robin Brown (ICS, University of Leeds): *Face/Off* and *The Matrix*; Stephen Hay (ICS, University of Leeds): *The Bicycle Thieves, Performance, Taxi Driver, Apocalypse Now, Blade Runner, Do the Right Thing, Raging Bull, Beauty and the Beast* and *Eyes Wide Shut*; David Lancaster (ICS, University of Leeds): *Bringing up Baby, Casablanca, Sunset Boulevard, Singin' in the Rain, Rear Window, Vertigo* and *William Shakespeare's Romeo + Juliet*.

All entries were written and/or edited by the authors. Therefore any faults of content are ours and ours alone.
The publishers would also like to thank the film companies for the use of their stills. Every effort has been made to trace copyright holders of material produced in this book. Any rights not acknowledged here will be acknowledged in subsequent printings if notice is given to the publishers.

INTRODUCTION

Keys and Canons

When we first put together the idea for writing this book we were confronted with the tricky 'canon' question. Were we in fact – in a rather unfashionable non-postmodern way – trying to produce a canon?

Well . . . yes!

'The canon' was a term originally used to describe a list of books accepted by the Catholic Church. Later, it came to mean a list of recognised, genuine works by a particular author. More recently, it has become a vaguely defined but frequently cited list of works that 'everyone' agrees that everyone else should know – e.g. the literary canon.

How does a canon of films emerge?

Functionally, it is often really useful to have an agreed group of films that everyone else will 'take as read', a common reference point. If you are discussing popular music, it is reasonable to assume that everyone has heard – or ought to have heard – of the Beatles. You cannot start from scratch every time.

But, the canon is self-perpetuating. Good films get left out and bad films are kept in. We study a film because it is a film we study (and because it influenced other films we study).

Pragmatically, we need to impose order on a disparate field of study. You cannot study every film. You can sort them into sets, even 'Milestones and Monuments' (as Ernst Gombrich put it when discussing the visual arts).

The big questions remain. Who decides what goes into the canon? How does a text become canonical? What else can we do? If the idea of the canon is flawed, do we give up and stop studying cinema? If we cannot make perfect choices, do we make none at all?

Between 1915 and 1960 in excess of 20 000 feature films were produced in the USA alone. Some of these films are frequently chosen for discussion and analysis; most others are ignored. Some films are frequently cited as examples. Some films are held to be influential, historical or even just spectacularly typical – whilst most are forgotten. It is not just academics and critics: film-makers themselves help form the canon by remaking 'classic' films, by alluding to them, even parodying them. You cannot parody a film that the audience has never heard of. By parodying it you in fact reinforce a film's importance.

The final reason for canonical activity is evaluative (and therefore selective). Someone decides which is best. What are the criteria? What values do we use to decide? Who gets to make the decisions? The reader is entitled to ask how *we* chose the films for this book.

We have chosen films that everyone who claims to know anything about the history and the theory of cinema will be expected to know (by other people who *do* know something about the history and theory of cinema). It is not a perfect selection, but we all have to start somewhere. Even people who oppose the canon will still expect you to have the basic film knowledge that includes these films. It is a grounding, a common pool of references in which we can base our investigations into cinema. Secondly, it is important to know the films that have been influential – films that have clearly influenced the films that contemporary film-makers are making today.

We have tried to keep this volume focused on its introductory remit and make it reasonably representative – for example, only one or two films per director, apart from Hitchcock, and at least the beginnings of an attempt at a geographical spread.

On a practical level, we have tried to discuss only films that are readily available on video/DVD. Thus there are only a couple of women directors represented but plenty of stars. There are few non-Western films, although we have tried to illustrate the influence of international cinema even on the Hollywood hegemony.

For justifiable yet deeply regretted omissions we send our heartfelt apologies to: the Lumière Brothers and George Méliès along with many other notable omissions including Rainer Werner Fassbinder, Abel Gance, King Vidor, William Hanna and Joseph Barbera.

The films discussed in this volume are also very good films. They were made to be enjoyed (not always as pure entertainment but certainly to engage the viewer). We who 'study' film sometimes forget to enjoy. Don't let that happen to you!

The study of film is democratic and organic – it (like cinema itself) is pointless without an active audience. Come and join the project at www.international-film.org.

Reading Film Texts: The Key Concepts

This book is designed as a companion volume to *Introducing Film* (Roberts and Wallis, 2001), which introduces the different concepts and theoretical approaches to the study of film. We strongly recommend that the student who is new to film start with a comprehensive introduction to the methods of reading a film than can be provided there.

At a very basic level, the study of film can be boiled down to four areas of focus:

- the text (the content and meaning of the film itself);
- the makers (discussions of the craft and motivations of the people who combined to produce the text as well as how the audience 'makes meaning' of the text);
- the institutions (the organisations that 'produce, distribute and exhibit' the text);
- the social, political and historical context of 'the text'.

The reader will discover (*a*) that we try to focus on areas of analysis that correspond to these basic areas and (*b*) that these areas inevitably overlap and influence each other.

Many readers may find the following list useful, as it briefly defines some of the key terms that you need to be familiar with when using *Key Film Texts*.

Auteur is the French term for author. The auteur is (usually) a director whose work is characterised by distinctive thematic concerns and a visual style that occurs across a body of films. Auteur criticism looks at films as the personal creative expression of the director, which is controversial given that film is a collaborative art form. François Truffaut and his fellow critics writing for the French film journal *Cahiers du cinéma* developed 'auteur theory' in the 1950s. Truffaut's *politiques des auteurs* called for a shift in creative responsibility from screenwriters to directors. In spite of the obvious flaws in the theory, auteurism has remained popular (except with screenwriters – witness the threatened strike of 2001). It is popular with theorists because it raises the status of film from popular culture to art form, and popular with industry executives as a means of selling films. Purists may argue that auteur theory is nonsense, but audiences will still go to see 'a Martin Scorsese picture'.

Genre simply means type, and films have been produced, written, directed and marketed according to generic conventions from the very early days of cinema. Genre, like auteur, is a successful means of selling films to the public by giving them something recognisable: thus genre works on audience expectations. Genre provides both film-makers and audiences alike with a kind of shorthand (iconography). We recognise the characteristics of a particular genre – i.e. settings, costumes, locations, stars, music and narrative patterns – and therefore themes, characters and plot lines do not have to be explained in laborious detail. Genre study looks at variations and developments within particular genres over time. Of particular interest to the contemporary viewer is the postmodern tendency to blend characteristics from different genres.

Stardom is numinous, glamorous, intangible, yet keenly felt. It seems to be a natural, even primordial, force in film. NEVER FORGET – an enormous amount of effort goes into creating this force. The functional definition of a 'star' is clearly put by John Ellis in C. Gledhill (ed.), *Star Signs* (1992): 'a performer in a particular medium whose figure enters into subsidiary forms of circulation and then feeds back into future performances.'

Mise en scène is a theatrical term (from the French 'to put in place') that means placed on the stage. It was popularised in film studies by the French critics of the *Cahiers du cinéma* in the 1950s and has come to mean everything that is placed before the camera. Thus *mise en scène* includes setting, costume and make-up, lighting and position and movement within the frame.

Cinematography can be defined as everything to do with the camera. Thus discussions of cinematography include the choice of lens and film stock as well as the position of the camera in relation to the action (type of shot), camera height and angle and camera movement. Cinematography is a primary tool with which the film-maker can guide the way in which the viewer responds to the *mise en scène*.

Editing is the term used to describe the joining of shots (usually) to create a coherent narrative. Editing enables the film-maker to move between different periods of time and place as well as to construct scenes from a number of different camera positions. Mainstream cinema from the days of classic Hollywood and beyond has sought to make the editing process as invisible as possible so as to enable viewers to forget about the film process and lose themselves in the story. The techniques developed to achieve this became known as the continuity editing system whereby a number of rules are followed in order to orientate the viewer into the scene and make the transfer from one shot to the next apparently seamless.

Montage is a form of editing developed by the directors of Soviet cinema in the 1920s. Unlike continuity editing, montage is not concerned with making the editing process invisible but rather sees editing as the primary tool with which the film-maker can construct meaning. Montage usually involves rapid cutting between shots. Meaning is created through the *juxtaposition* of the images.

Sound in film can be broken down into two categories – that belonging to the world of the film, which is known as diegetic sound and includes things like dialogue and sound effects (e.g. footsteps), and non-diegetic sound, which is sound laid over the top, such as a voice-over or musical score.

Narrative consists of both the story and also the methods by which the story is told: by what means (*mise en scène*, cinematography, editing, sound) and in what order (structure). 'Classic narrative cinema/classic Hollywood narrative' refers to the narrative tradition that dominated Hollywood from the 1930s to the 1960s but that also pervaded Western cinema. Most contemporary mainstream cinema will share many elements of the classic Hollywood narrative, which is constructed around the following principles:

- Cinematic style focuses on creating verisimilitude.
- Events follow the basic structure of order/disorder/order restored.
- The narrative is linear.
- Events are linked by cause and effect.

- The plot is character led and thus the narrative is psychologically (and individually) motivated – usually towards the attainment of some goal or desire.
- The role of the hero is central.
- The narrative has closure.

Episodic narrative is an alternative to the classic Hollywood narrative with its focus on character-led story. The episodic narrative has its roots in the B-movie serials of the 1930s. Since the arrival of *Star Wars* (Lucas, USA, 1977), the episodic narrative tradition has made something of a comeback, as its structure (a series of loosely linked episodes) allows for frequent scenes of action/spectacle with the consequent excitement of cliffhangers.

Realism is a philosophical approach that claims that film's special strength is its relationship with the real world. Film, therefore, should prioritise content and subject matter over form. André Bazin – the founding father of the French New Wave – claimed that 'Film was reality's footprint' (see, for example, Italian neorealism, chapter 13). On a more 'realistic' level, we should note that the key to the commercial success of cinema is its ability not only to create fantasy but to make it appear real (the essence of verisimilitude – the 'appearance of reality').

Expressionism, as an antonym to realism, stresses the psychological and personal level of moving pictures. As such it is linked to expressionist movements in all of the arts – for example, German Expressionism (see chapters 2 and 5).

Formalism is an approach to film-making and film viewing that stresses the structure and construction of the artistic product.

Institutions and institutional constraints. Film-making costs a vast amount of money. Even a so-called low-budget movie will cost more than most people could borrow from a bank. Added to the sheer cost of production are the costs of distribution and marketing (the latter is often way in excess of the production budget). Thus the film requires backing from institutions – be they governments, studios or multinational corporations – and these institutions have certain ideas (either as policy or as ingrained methods of working) about what constitutes successful film-making. Note that we should not see institutional constraints as necessarily the forces of evil – particularly if they act as a constraint on pretentious or preposterous product that wastes everybody's time and money. Certain 'institutional' situations have been so powerful as to produce their own form of cinema (for better or worse). Three examples will help to explain this institutional phenomenon.

- *Classic Hollywood* refers to films made in Hollywood's studio era – that is, from 1930 until the Paramount Decision in 1948, which made it illegal for the studios to own all three areas of the film industry (i.e. production, distribution, exhibition), thus closing down the studio system as it had been known. Classic Hollywood style, which is centred around the classic narrative (see above), continued into the 1960s and is still present in its influence on mainstream cinema today.
- *The French New Wave* was an influential movement in French film-making from approximately 1959 until 1964. The French New Wave brought the work of two key directors onto the international cinema stage: Jean-Luc Godard and François Truffaut (see chapters 20 and 21). French New Wave cinema is characterised by cinematic innovation (that is, breaking the rules of classic Hollywood and the Tradition of Quality in French cinema of the 1950s) and its love/hate relationship with American genre films. It has remained important because of its influence on contemporary 'Hollywood' directors such as Quentin Tarantino (see chapter 37).
- *'The New Hollywood'* is a term used rather loosely to describe Hollywood after the studio system. Although this would officially date new Hollywood as starting after the Paramount Decision in 1948, working practices and product continued in classic Hollywood style well into the 1960s. It seems reasonable, therefore, to date new Hollywood from the point where these things significantly changed – that is, the advent of blockbusters, saturation release (and other marketing ploys) ushering in the first films to take over $100 million at the box office – for example, *Jaws* (Spielberg, 1975) and *Star Wars* (Lucas, 1977) (see chapter 28), which in terms of style, structure and distribution strategy seem to have initiated a new era in Hollywood that is significantly different from the classic.

1 *INTOLERANCE*

Griffith, USA, 1916

Production Details

Production company/studio	Triangle Productions and Wark Producing Corporation
Producer	D. W. Griffith
Director	D. W. Griffith
Cinematographers	Billy Bitzer and Carl Brown
Editor	D. W. Griffith
Screenwriters	Tod Browning and D. W. Griffith

Cast Includes

Olga Grey	*Mary Magdalene*
Mildred Harris	*Harem Girl*
Robert Harron	*The Boy*
Joseph Henabery	*Admiral Coligny*
Lloyd Ingraham	*Judge of the Court*
Lillian Langdon	*Mary the Mother*
Ralph Lewis	*Governor*
Howard Gaye	*The Christ*
Lillian Gish	*The Woman who Rocks the Cradle/the Eternal Mother*
Walter Long	*The Musketeer of the Slums/Babylonian Warrior*
Mae Marsh	*The Dear One*

FOCUS: Film History and Film as History

Any volume of 'key texts' stands accused of presenting a canon – to put it crudely, a list of recommended texts given precedence over others. Any putative canon compiler is confronted with the tricky problem of deciding where and when the canon starts. The authors of this volume – after considering the Lumière Brothers as well as Méliès and the British pioneers – decided to begin with D. W. Griffith.

Film as an entertainment medium was 20 years old by the time of Griffith's *Intolerance*. It was with this film that D. W. Griffith made the leap into film as an art form that was both artistically and politically important and influential.

D. W. Griffith (1875–1948) has been described as 'the father of film'. His claim to parentage is based upon not technological but narrative breakthroughs made long before *Intolerance*. In 1907 he moved from stage production to the movies. After a spell with the Edison Company he moved to Biograph. There, via hundreds of 'two-reeler' shorts, Griffith worked out the grammar and syntax of what would become internationally recognised and consumed mainstream cinema: establishing shots, dextrous use of close-ups to show character traits and engage the spectator, complex camera movement and the rules of cross-cutting. In effect he not only contributed to moving cinema away from the purely scientific (Lumière) and purely sensational (Méliès), but also developed the moving picture away from theatre into a new art form whose features depended on spatial and temporal mobility itself.

Griffith has a very strong claim to be the father of American film – that is, an institutionalised outlook predicated on the *selling* of 'the movies' as an engaging entertainment medium. His films were both engaging and well promoted. He had begun with short films based on popular melodrama, from which he had developed a strong grasp of what constituted engaging material for the audience. When his aspirations led to longer more complex narratives, Griffith held to his belief in strong character-led narrative.

Via *Judith of Bethulia* (1914), *The Birth of a Nation* (1915) and *Intolerance*, Griffith also lays claim to be the progenitor of Hollywood spectacle. In retrospect it seems odd that Biograph was nervous about the financial implications of making bigger and more spectacular films. After the four-reel *Judith of Bethulia*, it let Griffith go to Mutual. Griffith gathered his extraordinarily talented team of technicians and actors around him and, forming his own production company (Triangle – with Mack Sennett and Thomas Ince), took cinema to new heights of ambition.

It is entirely in keeping with the ambition of Griffith and his company that their first film was the longest and greatest (in terms of temporal, spatial and moral ambition) in the history of film to that point. *The Birth of a Nation* was also a film that courted controversy. It is unquestionably a masterpiece of film-making. However, it is also a film that overtly sanctions the actions of the Ku Klux Klan. The film was made at a time when America was experiencing an upsurge in Klan activity. Griffith's epic of American history began the continuing debate about artistic licence, which, as with *Battleship Potemkin* (see chapter 3) or *Olympia* (see chapter 7), is at its most intense and interesting when a liberal critic comes up against great film-making in dubious causes.

Griffith appears to have been genuinely – if naively – surprised by the reaction to *The Birth of a Nation*. Unsympathetic condemnation of his masterpiece led Griffith to create *Intolerance*. Griffith's scriptwriter Tod Browning went on to a directorial career that relied on the investigation of outsiders and the responses of mainstream society with films such as *Dracula* (USA, 1931) and the controversial *Freaks* (USA, 1932).

Intolerance is an epic dealing with the issue of intolerance and its effects in four historical eras. In ancient Babylon religious rivalry leads to the downfall of the city. In Jerusalem the Pharisees condemn Jesus Christ to death. In sixteenth-century Paris the Huguenots are slaughtered in the St Bartholomew's Day Massacre. In the contemporary USA deprivation leads to crime; social reformers, who believe they know best, destroy the lives of innocent young women through unfeeling reaction.

The two masterstrokes that Griffith brought to bear on these historical issue were:

- focusing on individual stories – for example, of the Huguenot lovers or the modern young woman and her 'beloved' against the historical background (thus engaging the viewer emotionally);
- intertwining the stories to create ideological connections but also to enrich the narrative structure.

What remains today is an impression of the sheer confidence of the team who created this movie. Griffith's company thought little about the vast amounts of attention (and money) spent on the sets. Technicians were brought from Italy, until then the home of the cinema epic, to 'create' Babylon. The Taviani Brothers' *Good Morning Babylon* (Italy/France, 1987) tells this story from the Italians' point of view. Bitzer and Brown were encouraged to take the camera (literally) to new heights and to hang the expense.

Contemporary criticism of this epic did not centre on its cost and boundless self-confidence but rather on the oversimplified morality of the piece and its overtly anti-war stance. The film was released as the controversy over America's entry into the First World War raged. Today we may be less in sympathy with *Intolerance* because of its very strengths. It is a very didactic and heavy-handed allegory. Critics, including David Thomson in *The Biographical Dictionary of Film* (1995), have pointed to the portentousness of Griffith's epics. After the financial disaster of this epic Griffith scaled down his vision and made rather more human-scale and engaging works – e.g. *Hearts of the World* (1918), *Broken Blossoms* (1919) and *Way down East* (1920).

The Griffith legacy – and indeed that of *Intolerance* itself – on the American industry and beyond is incalculable. Chaplin was inspired to go beyond his studio-bound formula comedies and joined Griffith in forming United Artists. In Soviet Russia Eisenstein viewed Griffith's epics and was inspired to abandon theatre and head for the cinema as a more emotionally and intellectually influential medium. A generation later Welles was inspired by Griffith's example to exhibit ostentatious virtuosity and demand that his crew push the possibilities of form in *Citizen Kane*.

Some Things to Watch out for and Consider

- Can you watch a film as 'art' divorced from its ideology?
- How could Griffith have made *The Birth of a Nation* and *Intolerance*?
- Is *Intolerance* of more than historical interest?
- After watching *The Birth of a Nation*, consider what we have gained and what we have lost in the last 80 years of narrative cinema. What have we lost since films began to 'talk'? What have we lost since silent film? Think about: *mise en scène*, editing and narrative structure.
- Does Griffith overstretch himself? Is film really the right medium for the epic?

Further Viewing

The Birth of a Nation (Griffith, USA, 1915)
The Battleship Potemkin (Eisenstein, Soviet Union, 1925)
October (Eisenstein, Soviet Union, 1928)
The Great Dictator (Chaplin, USA, 1938)

Gone with the Wind (Fleming, USA, 1939)
Citizen Kane (Welles, USA, 1941)
Barry Lyndon (Kubrick, UK, 1975)
One from the Heart (Coppola, USA, 1981)
Good Morning Babylon (Taviani Brothers, Italy/USA, 1987)

2 NOSFERATU
A Symphony of Horror (Eine Symphonie des Grauen)

Murnau, Germany, 1922

Production Details

Production company/studio	Prana-Film
Producers	Enrico Dieckmann and Albin Grau
Director	F. W. Murnau
Cinematographers	Gunther Krampf and Fritz Arno Wagner
Editor	F. W. Murnau
Screenwriter	Henrik Galeen
Art director	Albin Grau

Cast Includes

Max Schreck	*Count Orlok (Nosferatu)*
Gustav Botz	*Dr Sievers*
John Gottowt	*Professor Bulwer*
Ruth Landshoff	*Lucy Westrenka*
Max Nemetz	*Captain*
Georg H. Schnell	*Westrenka*
Greta Schröder	*Ellen Hutter*
Hardy von Francois	*Doctor in the Hospital*
Gustav von Wangenheim	*Thomas Hutter*

(NB in recent video releases names have been 'Stokerised')

FOCUS: Genre and the Influence of Art Cinema

Nosferatu begins in Bremen, Germany, in 1838. Knock, a property agent, assigns his employee Hutter to visit the remote castle of

Count Orlok. The mysterious Count wants to buy a house ('a deserted one'). The viewer will not be surprised to learn that *Nosferatu* was originally titled 'Dracula'. Bram Stoker's estate – suspicious of moving pictures – sued. All prints and even the original negative were ordered to be destroyed under the terms of a lawsuit by Stoker's widow. However the film – like the Count – surfaced in other countries in subsequent years and spawned many, many copies.

For the first third of the film the audience experiences very little that is remarkable in silent cinema; even the fluid camera style was typical of the time. However, as Hutter travels to Orlok's ancestral lands in the Carpathian Mountains (he continues to doubt superstitious warnings), the film begins to take on a sense of sensuality and deep unease. The scene in which the Count appears and leads Hutter into the shadows is an unforgettable moment of real cinematic menace. In the following scene Hutter cuts himself with a bread knife. The tension mounts as the knife lays in Hutter's palm under the searing gaze of the Nosferatu. The Count is thrilled by: 'Blood – your beautiful blood!' The Count is also visibly filled with lust for the young man's wife. He traps his visitor and begins his pursuit of Ellen.

This earliest vampire film contains many strikingly imaginative cinematic moments. At the inn, all of the customers fall silent when Hutter mentions Orlok's name. Outside, a snarling hyena appears. Hutter's hired coach refuses to take him onto Orlok's estate. The Count sends his own coach, which travels in fast motion, as does his scurrying ratlike servant. The production's special effects are disquieting. The speeding-up and slowing-down of motion (by varying the frames shot per second) and appearances and disappearances into and out of thin air are all techniques available to even the early pioneers. But they never used them to create shock or terror. Murnau also pioneered the use of a photographic negative image to produce white trees against a black sky.

Nosferatu was written by Henrik Galeen, a stalwart of the German cinema before and after the First World War. He had directed possibly the first Gothic horror movie, *Golem*, in 1915. The strategies, which may now be seen as clichés, were in 1922 writing the rulebook of the horror genre. As Rogert Ebert – the doyen of modern-day critics – puts it: 'To watch F. W. Murnau's 'Nosferatu' is to see the vampire movie before it had really seen itself. Here is the story of Dracula before it was buried alive in clichés, jokes, TV skits, cartoons and more than 30 other films. The film is in awe of its material. It seems to really believe in vampires.'

In the decades that have passed, many legends have grown around the film. The strangest is that Maz Schreck (the name means 'terror' in German) was not only a real vampire but the actual 'Nosferatu'. This story has recently been retold in *Shadow of the Vampire* (Merhige, USA, 2001).

The scenes on the ship carrying Orlok's coffins remain shocking today. As the crew become sick and die, one brave sailor opens a coffin to reveal a river of rats. The Count rises straight up, stiff and eerie, from one of the coffins.

Schreck plays the Count like a sad, doomed and diseased animal. Albin Grau, the art director, gave him batlike ears, claws and pointed fangs that are in the middle of his mouth like a rodent's. The film has had a profound influence on the more horrific and erotic of the remakes – e.g. Klaus Kinski's performance in *Nosferatu Phantom der Nachte* (*Nosferatu Phantom of the Night*) (Herzog, Germany, 1979) and the art direction in *Bram Stoker's Dracula* (Coppola, USA, 1992).

The film contains montage sequences – which have been falsely claimed as technical breakthroughs (see chapter 1), but which are powerful examples of editing as a storytelling device – for example, as Orlok advances on Hutter, in Bremen, Hutter's wife, Ellen, sleepwalks and cries out a warning that causes the vampire to turn away. After Hutter has realized his danger, he escapes from the castle and races back to Bremen by coach, while Orlok travels by sea. Murnau intercuts not two but three events: the coach, the ship and Ellen restlessly waiting.

Griffith had given the audience the pleasure of visual power – that is, the apparent ability to see more than the protagonists of the film. In *Nosferatu* Murnau explores a darker pleasure: the sheer (sexual) charge of seeing itself. Nosferatu is revealed to us as the bringer of doom but also as a figure of visual fascination. Ellen Hutter finally realises that the only way to stop a vampire is to distract him so that he stays out after dawn. Thus, according to the titles, she sacrifices herself to his lust to save humanity. Yet the pictures tell a darker and more complex story. Ellen's surrender to Orlok's gaze is highly sexualised. His response is one of uncontrollable lust. He perishes because he cannot tear himself away from her bedside. Our observation of their confrontation is, at least in part, voyeuristic.

With *Nosferatu* Murnau revealed himself as a stylist particularly of the mobile camera. This mobility creates a sense of searching not to empower the viewers but rather to take them into corners they do not feel they want to visit. Murnau was also a master of framing. The corners of the screen are filled and thus used more than was or is usual. The shot composition becomes 'unbalanced' and full of tension as the eye is drawn away from its usual focus.

Murnau went on to make *The Last Laugh* (1924): a subtle and moving tale with Emil Jannings as a hotel doorman devastated by the loss of his job. He was inevitably lured to the newly all-powerful Hollywood, where he signed for Fox in 1926. Murnau's American masterpiece was *Sunrise* (1927). Janet Gaynor won an Oscar for her work as a woman whose husband considers murdering her. His last film was *Tabu* (1931); he was killed in a car crash on the Pacific Coast Highway just before its première, his promising career cut short at 43.

Fritz Arno Wagner was a senior figure on the production, having made many films before. He went on to contribute to some of the great classics of Expressionist cinema, including Fritz Lang's *M* (Germany, 1931) and *Das Testament des Dr Mabuse* (*The Testament of Doctor Mabuse*) (Germany, 1933), as well as Pabst's *Kameradschaft* (*Comradeship*) (Germany/France, 1931). Gunther Krampf, the cinematographer who began his career with *Nosferatu*, went on to make over 50 films, including *Die Büchse der Pandora* (*Pandora's Box*) (Germany, 1929), *Kuhle Wampe* (Germany, 1932), Alfred Hitchcock's short *Aventure malgache* (Italy, 1944), and the Bolting Brothers' *Fame Is the Spur* (UK, 1946).

Like Murnau, Krampf was part of an international cinema of the 1920s into the 1930s, inspired by the figure of Erich Pommer at the UFA studio. A contender for Pommer's finest production would be *Der Blaue Engel* (*The Blue Angel*) (Germany, 1930), directed by Josef von Sternberg (with cinematographer Gunther Ritau and editor Sam Winston) and starring Marlene Dietrich. Like Murnau, the talent base of this international production soon went to Hollywood, as did Fritz Lang and so many others.

This talent exodus ultimately drained Europe and fuelled Hollywood – just as Nosferatu drained the blood of his victims. The great British director of the inter-war years Alfred Hitchcock also learned his trade in the international atmosphere of the German cinema in the 1920s. Hitchcock, once attracted across the Atlantic by David Selznick, played his own spins on the horror genre (see *Psycho*, chapter 24) as well as directing the ultimate voyeur movie with *Rear Window* (see chapter 16).

Some Things to Watch out for and Consider

* Is Murnau's *Nosferatu* scary in the modern sense? Ebert thinks not: 'It doesn't scare us, but it haunts us.'
* What are the genre characteristics of 'horror'? Have they changed over the decades?
* Why is there such an enduring popularity in horror and in vampires in particular?

Further Viewing

Dracula (Browning, USA, 1931)
Nosferatu Phantom der Nachte (Herzog, Germany, 1979)
Bram Stoker's Dracula (Coppola, USA, 1992)
Psycho (Hitchcock, USA, 1960)
Scream (Craven, USA, 1996)
The Blair Witch Project (Myrick and Sánchez, USA, 1998)
Sunrise (Murnau, USA, 1929)
Metropolis (Lang, Germany, 1927)
The Lodger (Hitchcock, UK/Italy, 1926)
Blackmail (Hitchcock, UK, 1929)
Rear Window (Hitchcock, USA, 1954)

Further Reading

T. Elsaesser, *Weimar Cinema and After* (London, 2000)
J. Hollows, P. Hutchings and M. Jancovich (eds), *The Film Studies Reader* (London, 2000)
S. Neale, *Genre and Hollywood* (London, 2000)
J. Ursini and A. Silver, *The Vampire Film* (New York, 1993)

3 BATTLESHIP POTEMKIN
(Bronenotsets Potemkin)
Eisenstein, Soviet Union, 1925

Production Details

Production company/studio	Goskino
Producer	Goskino
Directors	Sergei M. Eisenstein and Grigori Aleksandrov
Cinematographer	Eduard Tisse
Editor	Sergei M. Eisenstein
Screenwriters	Nina Agadzhanova and Sergei M. Eisenstein

Cast Includes

Aleksandr Antonov	*Vakulinchuk*
Beatrice Vitoldi	*Woman with Baby Carriage*
N. Poltavseva	*Woman with Pince-nez*
Grigori Aleksandrov	*Chief Officer Giliarovsky*
Sergei M. Eisenstein	*Ship Chaplain (stunt scene)*

FOCUS: Film History (Art and Institutional Constraints)

Eisenstein's *Battleship Potemkin* is a drama about a mutiny on board a battleship. It is based on a minor (even farcical) incident from the unsuccessful Russian Revolution of 1905.

As history the film is unreliable, although it is a fascinating insight into the social and political attitudes of *the period of its making* (i.e. the first decade of the Soviet regime). Soviet cinema

Battleship Potemkin. Courtesy of BFI Stills, Posters and Designs

was a product of the Soviet Union. In February 1917 – after popular uprisings in Russia – the Tsar abdicated. In October 1917 the rather ineffective 'Provisional Government' was removed from office by a coup engineered by the Bolsheviks (with popular support). The Bolsheviks – led by Lenin – were committed to the use of all available means of agitation and propaganda, especially the cinema. As Lenin noted in 1922: 'for us the most important of all the arts is cinema.'

The Soviet (Bolshevik) government nationalised the film industry in February 1918. It set up a special cinema section in the Commissariat of the Enlightenment, with Lenin's wife in charge. Life was hard – there was a civil war raging (which in 1919 it looked like the Bolsheviks would lose) – but young cadres flocked to the film industry.

Many of the young directors had a political allegiance to the Bolsheviks. The Revolution had given them their opportunity to *be* film-makers. As the established producers and directors fled west, so Lev Kuleshov along with Eduard Tisse and Dziga Vertov seized their chance at accelerated progress in the cinema. Many others, including Esfir Shub and Eisenstein, would follow in the early 1920s.

The early works of these new film-makers were notable for their economy of style and virtuoso editing technique. *Battleship Potemkin* is one of those brilliant, formal pieces of film-making produced in the Soviet Union between 1924 and 1929. It is a very, very clever film. In addition, the film is an exercise book in the editing technique known as *montage*.

Montage is simply a form of editing, *but* it is editing that emphasises dynamic, sometimes discontinuous, relationships between shots and the juxtaposition of images to create ideas not present in either one by itself. Thus the Soviet masters went beyond the cross-cutting developed a decade earlier by Griffith (see *Intolerance*, chapter 1).

There is a controversy about who deserves the credit for the discovery of the intellectual power of montage. Eisenstein certainly did not invent editing. He was not even the first film-maker/theorist to decide that editing was pre-eminent. That honour should rightfully go to Lev Kuleshov. It was Kuleshov who first used the term 'montage' in 'The Tasks of the Artistic Cinema' (1917): 'regularly ordered in time and space a cinema that fixes organised human and natural raw material and organises the viewer's attention at the moment of projection through montage.' Kuleshov returned from newsreel duty in the Civil War as a veteran of war and cinema (aged 20) to run his own workshop at the State Film School (GIK). He got so prestigious a position largely because he was the only experienced film-maker left in the Soviet Union. Making a virtue of the famine in film stock, he launched a series of experiments that led to the development of montage and the militant belief that the essence of cinema was in its editing.

Kuleshov, along with Vertov and later Eisenstein, was also a champion of cinema as cinema – not filmed theatre. Thus in a 1918 article 'The Art of Cinema' he wrote of 'cinema specificity' (*kinomatografichnost*). Editing was the activity that separated film from theatre. Beyond this ideological position, the particular style of editing – montage – was the result of a number of factors.

- *Practicality*. Very little film stock requires no waste (so keep the shot length short).
- *Newsreel experience*. This led to the realisation that images can be juxtaposed to create effects. There was no time or need for smooth transitions.
- *American influence*. Kuleshov recommended American film as a model for: 'how much plot you can get into a very short film . . . they strive to achieve the maximum number of scenes and maximum effect with the minimum waste of film'. In 'American-ness' (1922) Kuleshov stated that a 'genuine cinema is a montage of American shots'.

Sergei M. Eisenstein (1898–1948) was an artist as well as a film-maker. He was also the author of a massive amount of theoretical work. That is why his name is linked more closely to montage theory than the other early Soviet innovators. Eisenstein began his public career designing in the theatre. His friend Esfir Shub – who was editing Western films (including Chaplin and Lang) for the Soviet authorities – revealed to Eisenstein the power of cinema and led to him changing career. In 1924 Eisenstein wrote in 'Montage of Attractions' of a new approach: 'a free montage with arbitrarily chosen independent (of both the particular composition and any thematic connection with the actors) effects (attractions) but with the precise aim of specific thematic effect.'

Eisenstein's first film, *Strike* (1924), was planned as part of a trilogy – the history of the revolution. The three films are:

* *Strike*, the stirrings of revolutionary consciousness;
* *Potemkin*, the first revolution (1905), a historical drama about a mutiny on board a battleship;
* *October*, the film of the revolution.

His slogan was to be: 'art through revolution: revolution through art'.

Eisenstein's attempt to fulfil his revolutionary remit can be seen in the climactic 'Odessa Steps' sequence of *Battleship Potemkin*. It is certainly one of the most celebrated (and copied) sequences in the history of film-making. The good people of Odessa have been fêting the sailors who have risen against their cruel officers. A holiday mood has enveloped the crowd on the steps leading to the harbour – but the forces of repression are ready to strike.

Here is Eisenstein's own description of 'the steps' (from *Battleship Potemkin*, trans. G. Aitken (1968), p. 14):

movement – is used to express mounting emotional intensity.

Firstly there are close-ups of human figures rushing chaotically. Then long shots of the same scene. The chaotic movement is next superseded by shots showing the feet of soldiers as they march rhythmically down the steps.

Tempo increases. Rhythm accelerates. And then, as the downward movement reaches its culmination, the movement is suddenly reversed, instead of the headlong rush of the crowd down the steps we see a solitary figure of a mother carrying her dead son, slowly and solemnly going up the steps.

Because Eisenstein has such a clear sense of rhythm built into this sequence, he can insert images that appear unconnected – for example, members of the crowd filling the frame or moving in contrapuntal directions. He can also repeat sequences – for example, the mother falling as the pram teeters on the step, the pram's progress downwards and the final flourish of the Cossack officer's sword slash.

The coda to this section shows the power of associative montage. The guns of the battleship make their reply to the barbarity. They shell 'The Odessa Theatre – headquarters of the generals'. The stone lions, lying, sitting, standing, which decorate the theatre, are edited in sequence to produce an ideogram of a lion (representing the people) rising in defiance.

Battleship Potemkin has remained a famous – even controversial – film since it first appeared. Authorities in the UK and the USA viewed it as so powerful as to warrant banning for decades. To this day it remains a film to be studied by all film students, directors and so on. It is also consciously referred to in many films (e.g. Brian De Palma's *The Untouchables*, USA, 1987). Montage technique remains as an influence, in particular on action films, commercials and many videos for popular music performers.

Some Things to Watch out for and Consider

* Is *Battleship Potemkin* really such a good film, or is it just an important one?
* Why has *Battleship Potemkin* proved to be so influential?
* How successful is *Battleship Potemkin* as a piece of propaganda?

Further Viewing

The Birth of a Nation (Griffith, USA, 1915)
Intolerance (Griffith, USA, 1916)
The Man with the Movie Camera (Vertov, USSR, 1929)
Triumph of the Will (Riefensthal, Germany, 1933)
Olympia (Riefensthal, Germany, 1936)

The Untouchables (De Palma, USA, 1987)
Naked Gun 33⅓ (Segal, USA, 1994)

Further Reading

G. Roberts, *On Directors: Eisenstein* (London, forthcoming)
R. Taylor, *Film Propaganda* (London, 1999)
R. Taylor and I. Christie, *The Film Factory* (London, 1989)

4 THE GOLD RUSH

Chaplin, USA, 1925

Production Details

Production company/studio	Charles Chaplin Productions/UA
Producer	Charles Chaplin
Director	Charles Chaplin
Cinematographer	Rollie Totheroh
Editor	Charles Chaplin
Screenwriter	Charles Chaplin

Cast Includes

Charles Chaplin	*The Lone Prospector*
Mack Swain	*Big Jim McKay*
Tom Murray	*Black Larson*
Georgia Hale	*Georgia*
Henry Bergman	*Hank Curtis*

FOCUS: Genre/Auteur

In *The Gold Rush* Chaplin's most enduring character (the tramp) goes to the Klondike in search of gold and, against all the odds and any sense of logic, finds it – eventually. In typical Chaplin manner he also finds love, again in circumstances that defy belief. That the tramp succeeds more by luck than judgement makes the rags-to-riches story that much more appealing to audiences (then and now).

Although fans of Buster Keaton or Harold Lloyd might demur, *The Gold Rush* is arguably the best possible example of a silent screen comedy. It is also a towering achievement as a film in its own right. In 1958 an international jury in Brussels selected it as the second greatest film of all time. Only *Battleship Potemkin* was ranked above it.

It is due to this film (and many others) that Chaplin remains one of the key figures of world cinema. His career in some ways shaped the development of the Hollywood dream factory.

Charles Spencer Chaplin was born in London in 1889. He began his performing career in the music hall at the age of 5. He toured England and the USA with Fred Karno's 'London Comedians'. Whilst performing in the USA he was spotted by the film impresario Mack Sennett and joined the Keystone film company in 1914. Chaplin devised the character of the 'little fellow' or 'the little tramp' with what became his trademark baggy trousers, bowler hat, cane and incongruously carefully trimmed moustache. Unimpressed by the sloppiness of the production process of the time, he began directing himself. Chaplin quickly became a household name. He came to personify the power of stardom in Hollywood. In 1918 he signed the film industry's first million-dollar contract.

The Gold Rush is of a piece with Chaplin's world view – that the powerless are inherently good, and that all authority exists to be undermined. However, it has the advantage over his later films that the narrative is stronger than the moral message. The little tramp (described in the titles as 'a lone prospector' but clearly not dressed for the part) takes on the frozen wastes and ventures into Alaska looking for gold. Inevitably he reveals himself to be largely incapable of his task; also inevitably, he falls in love with the beautiful saloon girl, Georgia. He tries to win her heart with his singular charm.

The film is actually a series of set pieces. These individual parts are enormously well crafted and build to successful denouements. As a whole the film is overly episodic (compared say to the work of Griffith). The lasting legacy of the film is that it ushered in mature comedy. *The Gold Rush* is more than a series of visual gags. In addition, the performances are complex for such a genre (up to that point). Chaplin was doing for comedy what John Ford later did for that other popular but undervalued genre the Western (see *Stagecoach*, chapter 9).

The film is packed with moments of carefully staged and choreographed comic genius: entertaining the girls with the 'dance of the rolls', fastidiously eating a leather shoe, the extended sequence of the cabin tottering over a precipice – Chaplin's literal 'cliffhanger' – and so on and so forth.

Chaplin worked fast – how else could he have made hundreds of films? – but he was the ultimate craftsman. Twenty-seven times more film stock was shot than appeared in the final cut. The scene where the tramp and 'Big Jim' have a boot for supper took three days and more than 60 takes to get right. The boot was made of liquorice, and Chaplin (a diabetic) was later rushed to hospital suffering insulin shock.

Chaplin re-edited the film in 1942. That version, with his narration and music by Max Torr, is the one we see today. The music (nominated for an Oscar) might help a modern audience – but the narration is of a piece with Chaplin's later style. It is rather heavy-handed in its pointing to the moral message and therefore rather less engaging than the visuals.

The period from *The Gold Rush* (1925) to *City Lights* (1931) was the height of Chaplin's fame and film-making prowess. During this rich creative phase the tramp character became the centre of a style that combined pure comedy with an atmosphere of melodrama including moments of sentimental tragedy. The tramp character disappeared in 1936 as Chaplin made more overtly political films such as *Modern Times* (1936) and *The Great Dictator* (1940). These films contain moments of comic genius but they are very didactic. Chaplin's popularity began to wane – a most powerful example of the problems of using moving pictures to impart ideology.

The influence of the film (and Chaplin's 1920s work in general) is too broad and huge to detail. The mixing of slapstick and sentiment in his themes persists throughout film and television comedy today, as does the role of the underdog. The 'little tramp' is always surrounded by enormous bullies, but always survives by way of his wit and humour – just as Tom is always outwitted by Jerry, Popeye eventually triumphs over the brutish Bluto, and the roadrunner always evades the Wily Coyote.

On a more sophisticated level, it is obvious that Woody Allen (*Annie Hall*, chapter 29) owes much to Chaplin and the tramp character. Both are instantly recognisable 'types' who write, direct and appear in their own films. Both get a laugh the first time they appear in each scene because of their incongruity with the diegesis they desperately try to thrive in. Both are underdogs who survive on their intelligence and wits. Both are unlucky in love (on and off camera).

Some Things to Watch out for and Consider

- This film is unapologetically sentimental. Is that a bad thing?
- Have we gained anything by our determination to be cool?
- Why is the role of the 'underdog' figure so central to film comedy, past and present?
- How much did Chaplin gain or lose by the move from silent to sound?
- Compare and contrast the character of Chaplin's 'little fellow' with Woody Allen's 'Alvie Singer' in *Annie Hall* (Allen, USA, 1977).

Further Viewing

City Lights (Chaplin, USA, 1931)
Modern Times (Chaplin, USA, 1936)
The Great Dictator (Chaplin, USA, 1940)
The General (Keaton, USA, 1926)
It's a Wonderful Life (Capra, USA, 1946)
Annie Hall (Allen, USA, 1977)
Titanic (Cameron, USA, 1997)

5 *METROPOLIS*
Lang, Germany, 1927

Production Details

Production company/studio	UFA
Producer	Erich Pommer
Director	Fritz Lang
Cinematographer	Karl Freund
Editors	Erich Hunter and Fritz Lang
Screenwriter	Thea von Arbou

Cast Includes

Alfred Abel	*John Fredersen*
Gustav Fröhlich	*Frieder*
Brigitte Helm	*Maria/The Robot*
Rudolf Klein-Rogge	*Rotwang*
Heinrich George	*Grot*

FOCUS: Film as Art/Film as a Social Document

Metropolis is a film fantasy of the futuristic city and its mechanised society. Fritz Lang's visionary movie was not the first one to depict 'the future'. Méliès had done so a quarter of a century before. However, Lang was the first film-maker to try to represent a future world consistently – including social organisation, architecture, costumes and predictions of technological change.

The narrative – which follows an upper-class young man abandoning his life of luxury to join oppressed workers in a revolt – is often disjointed and the plot rather shallow. The 'special effects' do look rather quaint now. However, what is striking even to present-day viewers is the 'look' of the film. The production design is magnificent (see *Intolerance*, chapter 1). Lang was in part influenced by the German expressionist tradition popular during the 1920s (see *Nosferatu*, chapter 2): expressionism is divorced from the 'realism' of American cinema of the time. As a mode of representation, expressionism features distorted and dramatic sets, high contrast lighting and symbolic (rather than natural) acting.

Fritz Lang developed through his directorial career as a master of *mise en scène*. With Lang's work, the pictures really do tell the story. The experimentation of *Metropolis* was both made more intimate and conversely taken further in the masterful *M* (1931), where the setting creates an effect of entrapment. Lang (like Murnau) exported his style to Hollywood, particularly with seminal *film noir* pictures such as *The Big Heat* (USA, 1953) and *Beyond Reasonable Doubt* (USA, 1956).

Metropolis opens with images of pistons pumping and wheels spinning cut with the image of a ticking clock. We are viewing the internal workings of some huge machine. This is the first of many suggestions that the society of 'Metropolis' is mechanised, ordered and controlled. The subsequent images reinforce this idea. 'The Day Shift' is announced in white text against a black background and we then see two sets of workers waiting in ordered ranks before the huge, barred gate of a lift. The setting with its bars has a prison-like quality and this is enhanced by the uniform costume of the workers (black caps, black shirts, black trousers) and their position and movement. All have bowed heads and expressionless faces and when the gates open they move in a choreographed and synchronised manner. They are organised like soldiers but shuffle more and are slower, their bowed heads suggesting defeat. The rhythmic quality of their slow march echoes the movement of the pistons in the opening shots, indicating that they are part of the same mechanism.

These opening images combine to create the impression of slavery and imprisonment. The workers and their environment seem inhuman, totally devoid of individuality, freedom of choice or movement. The lighting at this point is high key, allowing us to see the details of the set. Once the bars of the lift have closed, the workers are taken down (symbolically) to 'The worker's city, far below the surface of the earth'. Here the setting, with its rectangular shapes, soaring pillars and sharp lines, presents us with the same inhuman quality. It looks both alien and magnificent, the effect enhanced by shafts of light and shadow criss-crossing the enormous structures, the height of which completely dwarfs the workers.

The next title introduces us to a contrasting setting: 'And high above a pleasure garden for the sons of the masters of Metropolis'. For the first time we see movement that looks spontaneous rather than rhythmic, as a scantily clad girl runs across the set pursued by Frieder, the hero of the film. The contrast to the inhuman quality of the workers' city is further enhanced by the first 'natural' images. We see a peacock and other exotic birds, plants and the flowing water of the fountain at the centre of the garden. The overwhelming impression created by the jewelled costume and naked flesh of the woman, the mermaid at the centre of the fountain, the game of chase followed by an embrace, is one of decadent pleasure. The garden in fact seems as clearly constructed for a purpose as the workers' city. The juxtaposition of these two contrasting settings clearly suggests that it is the slave labour of one group that provides the pleasure garden of the other. This message is then reinforced by the intrusion into the garden of a woman with a group of dirty bare-foot children. Her costume, plain laced-up dress and demure collar, sets her apart from the women of pleasure in the garden. Her face is both sad and pleading. Described by the text as the daughter of a worker, she appeals to the occupants of the garden to recognise the children as their 'brothers'. Her appeal has a profound effect on Frieder, whose privileged position as the son of the master of Metropolis is denoted by his pale aristocratic clothes. He follows her exit and makes his way to the underground areas.

Once underground, we see the workers in action, their choreo-graphed rhythmic movements making them at one with the great machine that they tend. We see a worker collapse at his station; the pressure gauge rises and there is an explosion. Workers' bodies fly through the air, which is swathed in steam. Out of the steam Frieder's symbolic vision of 'Moloch' – the Canaanite idol to which children were sacrificed – is slowly revealed. The great machine retains the same lines and overall shape but now we see at its centre a huge sphinxlike structure, the entrance to a temple of hell. The workers are now represented as bound slaves being whipped up the steps and thrown into the great demonic mouth at the heart of the machine. Slowly the images of sacrifice fade and we see the great machine once more, as the bodies of the dead and wounded are removed on stretchers and the work goes on. It is through the juxtaposition of such images that the tyranny at the heart of Metropolis is made clear. The children who appeared briefly in the pleasure garden will be sacrificed to the great machine to work until they die.

Lang cuts to the image of the skyline in the world above. Again the setting is elaborate and magnificent, dominated by skyscrapers and movement happening on many different planes, as cars, trains and aeroplanes traverse the city. This futuristic landscape was created in 1926. It is a tribute to the imagination of the set designers that it has been so much copied in films as recent as *Blade Runner* (Scott, USA, 1982) (see chapter 32), *The Fifth Element* (Besson, France, 1997) and *The Phantom Menace* (Lucas, USA, 1999).

In these opening scenes of *Metropolis* it is the different elements of *mise en scène*, setting, costume, position and movement within the frame and lighting that create very specific meanings. Lang uses settings and contrasts between settings with particular effect: they do more than present us with a landscape of the future; they embody messages and values that enable us to understand and make judgements about the nature of society in *Metropolis*.

Metropolis is a visually arresting film. It is also sociologically and historically interesting. The film is a vision of 'the city' (as inspired by a particular city after Lang's visit to New York). It is a vision of 'the future' – and not an entirely happy one. The dystopian elements of *Metropolis* may well be a product of post-world war disillusion. They may also be read as a critique of capitalism. It is interesting – if somewhat fanciful – to see Lang's vision as prefiguring the excesses of the totalitarian regimes to come.

Some Things to Watch out for and Consider

- How and why has *Metropolis* proved so influential?
- How realistic a vision of the present and/or future does it present?
- How optimistic a film is it?
- What might the film have gained or lost from being made (or remade) in colour and/or with sound?
- How might Tim Burton's *Batman* movies be indebted to *Metropolis*?

Further Viewing

The Cabinet of Dr Caligari (Wiene, Germany, 1919)
Dr Mabuse the Gambler (Lang, Germany, 1922)

M (Lang, Germany, 1931)
Blade Runner (Scott, USA, 1982)
Batman (Burton, USA, 1989)
Batman Returns (Burton, USA, 1992)
The Fifth Element (Besson, France, 1997)

6 THE MAN WITH THE MOVIE CAMERA

(Chelovek s kinoapparatom)

Vertov, Soviet Union, 1929

Production Details

Production company/studio	The Ukrainian Photo and Cinema Administration
Producer	The Cine-Eye Group
Director	Dziga Vertov
Cinematographer	Mikhail Kaufman
Editor	Elizaveta Svilova
Screenwriters	Dziga Vertov and the Cine-Eye Group

Cast Includes

Mikhail Kaufman and the people of Moscow, Kiev and Odessa

FOCUS: Documentary/Propaganda

Dziga Vertov's *The Man with the Movie Camera* is a remarkable film. It is unlike anything that came before or after it in Vertov's œuvre, Soviet cinema or indeed the history of film. The film is a documentary made by one of the most prolific and vociferous defenders of non-fiction (or 'unplayed') film. 'Unplayed film' (*neigrovaia fil'ma*) was the contemporary Soviet term for the genre. Vertov used the term 'unplayed' to highlight his 'Cine-Eye' Group's approach to *using* factual material. Thus it is the difference *in the material itself* from scripted drama that is important. Vertov's own phrase was 'life caught unawares' (*zhizn' vrasplokh*). Vertov saw documentaries as the *only* valid form of film. *The Man with the Movie Camera* is a statement of commitment to the documentary approach. It is also a 'box of tricks' that serves as an essential example of Soviet montage and a catalogue of the possibilities of filming technique.

Vertov and his editor Elizaveta Svilova constructed the film from material 'captured' by the Cine-Eye team during the turbulent years 1924–8. It is a document of a period of transition in the history of the Soviet Union, of modernism and Constructivism – indeed of the cinema itself. *The Man with the Movie Camera* can also be viewed as a cinematic affirmation of the Stalinist policies about to unfold: crush resistance in the countryside, urbanise, industrialise, purge opposition.

The Man with the Movie Camera was previewed by the Ukrainian Photo and Cinema Administration (VUFKU) in the autumn of 1928. It had its first public showings in Kiev on 8 January and in Moscow on 9 April 1929. The film was then quickly shelved in the Soviet Union whilst going on to some critical success (or at least interest) after screenings in Berlin, Paris and London. It stands as one of the most important films in the history of documentary cinema. It is also a creative masterpiece.

To talk about 'plot' with reference to a non-fiction film, particularly this most militant of non-fiction films, may seem perverse. However, in general terms non-fiction film does require a narrative role/structure. Early documentary-makers, e.g. Robert Flaherty, were attracted to the classic genre of the journey. The other favoured structure, particularly when attempting to present the chaotic activity of the city, was 'a day in the life'. The most famous example of this approach is Walter Ruttmann's *Berlin: Symphony of a Great City* (*Berlin: Die Sinfonie der Grossstadt*) (Germany, 1927). Among the many concepts and conventions that Vertov plays with in his film is the diurnal narrative and indeed narrative itself.

The Man with the Movie Camera does have a plot. It is typical of the playful nature of the film that it initially appears to be structured around a (generic) 'day in the life' format. In this case we appear to be watching the cameraman's day as it connects with a (constructed) city. The breaks from this narrative are largely cutaways to show the process of the energy production that makes all the activity possible. The film continually pulls the viewer away from the possibility of too simplistic a reading. Most obviously, the diegesis is clearly constructed from footage from several sites. Not only is there a lack of geographical continuity, but temporal continuity is also broken deliberately and ostentatiously. Sequences, or more usually fragments of sequences, are repeated and utilised in different juxtapositions.

One third of the way into the movie narrative is halted as the film itself 'stops' for an educative exercise in editing technique. From that point on 'day in the life' reading becomes increasingly difficult. All human life is here from birth to death via childhood, marriage, divorce, work, rest and play. The last three activities are a key to Vertov's message. The overall structure of the film does lend itself to the more ideological view of the 'day' as one third rest, one third work, one third (constructive) leisure.

The moving images begin with a cameraman 'mounting' a giant camera to survey 'the city'. The 'man with the movie camera' (i.e. the cameraman) enters a cinema that is being prepared to show the film *The Man with the Movie Camera*. The audience enters, the band waits and then begins to accompany the film.

A woman is dreaming of the city (still asleep). Various scenes of inactivity (including sleeping cab drivers and babies) illustrate this. Machinery stands idle. A car arrives at an apartment block to pick up the cameraman. He films an onrushing train and appears to be caught on the track. The woman awakes, dresses and washes. The city begins to awake. A vagrant stirs and laughs at the camera. On Tverskaia Street in Moscow, previously deserted, people appear.

The cameraman begins his tour through the city that is now bustling. Meanwhile miners work to dig the coal that fuels the activity of the factories that spring into action. The machinery, which had previously been still, is now working. The cameraman films a street market and means of transport including buses, trams and aeroplanes. He strides through the crowds. He observes the opening of shops and the activity of a policeman on traffic duty. At the Main Railway Station in Kiev cabs await passengers. The cameraman pursues them, filming groups of passengers. Their images, and others including laughing children, are frozen – and brought to life – by the film editor in her laboratory.

Activity in the city continues: people marry and divorce; a funeral takes place and a birth. The pace of life speeds up. A woman's eye (that of the editor) blinks and surveys the skyline. Her gaze swoops down on the streets. An accident has occurred and the cameraman follows the ambulance to the site. Then he films a fire engine on an emergency call.

The editor cuts together the activities of a beauty parlour and manual labour. Whilst she edits, other women sew. Machine operators become like machines. Miners continue to quarry. The activity becomes more and more frenetic, until the machines come to a halt. The workers wash and change. Workers engage in healthy activities on the beach. A magician entertains children and the camera does magic tricks of appearance and disappearance too.

The cameraman films the production of a wall newspaper and is drawn to an item about sport. The fit and happy Soviet workers engage in exercise. The cameraman takes his equipment for a swim.

The cameraman enters a bar. The camera becomes drunk. It staggers past a 'Candles and Icons' store. No Soviet audience would fail to understand the message that religion and intoxication are closely linked. As an antidote, 'the man with the movie camera' marches purposefully to the Lenin Workers' Club (in Odessa). Workers read, play chess and listen to the radio. A musical performance utilising household items takes place on screen.

Back in the cinema the audience is watching as the camera, much to its amusement, takes on a life of its own. It also enjoys a montage of dancing and music making. Crowds mass on screen as the audience looks on. Giant cameras dominate the city as the Bolshoi Theatre implodes. Time speeds up. Images from earlier in the film return with increasing rapidity. The pace continues into a blur until the camera closes its 'eye'.

This torrent of action and cinematographic magic would be enough – if not too much – for any audience. But there is more to *The Man with the Movie Camera* than meets the (unsuspecting) eye – much more. Vertov was not only an inventive cinematic artist. He was also a political film-maker. *The Man with the Movie Camera* is his masterpiece as a political film (however flawed or unsuccessful in its propagandistic role) (see *Olympia*, chapter 7). Vertov was a film-maker committed to a political position (Marxism-Leninism) and to a rigorously thought-out documentary practice.

> **Some Things to Watch out for and Consider**
>
> • What is the point of documentary? How might its uses and forms have changed since the 1920s?
> • How objective can documentary ever be? Can it ever tell the whole truth?
> • If you were the subject of a documentary, how would the presence of the camera affect your behaviour?

Further Viewing

Nanook of the North (Flaherty, USA, 1922)
The Cameraman (Keaton, USA, 1928)
Olympia (Riefensthal, Germany, 1938)

Further Reading

G. Roberts, *Stride Soviet* (London, 1999)
G. Roberts, *The Man with the Movie Camera* (London, 2001)
B. Winston, *Claiming the Real* (London, 1996)

7 OLYMPIA
Part I. Fest der Völker (Festival of the Nations)
Part II. Fest der Schönheit (Festival of Beauty)
Riefenstahl, Germany, 1938

Awards

Venice Film Festival: Winner – Mussolini Cup for Best Film (tied with *Luciano Serra* pilota, scripted by Mussolini Jr)

Production Details

Production company/studio	Olympia Film
Producer	Leni Riefenstahl
Director	Leni Riefenstahl
Cinematographer	Leni Riefenstahl (plus 22 uncredited cameramen)
Editor	Leni Riefenstahl
Screenwriter	Leni Riefenstahl
Art director	Leni Riefenstahl

Cast Includes

Josef Goebbels	*Himself (spectator)*
Hermann Göring	*Himself (spectator)*
Adolf Hitler	*Himself (declares Games open)*
John Lovelock	*Himself (New Zealand 1500 metres runner)*
Ralph Metcalfe	*Himself (American sprinter)*
Dorothy Odam	*Herself (British high jumper)*
Jesse Owens	*Himself (American sprinter)*
Fritz Schilgen	*Himself (he lights Olympic flame)*

FOCUS: Documentary/Propaganda

Cinema itself began with the capturing of realty – i.e. the Lumières filming their own workers leaving the factory in 1895. Audiences were only too ready to be impressed by early shorts of real 'events', major or minor. After the rise of fiction features, the public continued to expect some form of news coverage in their cinema programmes. 'Documentary' as a term was coined by John Grierson in 1925. As a theorist, film-maker and (mainly) producer, Grierson presided over the growth of the 'documentary movement', which had at its heart a functional/educative momentum. Grierson's own manifestos were not unlike those of Vertov's group in the Soviet Union (see chapter 6), though rather more prosaic. He too believed that cinema should not be shackled to the studio and the telling of fictional stories. The real world had drama enough and lessons to be learnt: 'Cinema is neither an art form nor an entertainment. It is a form of publication. I look upon it as a pulpit.'

For the average film-goer the film-maker who most personified the (Griersonian) documentarist position in the West was Robert Flaherty. This Michigan-born adventurer chose the moving image as a method of capturing evidence of the peoples he encountered on his travels. Flaherty – as an explorer – aimed to bring pictures of parts of the 'real world' to audiences unable to visit the exotic locations themselves. There were a whole host of political subtexts to this activity – not least around the value judgements of what and who constitute the exotic. Nonetheless, Flaherty and others positioned themselves in a 'liberal–humanist' tradition that (ostensibly) offered up information for educational purposes not for 'propaganda'.

Leni Riefenstahl as a documentary director in Nazi Germany – like Vertov and Shub in the Soviet Union – was working in an overtly politically charged milieu. Thus it would be unreasonable to expect her to not make 'political' films. However, whereas Vertov was trying to confront his audience with a (politicised) reality, with *Olympia* Riefensthal bamboozles the viewer with soft-focus Fascist pornography.

Leni Riefenstahl – birth name Berta Helene Amalie Riefenstahl – was born in Berlin on 22 August 1902. A striking beauty, she began her entertainment career as a dancer and began film acting when she attracted the attention of film director Arnold Fanck. She subsequently starred in some of Fanck's 'mountaineering' pictures such as *The White Hell of Pitz Palu* (1929) and *Storm over Mont Blanc* (1930). With Fanck's backing, Riefenstahl began directing films. Her ability to produce epic visuals earned her acclaim, and awards for her films, across Europe.

Riefenstahl received the commission for *Triumph of the Will* (1935) because Hitler was impressed by her 1932 directorial effort, the suitably German-Romantic and melodramatic *The Blue Light* (1932). *Triumph of the Will* ostentatiously documented the Sixth Nazi Party Congress in Nuremberg. Adolf Hitler was portrayed as the saviour of Germany. It was her work on *Triumph of the Will* that would come back to haunt her after the Second World War. After the war Riefenstahl declared that her work was mere documentary. Many colleagues testified to her naivety at the time, claiming she really did not know what kind of people she was dealing with. Nonetheless, Riefenstahl spent four years in a French detention camp after the war as punishment for her part in glamorising the Nazi regime.

After *Triumph of the Will* Riefenstahl went on to direct *Olympia* (1936). She was commissioned by the Olympic Committee to make a feature film about the 1936 Berlin Games. She saw the Olympic Games as a once-in-a-lifetime chance to glorify the beauty and grace of the human body. The Nazi Party saw the event as a giant parade to the glory of National Socialism. The disturbing subtext of the film is that Riefenstahl did not perceive a dichotomy between the two visions.

Joseph Goebbels – Nazi Minister for Propaganda – was acutely aware of the opportunity provided by the Olympics to publicise the regime on an international stage. No cost was too high to create an impression. Thus the budget for the film was left open and Riefenstahl was invited to give free rein to her taste for the epic. The director/producer employed 200 cameramen and several hundred technicians. Over 250 hours of film were shot. Riefenstahl took over 19 months to edit her film into a two-part, 200-minute documentary.

The opening of the film is a most impressive visual spectacle. In Part I Riefenstahl marries her ability to capture spectacle with a genuine sense of drama. She captures the theatrical power of high-level competition, especially in the coverage of the Marathon. Ironically, the sequences that best capture the awesome power of the human body achieving exceptional physical performance feature Jesse Owens (a black athlete). The events in Part II (boating and so on) are not well suited to bravura film-making and rather too much time is spent in vacuous tableaux.

The games – and therefore the filmic record – were intended as a hymn of praise to the glories of Aryanness. Jesse Owens – a black American – rather spoiled things by winning the main event gold medals. To Riefenstahl's credit, she did not edit out Owens's achievements. She did, however, choose not to show Owens receiving his gold medals.

Much like Esfir Shub and her work on historical documentary in the Soviet Union, Riefenstahl is a seminal influence on the structure and language of a particular form of 'documentary' visual presentation. The techniques she employed – e.g. rhythmic cutting between multi-camera set-ups and tracking the move-ment of athletes – turned into the grammar of television sports broadcasts.

In her life as in her films, Riefenstahl was always rather selec-tive in her presentation of truth. Despite her protests to the contrary, Riefenstahl was considered an intricate part of the Third Reich's propaganda machine. Some critics have considered *Tiefland* (1954) to be Riefenstahl's cinematic statement on her rejec-tion of Hitler and the Nazi regime. Unable to get financing for any features, she worked as an acclaimed still photographer in Africa during the 1960s. In 1992 she published her autobiography, *Leni Riefenstahl: A Memoir*, and was the subject of a sceptical documen-tary, *The Wonderful, Horrible Life of Leni Riefenstahl* (Muller, 1993). She did not make a film for almost 50 years. In 2000 Riefenstahl completed a documentary film about an African tribe, thus, ironi-cally, joining the anthropological tradition of documentary begun by Flaherty.

Some Things to Watch out for and Consider

- Should broadcasters or distributors make Riefenstahl's (possibly attractive) films available to the unprepared public?
- Much of *Olympia* is beautifully filmed and engaging to watch. Can we divorce the visual pleasures of the film from the horror of the regime that produced it?
- Can we make the same answer in respect of *Triumph of the Will* (or *The Man with the Movie Camera*)?
- Is watching *Olympia* a more or less historically and/or educationally useful activity than watching *Night and Fog* (Resnais, France, 1955) or *Schindler's List* (Spielberg, 1993)?

Further Viewing

Triumph of the Will (Riefenstahl, Germany, 1932)
Nanook of the North (Flaherty, USA, 1922)
Tabu (Flaherty and Murnau, USA, 1931)
Night Mail (Wright and Watt, UK, 1936)
The Cabinet of Dr Caligari (Wiene, Germany, 1919)
Metropolis (Lang, Germany, 1927)
M (Lang, Germany, 1931)
The Great Way (Shub, Soviet Union, 1927)
The Man with the Movie Camera (Vertov, Soviet Union, 1929)
Today (Shub, Soviet Union, 1930)
Night and Fog (Resnais, France, 1955)

Further Reading

R. Taylor, *Film Propaganda* (1999)
D. Welch, *Film Propaganda and Third Reich* (1986)
B. Winston, *Claiming the Real* (1996)
B. Winston, *Lies, Damn Lies and Documentary* (2001)

8 BRINGING UP BABY

Hawks, USA, 1938

Production Details

Production company/studio	RKO
Producer	Howard Hawks
Director	Howard Hawks
Cinematographer	Russell Metty
Editor	George Hively
Screenwriter	Dudley Nichols

Cast Includes

Katherine Hepburn	*Susan Varica*
Cary Grant	*David Huxley*
Charlie Ruggles	*Horace Applegate*
May Robinson	*Aunt Elizabeth*
Barry Fitzgerald	*Mr Gogarty*
Walter Cattlet	*Constable Slocum*
Fritz Feld	*Dr Lehram*
Leona Roberts	*Hannah Gogarty*
George Irving	*Alexander Peabody*
Virginia Walker	*Alice Swallow*

FOCUS: Auteur Theory

Howard Hawks is the most deceptive of the great directors of the Hollywood Golden Age. His films, which encompass action/adventure, Westerns, musicals and comedies, are so appealing and effortless that for years it was assumed he was an unimportant, if commercially successful, workhorse. In the 1950s, however, when the *Cahiers du cinéma* critics (see chapters 20 and

21) were scouting round for evidence to support their auteur theory, they pounced on this director with glee and, in effect, 'outed' him.

Drag Hawks 'the entertainer' out of the closet, they – or at least Godard – argued, and you will discover the real Hawks, the artist, who created a body of films that express a common collection of concerns irrespective of their subject matter or the apparent simplicity of their style. *Bringing up Baby*, Hawks's contribution to the 1930s 'screwball' genre, is a fine example of how the master uses comedy to explore one of his recurring themes: the need for people who embody widely differing values to reconcile those values before they can come together as lovers or friends. In addition, this madcap farce demonstrates the director's distinctive approach to film storytelling itself, to symmetry, pattern and shape.

There are two main characters in this movie, two spiritual opposites. The first is Dr David Huxley (Cary Grant), a young zoologist who is obsessively dedicated to his work, the rather glum task of rebuilding a gigantic brontosaurus skeleton. As the film opens, we discover Huxley in his museum, bespectacled, contemplative, as potentially dead as his dead dinosaur; the imagery encourages us to see that this man's life is all work and no play.

Step forward the second major character: the maniacally playful heiress Susan Vance (Katharine Hepburn), David's mirror image and the living embodiment of his worst nightmare. Their first meeting, where they have a bizarre altercation over the ownership of a golf ball, sets the keynote for all the mayhem that follows: David tries in vain to be adult, logical, self-controlled; Susan, by contrast, is childlike, logical only in the way the Mad Hatter is logical, and she has no need for control of any description.

After this one-woman Exocet missile has inveigled the distraught doctor into helping her transport Baby, a pet leopard, to Connecticut, the confusions increase and the collisions between the two start to spiral; the spiral emits comic sparks, and the sparks tell us that these two fancy each other rotten.

The horseplay, then, is foreplay, but at a deeper emotional level this film takes David on a journey away from the dead, indoor dinosaur towards Susan's vitality, open-air joy and sense of fun. Finally, when all the misunderstandings have been resolved and the young woman has aided Huxley's work by getting him a large donation for his research, the two lovers are united: David has discovered his inner clown, thanks to his walk on the wild side; Susan may not have changed as such, but she has taken a significant step towards David's world, towards appreciating the value of his professional life. The lovers, then, end up in partnership, like two contrasting bookends, both very different from, but each in complete balance with, the other.

This movement towards spiritual symmetry can also be seen in the relationship between John Wayne and Montgomery Clift in Hawks's best Western, *Red River* (1948), and it is an important element in the two films he made with Humphrey Bogart and Lauren Bacall: *To Have and Have Not* (1944) and *The Big Sleep* (1946).

The emotional concerns of *Bringing up Baby* are also reflected and communicated in its narrative pattern. The overall shape is circular, starting with Huxley alone in his museum, then returning to the same location at the end, except this time Susan, not David's dreary fiancée, has occupied the space. Within this frame are numerous interconnecting contrasts, which contribute to the story's meaning in the way an increasingly complex chord structure enriches a piece of music.

For example, throughout this film, Hawks compares city with country, interior and exterior, night with day, order with chaos. At the same time, he gets plenty of anarchic fun out of the tension between the 'real' and the 'social' self. To take just one example: notice how David in particular keeps tearing, soaking or changing his clothes, as if what he feels he is on the inside, and what he believes the conventions require him to be on the outside, are locked in a loony death struggle.

The result of all this is wonderful, liberated (and liberating) comedy. Yet, even though *Bringing up Baby* is the moviegoing equivalent of running away and joining the circus, bear in mind that its laughter and energy are rooted in serious issues about how we can live fully, freely – and in harmony with one another.

Note how all the nonsense (or non-sense) is firmly rooted in logic; be aware of comparisons and contrasts within scenes and between shots; consider how all these things influence your responses. In other words, use your enjoyment of this extremely enjoyable movie to help you to work out *why* you enjoy. You need to watch any movie by Howard Hawks like, well, a hawk.

Some Things to Watch out for and Consider

- Think about narrative devices. Ask yourself:
  - What roles do the animals play?
  - How do recurring lines of dialogue enhance and develop the story?
  - What is the significance of the dinosaur bone?
- Think about Cary Grant and Katharine Hepburn. Ask yourself:
  - How does the way they physically move contribute to our understanding of their characters and relationship?
  - How do their voices and speech patterns help us to understand who they are?
  - How does Hawks's camera framing tell us how their relationship is developing?
- Try writing your own script for the scene we do not see – the one that results in David sitting in Susan's car covered in chicken feathers. Justify your approach with evidence from the film.
- Reconstruct the story, but from the point of view of George the dog (seriously!).

Further Viewing

The Awful Truth (McCarey, USA, 1937)
His Girl Friday (Hawks, USA, 1940)
To Have and Have Not (Hawks, USA, 1944)
The Big Sleep (Hawks, USA, 1946)
Red River (Hawks, USA, 1948)
What's Up, Doc? (Bogdanovich, USA, 1972)

Further Reading

G. Mast, *Howard Hawks: Storyteller* (Oxford, 1982)
J. McBride, *Hawks on Hawks* (Los Angeles, 1982)
T. McCarthy, *Howard Hawks: The Grey Fox of Hollywood* (New York, 1997)

9 ***STAGECOACH***
Ford, USA, 1939

Awards

Academy Awards: Winner – Best Original Music and Best Supporting
  Actor (Thomas Mitchell)

Production Details

Production company/studio	Walter Wanger Productions
Producer	Walter Wanger
Director	John Ford
Cinematographer	Bert Glennon
Editors	Otho Lovering and Dorothy Spencer
Screenwriters	Dudley Nichols from an original story by Ernest Haycox
Music	Borris Morros

Cast Includes

John Wayne	*The Ringo Kid*
Claire Trevor	*Dallas*
Thomas Mitchell	*Doc Boone*
Andy Devine	*Buck*
George Bancroft	*Curly Wilcox*
John Carradine	*Mr Hatfield*
Donald Meek	*Mr Samuel Peacock*
Louise Platt	*Lucy Mallory*
Berton Churchill	*Mr Gatewood*

FOCUS: Genre, Stardom and Classic Hollywood Narrative

Westerns have a long history in cinema. Indeed, it is generally
agreed that the first American narrative film, Edwin S. Porter's

silent *The Great Train Robbery* (1903), was a Western. Before *Stagecoach*, Westerns were generally not quality films. They were made quickly and cheaply for a largely male audience. Their appeal lay in the gunfights, chases and spectacular scenery. They were 'B' features known within the industry as 'horse operas'. John Ford cut his teeth as a director on such Westerns. By the late 1930s he already had 100 films to his credit, but he had not made a Western since *Three Bad Men* in 1926. In effect his status as a director had risen, so that he did not need to make Westerns anymore. He was perceived by David O. Selznick, one of the most powerful and respected producers in Hollywood at the time, as a director of quality pictures. The fact that Selznick wanted to work with Ford indicates clearly Ford's status in 1939. The fact that Selznick pulled out when Ford insisted on making a Western indicates equally clearly the lowly status of the Western. Ford maintained his commitment to the project, determined to make a classic Western (a term that at the time was itself contradictory). *Stagecoach* was made and the Western genre was reborn and given a respectability it had never had before.

In viewing this film, then, we need to consider what John Ford brought to the genre. A clue is to be found in the fact that, when it was released, *Stagecoach* was described in the trade press not as a 'Western' at all but as a 'Melodrama'. Ford and his screenwriter Dudley Nichols chose to focus on people rather than gunfights and horses, and they deliberately broadened the appeal of the story beyond the traditionally male spectators of Westerns by developing the love interest and including the birth of a baby. The film contains the characteristics we would expect of the Western genre – for example, the Indian attack and the shoot-out between Ringo and the Plummer brothers at the end – but the real focus is character and character development. The perilous journey across the hostile Western landscape is a device that allows Ford to examine how the characters interact/develop once removed from the safe confines of society and its civilised values.

As well as being the classic Western, the template from which the rest were to follow, *Stagecoach* is also a perfect example of the classic Hollywood narrative.

- The narrative follows a conventional structure where we clearly see a beginning, middle and end (in that order).

- Events are linked by a cause-and-effect relationship that makes motivation clear to the audience – for example, at the start of the film we have a cause, which is the murder of Ringo's family. This causes (and affects the value of) the shoot-out at the end of the film.
- The story is character driven and we understand what drives the characters.
- The role of the hero is important; he instigates much of the action and brings about resolution at the end.
- We see economy of storytelling, where each event serves not only to illuminate character but also to move the story along by triggering the next event. The birth of Lucy's baby is a good example of this. The enforced wait amid the ever-increasing threat of Indian attack is juxtaposed with the images of birth and new life. The humanity (or lack of it) of each of the characters is revealed through his or her responses to both the increasing danger and the baby. For Dallas and Doc, it provides them with redemption and an opportunity to shine. For Gatewood, it reveals the true depths of his selfishness. As well as illuminating the characters in this way, the scene triggers further crisis because they cannot move Lucy.
- The film has a clear sense of closure, where nothing is left dangling or unexplained.
- Apart from the scene of the Indian attack, the film follows the rules of continuity editing – the process of piecing the film together so that the joins are invisible, spatial continuity is maintained and the viewer can easily follow the story.

Film theorist André Bazin wrote that: 'Stagecoach is like a wheel, so perfectly made that it remains in equilibrium on its axis in any position.' The structure of the film is certainly very formal. The story takes place over two days and is divided into carefully balanced episodes – for example, the 12-minute opening scene in Tonto, where the characters boarding the stage are carefully and comprehensively introduced, is balanced by the arrival in Lordsburg, where they disembark and their various goals are quickly resolved.

Much of the richness of the narrative comes from the mixing of such different characters each with their different but clearly defined goals. The characters can in fact be divided into groups. In one we see the apparently respectable people – Lucy Mallory, Gatewood (actually an embezzler) and Hatfield, whose chivalrous aspiration to protect Lucy marks a return to former values and an abandonment of his selfish gambling. In the second group we have the apparently disreputable characters – the drunken Doc Boone, Dallas the prostitute and Ringo the outlaw. The progression of the narrative will challenge these appearances. Doc, Dallas and Ringo each finds redemption through his or her humanity. Lucy's snobbery is momentarily lifted, only to return when she rejoins society. Hatfield dies having recovered his chivalrous Southern code (his death symbolising the death of the lifestyle and values of the South that he represents). It is Peacock, the solemn whisky-drummer, who presents us with the simplest moral of the film. 'Let us have a little Christian Charity toward one another.' Buck and Curly outside the coach act like a chorus on the moral debate within. These nine disparate characters are held together by two main narrative strands: the perilous journey across a hostile landscape and Ringo's revenge plot, both staple elements of the genre.

Stagecoach represents a significant development for women characters. In both Lucy and Dallas we have rounded and interesting characters, but they are still polarised into two available roles for women: the good wife and mother (Lucy) and the 'fallen' social outcast (Dallas). What is interesting is Ford's treatment of these roles, which encourages us to sympathise more with the prostitute than with the good woman. But what does Dallas achieve with all our sympathy? Promotion to the other female role – good wife and mother. In such limited possibilities for women, the film reflects the time in which it was made.

Stagecoach also introduced two major stars to the screen – John Wayne and Monument Valley – thus it can be credited with creating much of the iconography of the Western. Wayne had made a large number of instantly forgettable 'B' features, but it was his role as Ringo that brought him to stardom. From the moment that Wayne (as Ringo) stopped the coach, his persona and the characters he played began to fuse into the iconic image that is 'John Wayne'.

The functional definition of a 'star' is clearly put by John Ellis in C. Gledhill (ed.), *Star Signs* (London, 1992): 'a performer in a particular medium whose figure enters into subsidiary forms of circulation and then feeds back into future performances.' Richard Dyer has made major contributions to theorising the star via two seminal studies, *Stars* (1980) and *Heavenly Bodies* (1986). For Dyer the star image has four components:

- what the industry puts out;
- what the media say;
- what the star says and does;
- what the audience or spectator selects.

Following Wayne's career from *Stagecoach* through a host of films (all basically Westerns) via *The Searchers* (see chapter 18) and on to *The Green Berets* (Wayne, USA, 1968) would furnish the viewers with their own classic narrative of stardom.

Some Things to Watch out for and Consider

- How does the film-maker so concisely but effectively inform us about each of his characters in the opening sequence of the film?
  - For each character look at: costume; performance; dialogue; music.
  - Can you group the characters according to class? What are their feelings/prejudices towards each other?
- Compare this opening scene to the first stop at Dry Fork and the scene when Lucy's baby is born. How does Ford use these scenes to develop his characters and the interactions between them?
- Ringo's unique status as hero is partly marked out by the fact that he joins the coach separately and dramatically by holding it up.
  - What aspects of the cinematography increase the drama of Ringo's appearance?
  - What do we already know about Ringo's history?
  - What do we already know about Curly's and Buck's feelings/sympathies towards him?
- Ringo's code of honour demands that he seek revenge for the murder of his father and brother.
  - Consider how the film encourages us to sympathise with him.
  - Why do you think it is Ringo the murderer who escapes to freedom and a new life at the end of the film, whilst Gatewood the thief is captured and punished. How do you feel about their respective endings?
  - Compare Ringo's role as the Western hero with that of other Western heroes – e.g. Ethan in *The Searchers* (Ford, USA, 1956) (see chapter 18) and William Munny in *Unforgiven* (Eastwood, USA, 1992) (see chapter 38).

- Genre films work by creating a fine balance between fulfilling audience expectations and creating something new.
  - What aspects of this film do you find predictable and formulaic?
  - What aspects do you find surprising and original? Remember that the film is over 60 years old and has been much copied.
- Consider what messages and values are presented about:
  - gender
  - white people
  - Mexicans
  - Indians

Further Viewing

High Noon (Zinneman, USA, 1952)
Shane (Stevens, USA, 1953)
The Searchers (Ford, USA, 1956)
A Fistful of Dollars (Leone, Italy/Germany/Spain, 1964)
Unforgiven (Eastwood, USA, 1992)

Further Reading

R. Dyer, *Stars* (London, 1980)
R. Dyer, *Heavenly Bodies* (1986)
C. Gledhill (ed.), *Star Signs* (London, 1992)
G. Roberts and H. Wallis, *Introducing Film* (London, 2001)

10 *CITIZEN KANE*
Welles, USA, 1941

Awards

Academy Awards: Winner – Best Writing, Original Screenplay (Herman
 J. Mankiewicz and Orson Welles); Nomination – Best Actor (Orson
 Welles), Best Cinematography, Best Director and Best Film Editing
New York Film Critics Circle Awards: Winner – Best Film

Production Details

Production company/studio	Mercury Productions / RKO Radio Pictures
Producer	Orson Welles
Director	Orson Welles
Cinematographer	Gregg Toland
Editor	Robert Wise
Screenwriters	Herman J. Mankiewicz and Orson Welles
Music	Bernard Herrmann

Cast Includes

Orson Welles	*Charles Foster Kane*
Joseph Cotton	*Jedediah Leland*
Dorothy Comingore	*Susan Alexander*
Agnes Moorehead	*Mrs Mary Kane*
Ruth Warrick	*Emily Norton Kane*
Ray Collins	*Boss James 'Jim' W. Gettys*
Erskine Sanford	*Herbert Carter/Newsreel Reporter*
Everett Sloane	*Bernstein*
Paul Stewart	*Raymond*
George Coulouris	*Walter Parks Thatcher*
Herman J. Mankiewicz	*Newspaperman (uncredited)*

FOCUS: The Canonical Text

Citizen Kane has been marketed recently as both 'the classic story of power and the press' and 'the greatest film of all time', thus claiming 'classic' and canonical status for itself. The makers of the film, pre-eminently Orson Welles and Gregg Toland, as well as the studio (RKO) were consciously and unapologetically attempting to create a 'great' movie from the very inception of the project. So what can be said about a film created from such lofty ideals (and massive hubris) that the members of the British Film Institute have voted 'the greatest film of all time' (at least since 1960) and that topped the *Sight and Sound* poll of movies most admired by film-makers and film critics in 1962, 1972, 1982 and 1992?

Citizen Kane is one of 'those' films. Students of film are expected to have seen it, expected to have something to say about it and are probably somewhat intimidated by its status. In other words, beyond its own marketing claims, it really is unarguably a 'classic' (part of the canon). An entry in *Key Film Texts* can only begin to explain the hold that *Citizen Kane* holds on cinema history.

The fame of *Citizen Kane* is a product of two factors:

* controversy surrounding its release;
* the filmic qualities of the picture itself.

Citizen Kane, directed by and starring Orson Welles, was released in 1941. Welles was only 25 at the time, and this was the first feature film he ever made. The fact that he was given *carte blanche* (and final edit) on the film by RKO executive George Schaeffer led to phenomenal jealousy in the Hollywood 'community'.

It is generally accepted (and was generally assumed at the time) that the film was based on the real life of American newspaper baron William Randolph Hearst. It is an essentially unflattering portrait of the great entrepreneur. Hearst, with the help of his enormous media empire, did his level best to suppress the film. All mention of it was banned in Hearst's many papers and radio stations. At one stage, the movie industry got so terrified about a media backlash against Hollywood that a group of studio bosses offered RKO money simply to burn the negative. Even when the film was released, it achieved only a limited distribution because it was boycotted by circuits owned by the

Citizen Kane. RKO (courtesy of BFI Stills, Posters and Designs)

'big five' studios. The *Citizen Kane* story is most entertainingly (and largely accurately) told in a high-class TV movie *RKO 281* (Ross, 1999).

Yet *Citizen Kane*, so efficiently suppressed, came to have such an enormous reputation. The reason – beyond the natural urge of cinema-loving critics and audiences (particularly students) to rediscover, protect and eulogise an 'art' film so crushed by the power of mammon – is that *Citizen Kane* is a phenomenally good movie. *Citizen Kane* is innovative. The film is a box of tricks, because Welles certainly saw cinema as precisely that. But *Kane* is more than 'clever'. It is universal in its themes, effective and massively influential.

Citizen Kane is a film that combines cinematic craft with human storytelling to provide something that – like *Battleship Potemkin* (see chapter 3) before it – breaks with the easy attraction of filmed theatre. It is a *film*, which exploits practically every cinematic technique that Welles and Toland had at their disposal. Welles challenged his colleagues to invent new ways to create a sense of physical and psychological reality on the screen. Yet, when you watch the film, no matter how much you try to pay attention to the cinematic craft, you will still get caught up in the human storyline. Therein lies the essential brilliance of *Citizen Kane*.

There is so much to see in this greatest of all Hollywood movies that the rest of this entry merely aims to start you watching.

Some Things to Watch out for and Consider

- *Narrative structure.* The film begins at the very end with the death of its major protagonist. It then proceeds to try and piece together his life as though it were a giant jigsaw puzzle (a recurring image in the film)
- *Camerawork*: in particular the use of deep focus photography (utilising depth of field to keep all planes in focus) and the dramatising effect of extreme camera angles and camera movement.
- *Editing:* how the passage of time is condensed so that the enormous and intricate sweep of the film can be communicated economically and without the audience losing track. Note the use of sound bridges.
- *The use of* mise en scène *as opposed to montage technique:* lengthy shots in which the action takes place within the frame. Viewers are required to search and read with their own eyes. Also note when Welles and Wise chose to abandon this technique and utilise shorter shot durations or varied the rhythm of the editing.
- *Lighting:* chiaroscuro technique with painterly use of light and shadow – lit more like a stage or an opera set.
- *Make-up:* notice how Kane (in particular) ages throughout the film.
- Is the ultimate aim of the narrative to explain the significance of Kane's dying word: 'Rosebud'? If not, what is the function of 'Rosebud' in the film?
- Finally, a serious question: is *Citizen Kane* 'the greatest movie of all time'? (How could we watch it without all the 'canonical' baggage anyway?)

Further Viewing

The Magnificent Ambersons (Welles, USA, 1942)
Chimes at Midnight (Welles, Spain/Switzerland, 1966)
Apocalypse Now (Coppola, USA, 1979)
Wall Street (Stone, USA, 1987)
Pulp Fiction (Tarantino, USA, 1994)
RKO 281 (Ross, USA TV, 1999)

11 CASABLANCA

Curtiz, USA, 1942

Awards

Academy Awards: Winner – Best Film; Nomination – Best Actor (Humprey Bogart), Best Supporting Actor (Claude Raines), Best Director and Best Screenplay

Production Details

Production company/studio	Warner Brothers
Producer	Hal B. Wallis
Director	Michael Curtiz
Cinematographer	Arthur Edeson
Editor	Owen Marks
Screenwriters	Julius J. Epstein, Philip G. Epstein and Howard Koch (from a novel by Murray Burnett and Joan Allison)
Art director	Carl Weyl
Music	Max Steiner

Cast Includes

Humphrey Bogart	*Richard Blain*
Ingrid Bergman	*Ilsa Lund*
Paul Henreid	*Victor Laszlo*
Claude Rains	*Louis Renault*
Conrad Veidt	*Heinrich Strasser*
Sydney Greenstreet	*Ferrari*
Peter Lorre	*Ugarte*
Dooley Wilson	*Sam*

FOCUS: Themes and Issues

Casablanca is a magical entertainment; it forms bonds between strangers. When you buy or borrow a video copy of the film, the assistant will hand over the box with a conspiratorial smile. 'Good choice,' he or she will whisper, as though you shared a similar taste in chocolates. This movie inspires that kind of thing: it is a holiday of the heart, a guy-loses-girl love story told with froth and zing; its pleasures appear to defy analysis. If you still await your first viewing, then lucky, lucky you.

All the same, there are some conundrums sloshing around in the champagne. First, for a love story, the film spends comparatively little time examining the Bogart–Bergman relationship as an active question in the present; it is much more interested in defining their love in terms of what once happened (the idyll of Paris) and how current feelings will influence the future (who gets the letters of transit and skedaddles out of the city). Secondly, an inordinate amount of time seems to be spent on subsidiary characters, like Claude Rains and the flotsam and jetsam floating on the surface of Rick's Café. This is odd, to say the least: it is as if *Gone with the Wind* (Fleming, USA, 1939) was constantly losing sight of the central Rhett and Scarlett relationship and getting distracted by minor details, like Aunt Pittypat's quince bottling or something. In short, *Casablanca* seems to be employing different methods for different purposes. The question is what those purposes are.

There is no denying this movie is a romance, but that does not mean it revolves exclusively around the Bogie–Bergman double act, like it would in a Howard Hawks story, for example. To refocus your sensibilities, push the two stars to the back of your mind and try to see *Casablanca* as an early 1940s version of *Star Wars* (Lucas, USA, 1977) (see chapter 28). Here, the nasty Nazi Conrad Veidt is Darth Vader, who represents the Evil (in this case, Fascism) threatening to take over the world; opposing him is the funky Jedi Knight Victor Laszlo (Paul Henreid) and bang slap in the middle is Rick (Bogart), our tuxedo-clad, and rather mature, combination of the idealistic Luke Skywalker and the cynical Han Solo.

Now *Star Wars* is clearly not interested in any one relationship between any one pair of characters; all the people in the story, all the concerns, are tributaries feeding into the great theme, which is the fairy-tale moral quest, where the hero undergoes a series of trials that reveal his latent powers and make him worthy of the final showdown with Evil. In the case of Luke Skywalker, he has to discover his true nature, his Jedi Knightness; Bogie, by contrast, has already been a Jedi Knight, back in Paris in his glory days as an anti-Fascist. The narrative aim of *Casablanca* is to help him rediscover the fact, to break out of his shell of Solo-style cynicism and selfishness. Read in this fashion, the film is not centred on Ingrid at all – that is, on *who* the hero gets or whom he does not get. The meaning is rooted in *what* he gets, his reconversion to struggle, commitment and faith.

In this context, Bergman is Obi-Wan Kenobi, Humph's spiritual mentor, but one without a beard and with a vastly superior dress sense. As you watch the two leading players strut their stuff, consider how their love consistently connects with other varieties of love: love of justice, kindness, right doing and right being. Just as Obi-Wan educates Luke in the ways of the Force, which really works only when you trust to your innermost feelings, so Ingrid takes Bogart through a series of moral exercises, which are rooted in a concept of spiritual integrity and revolve round the question: Are you on the 'Dark Side' or are you with us? The whole rigmarole over the letters of transit should be viewed in this context. Try to see the love scenes as moral tests, not as the usual lips-to-lips business, and view the finale at the airport as Rick finally regaining a fully working light sabre, not losing the girl.

Casablanca is a product of the Second World War; it breathes the air of a global peril when sides had to be taken. In consequence, its story speaks, not just of love between individuals, but of the wider love of humanity, of a pressing psychological need to stand shoulder to shoulder with others against the black clouds that loom over the world. Tragically, this problem did not come to a halt in 1945; the question of evil remains constant throughout the generations, although its forms change. This perhaps is the secret of *Casablanca*'s enchantment; it appeals to our hunger for a righteous cause, for a vision of something wider and more heroic than ourselves. It binds together you, me and (hopefully) every individual in the audience, because it dramatises a fundamental truth – that the self-absorbed business of kisses and sighs is never enough, that the human journey needs to be sustained by something grittier, more transcendent and in the end more beautiful: a case of do or die, a romance of valour.

Some Things to Watch out for and Consider

- Think about the magical quality of place in this film. Ask yourself:
    - What does America represent?
    - What does Casablanca itself represent?
    - What does Paris represent for Ilsa and Rick?

- Think about some of the other characters. Ask yourself:
  - What is the significance of Claude Rains and Bogart walking off into the mist at the beginning of their 'beautiful friendship'?
  - How do the reactions of Rick's café staff help us to track the moral journey of the hero?
  - What is the importance of the Bulgarian couple in setting Rick back on the right course?
- Try retelling this as a twenty-first-century story, where Conrad Veidt is the representative of a sinister multinational corporation that is seriously threatening the environment.

Further Viewing

Gone with the Wind (Fleming, USA, 1939)
Passage to Marseilles (Curtiz, USA, 1944)
To Have and Have Not (Hawks, USA, 1944)
Play it Again, Sam (Ross, USA, 1972)
Star Wars (Lucas, USA, 1977)

Further Reading

A. Harmetz, *Round up the Usual Suspects: The Making of Casablanca* (London, 1993)
C. Hirschhorn, *The Warner Bros Story* (New York, 1979)
J. C. Myers, *Bogart: A Life in Hollywood* (Boston, 1997)

12 GONE WITH THE WIND

Fleming, USA, 1939

Awards

Academy Awards: Winner – Honorary Award for William Cameron Menzies (for outstanding achievement in the use of colour for the enhancement of dramatic mood in the production of *Gone with the Wind*), Best Picture (David O. Selznick), Best Actress (Vivien Leigh), Best Art Direction (Lyle R. Wheeler), Best Colour Cinematography (Ernest Haller and Ray Rennahan), Best Director (Victor Fleming), Best Film Editing (Hal C. Kern and James E. Newcom), Best Supporting Actress (Hattie McDaniel), Best Writing, Screenplay (Sidney Howard) and a Technical Achievement Award (Don Musgrave) 'for pioneering in the use of coordinated equipment in the production'; Nomination – Best Actor (Clark Gable)

Production Details

Production company/studio	Selznick International/MGM
Producer	David O. Selznick
Director	Victor Fleming and George Cukor (uncredited)
Cinematographer	Lee Garmes (uncredited) and Ernest Haller
Editor	Hal Kern
Screenwriter	Sidney Howard (from a novel by Margaret Mitchell)
Production designer	William Cameron Menzies

Cast Includes

Clark Gable	*Rhett Butler*
Vivien Leigh	*Scarlett O'Hara*

Leslie Howard	*Ashley Wilkes*
Olivia de Havilland	*Melanie Hamilton Wilkes*
Hattie McDaniel	*Mammy*
Butterfly McQueen	*Prissy*
Everett Brown	*Big Sam, the Foreman*
Ona Munson	*Belle Watling*
Cammie King	*Bonnie Blue Butler*

FOCUS: Film History (Hollywood as Institution)

Gone with the Wind was not a typical, film-a-week studio production. It was advertised as: 'The most magnificent picture ever!' This
was meant from the start to be an epic: big, broad, expensive and
long. It won nine Oscars and is generally held to be the most popular American historical film ever made. It is still on the list of the
top 20 money-making films of all times (and would probably
remain first if inflation were taken into account). It opened in the
USA in the second week of December 1939. By New Year's Day
Selznick's 'blockbuster' had sold a million dollars' worth of tickets.
In London, it opened in 1940 and played for a record 232 consecu-
tive weeks. In 1976 the American TV première of *Gone with the Wind*
was the highest-rated single network programme ever broadcast.

    Gone with the Wind was adapted from a novel by Margaret
Mitchell, an Atlanta newspaper reporter. Her lengthy book was
based on stories of the old South that she heard as a child. The story
was published in 1936 and immediately became a best-seller, going
on to break sales records and attracting the Hollywood studios.
Gone with the Wind had the potential – if carefully scripted and especially marketed – to cross demographic barriers in the audience. In
particular, it had the potential to be both a men's and a women's
picture at the same time: a war story and the heroic figure of Rhett
Butler for the men; epic romance and the emotional Scarlett O'Hara
for the women. The film was produced by David O. Selznick in
conjunction with MGM. Selznick not only identified the novel's
huge potential as a top box-office film; as a long-time industry
insider he also negotiated a lot of personal control over production.

    Once Selznick had bought up the rights to the book, he had to
set about casting the picture. Gable was an obvious choice for
Rhett, but Selznick gained a publicity coup by basically publicly
auditioning America for an actress to play the part of Scarlett. In
the search for Scarlett, 1400 candidates were allegedly screen

tested. Selznick really spun the drama out. On 10 December 1938, Selznick shot the famous burning of Atlanta sequence with stunt doubles standing in for Gable and the still uncast Scarlett O'Hara. According to the legend, in the light of the flames of the Atlanta set, Selznick's brother, an agent, introduced him to his new client Vivien Leigh. Leigh was cast on the spot.

You will notice that the name Selznick is cropping up regularly in this story. David O. Selznick was not the director. He controlled the film – the casting and so on – before assigning a director. He fired the first director – George Cukor – on the pleadings of Clark Gable (who thought Cukor was a 'woman's director'). Victor Fleming replaced Cukor, but Selznick continued his hands-on style, including overseeing the set-ups of every shot. It is not entirely unreasonable to cast Selznick as 'producer as auteur' – but we should not underestimate the role of William Cameron Menzies – the production designer – and the influence of Selznick's brother Myron.

The production proceeded on an epically expensive scale: 59 leading and supporting players, 2400 extras, 90 sets; women's costumes alone cost $100 000 to buy. Selznick aimed at some form of authenticity. Dozens of historical advisers were brought in, plus a Southern dialogue coach, an expert on Southern etiquette and a historical architect specialising in the American Civil War period. Production costs topped $3.5 million (or $200 million in today's money), with another half a million spent on prints, publicity and advertising.

Even stripping away the hype (part of its allure, after all), *Gone with the Wind* remains triumphant. However much it cost to make – it made money. However shallow the supporting cast – the stars are stellar and compelling. However long and sprawling the movie may be – it remains, like *Casablanca (see* chapter 11) or *Star Wars* (see chapter 28), a testament to the power of mainstream commercial cinema as an engaging storytelling medium and enduring cultural product.

Some Things to Watch out for and Consider

* When watching the film – as with *Stagecoach* (chapter 9), *The Seven Samurai* (chapter 17), *Apocalypse Now* (chapter 30) and so many others – you should consider how movies portray and mythologise historical events and periods.

- 'Hollywood' is often assumed to produce 'realist' films – yet *Gone with the Wind* contains many expressionist flourishes – not least in the sets and lighting. Fleming made *The Wizard of Oz* in the same year – with apparently rather more justification for stylised *mise en scène*. Why do you think the filmmakers chose to move away from realism for this epic?
- Beyond being a ripping good yarn, *Gone with the Wind* does contain some very disturbing portrayals of black people and a deeply condescending view of the role of women. Is this simply 'telling it like it is' in the pre-Civil War South?
- If (heaven forefend!) you were remaking *Gone with the Wind* for a twenty-first century audience, who would you cast as Rhett and Scarlett? (Would it be easier to remarket the original? Why?)

Further Viewing

Treasure Island (Fleming, USA, 1934)
The Wizard of Oz (Fleming, USA, 1939)
The Birth of a Nation (Griffith, USA, 1914)
Do the Right Thing (Lee, USA, 1987)

13 THE BICYCLE THIEVES
(Ladri di biciclette)
de Sica, Italy, 1948

Awards

Academy Awards: Winner – Best Foreign Film
British Academy Awards: Winner – Best Film
Golden Globe: Winner – Best Foreign Film
National Board of Review, USA: Winner – Best Director and Best Picture
(any language)
New York Film Critic's Circle Awards: Winner – Best Foreign Language
Film

Production Details

Production company/studio	Produzioni De Sica/SA, Mayer Distributors ENIC
Producers	Vittorio de Sica and Umberto Scarpelli
Director	Vittorio de Sica
Cinematographer	Carlo Montiori
Editor	Eraldo Da Roma
Screenwriters	Cesar Zavatinni, Oreste Biancoli, Suso D'Amico, Vittorio De Sica, Adolfo Franci, Gherardo Gherardi, Gerardo Guerrieri and Luigi Bartolini (novel)

Cast Includes

Lamberto Maggiorani	*Antonio Ricci, the Father*
Enzo Staiola	*Bruno Ricci, the Son*
Lianella Carell	*Maria Ricci, the Mother*
Gino Saltamerenda	*Baiocco*
Vittorio Antonucci	*The Thief*

FOCUS: Italian Neo-Realism; Realism; *mise en scène*

Ever since its first release, *The Bicycle Thieves* has been hailed as an important work: an 'essential' illustrative text for film theory – namely, film realism. Over the years it has been cited in many of the regularly solicited lists of critics' most 'important', 'influential' or 'favourite' films. Whether or not *The Bicycle Thieves* is truly great cinema cannot of course be proved, but it remains a key piece of film history, representing perhaps the best all-round illustration of an influential school of thought or at least a highly principled approach in the creation of drama for the screen. Although not the first, it can, nevertheless, lay claim to being the most well-known and popular/populist example of the 1940s cinema known as Italian neo-realism. Three major Italian directors are most associated with neo-realism: Luchino Visconti (*Ossessione*, 1942), Roberto Rossellini (*Rome, Open City*, 1945), and de Sica. The core neo-realist 'movement' itself was short lived. Visconti, an aristocratic Marxist who spent the 1930s working in Paris with Jean Renoir, is best known for *Ossessione* (made in Hollywood as *The Postman Always Rings Twice* in 1946 by Tay Garnett and in 1981 by Bob Rafelson), but after the neo-realist *The Earth Trembles* (*Terra trema*, Italy, 1948) he turned to a grander, operatic style of production. Roberto Rossellini made a great critical impact with both *Rome, Open City* (1945) and *Paisan* (1946), but, following *Germany, Year Zero* (1947), he gave up neo-realism, and ended up more involved with television during the 1950s. De Sica had already made an impression with realist work directing non-professional actors in 1942 with *The Children Are Watching Us*, but his great contribution to neo-realism was limited to *Shoeshine* (1946) and *The Bicycle Thieves*, which both dealt with the shocking poverty in post-war Italy. Into the 1950s and 1960s, he moved more into acting (his first vocation) than directing, although he achieved great critical acclaim again with occasional subsequent works, most notably the epic study of anti-Semitism in Fascist Italy, *The Garden of the Finzi-Continis* (1971).

The Bicycle Thieves is an unashamedly political film and the very realism itself that it adopts can be seen as political. The neo-realist films of the mid- to late 1940s were made in deliberate reaction against the films of the 1930s and 1940s (especially in the formerly Fascist Italy), which had been epitomised by glossy escapism. The neo-realist films offered a grim reality in which the directors countered past politics and past cinematic styles 'truthfully' to try and depict the social problems of post-war Italy. They were also a rebuttal of the glamorous excesses of the Technicolor (American) dream factory. These films sparked off the now clichéd phrase 'gritty realism', which is used to identify 'documentary style', a clear aim served well by the films' contemporary documentary trademark of black and white film stock – a stylistic short cut for 'truth'. The films all contained a social/political message in their stories. They are all typified by location shooting, non-professional actors and documentary-style camerawork – a combination of static and hand-held work, made possible by newer lightweight American newsreel cameras. Following the action in this manner placed an emphasis on the subject that reduced the sense of a director calling shots. Subject matter focused of course on everyday subjects and ordinary people, rejecting the glamorous and extraordinary. The use of non-professionals created a sense of real characters undiluted by the impact of recognisable stars. (de Sica rejected having Cary Grant as Ricci in order to have a larger American budget.) The style of Italian neo-realism might be regarded as having no style at all. The pursuit of an impression of truth sought to avoid drawing attention to the director's technique. Despite favouring *mise en scène* over the artifice of montage, it remains opposed to expressionism too, where the director's hand becomes strikingly obvious through the overt dramatisation of visual filmic elements. Italian neo-realism is counter to formalism, which might seem like an antithesis to realism in general. In it, content is always more important than style. Realist film-making claims a relationship that is less with the director and more with the world that exists in front of the camera. The subject is everything.

The Bicycle Thieves is the story of a man who has his bike stolen. An Italian worker during the post-war depression, he gets the chance of work putting up posters on condition that he acquires a bicycle, which he does, but only after his wife has had to sell the sheets from their bed – a wedding present. In Ricci's state of complete poverty, the bicycle assumes absolutely vital status, as the key not only to his survival in employment, but to the very survival of his own dignity, his marriage and his whole family. The optimism and pride of his newly found job (with uniform) after he had redeemed the bike are shattered soon after when it is stolen in the street while he is at work (pasting up an image of Rita Hayworth in *Gilda*). Without his bike, our 'hero' will be unable to support his family. From then on, as an audience, we just tag along with the fruitless search and observe Ricci being slowly broken by the desperation of his plight. When the bike is stolen, he first ignores Bruno's question about it, but soon resorts to lying. His preoccupation so consumes him that he neglects his son, who ends up getting unwelcome attention from a suspect character in a market. By the end, Ricci does not even notice Bruno fall headlong in the rainy muddy road, and is so utterly at a loss that he desperately visits a fortune-teller, whose useless 'visions' he had condemned earlier. The plot is slight, but the film is rich in meaningful detail. If de Sica wants to express his view of the Church's decayed values, he simply leaves a pile of crucifixes strewn on the floor, in the background, as Ricci and Bruno pass by. He rejects dramatic music to heighten moments such as the theft of Ricci's bicycle, and above all he prefers to extract emotion out of simple pathos within action that avoids looking too constructed.

The Bicycle Thieves is uncompromising in its portrayal of poverty. Bruno is seen fighting constantly just to stay clean: cleaning mud from his trousers, beating dust from his father's hat, wiping his face with a handkerchief. Moments of uplift are followed swiftly by a bitter pill: cheerful accordion music turns out to be little children begging. Ricci's treating Bruno to his cheap *mozarrella in carozza* in a restaurant (sitting near a rich, groomed little boy) feels like the last supper, before their crucifixion. de Sica's film noticeably rejects the (Hollywood?) easy way out of blaming 'bad guy' individuals for Ricci's plight. People are sympathetic: the policeman, employment officials and even the man whose bike is stolen by Ricci in his desperate moment of madness. As for Ricci himself, goaded on by his environment (as a distant chanting football crowd seems to urge him on to his attempted theft), we are left in no doubt that his theft is no crime, simply the final humiliation. By then, de Sica's job is almost done, largely without resorting to heavy-handed statement, and all that remains is to show us the other thieves: Ricci and Bruno disappear into a crowd. Music and soundtrack fade as the screen fills with faceless people walking away from the camera, silent and anonymous. There, but for the grace of God, go the other bicycle thieves.

Some Things to Watch out for and Consider

- Does a great film have to be an optimistic film?
- Compare and contrast montage with *mise en scène* in film-making.
- How might Eisenstein have shot *The Bicycle Thieves* and De Sica *Battleship Potemkin*?
- Is it really possible to speak of the 'style of no style'?
- In what ways does Ken Loach's *Kes* (UK, 1969) continue the traditions of neo-realism?
- How completely are you able to suspend disbelief?
- Is the music in *The Bicycle Thieves* really justified within the ideals of neo-realism?
- What connects (and separates) *Dogme* (see chapter 45) from neo-realism?

Further Viewing

Obsession (*Ossessione*) (Visconti, Italy, 1942)
Rome, Open City (Roma, città aperta) (Rossellini, Italy, 1945)
Paisan (Rossellini, Italy, 1946)
Shoeshine (*Sciuscia*) (de Sica, Italy, 1946)
The Leopard (*Il gattopardo*) (Visconti, Italy, 1963)
This Sporting Life (Anderson, UK, Italy, 1962)
Kes (Ken Loach, UK, 1969)
The Postman Always Rings Twice (Rafelson, USA, 1981)
The Idiots (Von Trier, Denmark, 1997)

14 SUNSET BOULEVARD

Wilder, USA, 1950

Awards

Academy Awards: Winner – Best Screenplay; Nomination – Best Picture, Best Actor (William Holden), Best Actress (Gloria Swanson) and Best Director

Production Details

Production company/studio	Paramount
Producer	Charles Brackett
Director	Billy Wilder
Cinematographer	John Seitz
Editor	Doane Harrison
Screenwriters	Charles Wilder and Billy Brackett
Art director	Hana Drier

Cast Includes

William Holden	*Joe Gillis*
Gloria Swanson	*Norma Desmond*
Erich von Stroheim	*Max*
Nancy Olsen	*Betty Schaeffer*
Fred Clarke	*Sheldrake*

With: Cecil B. DeMille, Buster Keaton and Hedda Hopper (as themselves)

FOCUS: Issues of Stardom and Celebrity

Sunset Boulevard is similar to 'Odo the shape-shifter' in *Star Trek: Deep Space Nine*: at first glance, its structure and meaning seem so solid, but, look away for a second, or return to the film at different points in your life, and you discover that what you thought was certain has turned into something else entirely. Is this a movie that exposes the despair beneath the glitter of 'Tinsel Town', or does it merely use Hollywood as a metaphor for deeper questions about human aspirations and needs? Is it big, splashy and romantic, or is it bitterly cynical? For first-time viewers, only one thing can be said for sure: this great Billy Wilder masterpiece is a *film noir*, where all the characters are detectives, trying to solve the mystery of themselves. The rest is up to you, or who you are, or who you think you are.

It must be noted, however, that this book is not copping out and abandoning you to the shadows. In order to guide your thinking and response to this amazingly rich film we have been persuaded to purchase the exclusive rights to some yellowing scraps of paper, which were discovered stuffed down the back seat of Norma's old limousine when the Desmond mansion was demolished in the 1960s. These fragments are believed by experts (i.e. us) to be the only surviving pages of a much longer testament written by Max (Norma's devoted butler), who outlived the silent movie queen by a number of years and who lived on alone in the house, which the faded star bequeathed to him in her will.

Read Max's testament and compare it with your own responses to the film. Specific points to consider are offered at the end.

Max's Testament

... so not too long, I'm afraid, Mr von Mayerling; those were his exact words, and who am I to argue with the medical profession? I must write my final thoughts, here in the cobwebbed kitchen of the house I still think of as yours, Norma, as ours, just as the monkey was ours, our poor chimp-child who was buried on the very day when our nemesis turned his car into our driveway.

Yes, I must write. There are so many fleeting feelings to be captured, and what feelings we had together, you and I. When a life perishes, so does a world ...

... it was Gillis's fault. He was like the prince who enters the tangled forest, discovers the princess and wakens her to new life. I knew as soon as you scanned him with your eyes – and, just then, you were not thinking of that new suit, my dearest – that the sleep we had shared was over. What did he want? If it had only been your money, I would have understood. Yet that New Year's Eve when he ran away and came back – damn him, he was *kind*. Or so you told me. You were always confident that you had him in your power; the flick of a dollar bill, you said, that was all it took. Yet did he hope for something more from you? And what was it you hoped from him?

... I told Gillis, I warned that interloper: 'Madame has her moments of melancholy.' He did not listen, or care; he thought me a mere ghoul. Yet in my own mind I was an emperor. To serve you – you had brushed my face with your hand, who had melted into my camera, who had shown me the face of life at 16 transcendent frames a second, even though you later withdrew your enchantment and propelled me into the outer darkness – to serve you was to know the true intimacy of distance. Later, I was sometimes asked why I, the once great Max von Mayerling, had been prepared to be your lackey. I did not weary myself by telling them the truth: that I was nothing without the idea of you; and you were nothing without someone who remembered how great the idea had been.

Yet that idea: it bound us together, did it not, although we confused the reflected light of stardom with the inner illumination of love. That was our triumph and our doom, my darling: you devoted your energy to gaining, then attempting to regain, that world, not to mastering your heart. I merely wished to realise myself in you at whatever cost to my soul.

... and throughout those long years, before the gunshot rang across the swimming pool (how I would have loved to have squeezed the trigger!), I knew, even if you did not, that we had cast ourselves adrift in a golden boat, with advancing age lapping at our bows. Each day in this house, we grew madder together, yet, when the parasites finally swarmed through the corridors, it was only your madness they released fluttering into the sun. They did not notice me calling out 'Action!' They failed to notice that, in that one word, I was reviving the old, happy balance of our relationship, the balance between the watcher and the watched. I walked down that stairway with you, in spirit at least; I accompanied you in madness, right to the very end.

Oh, I have lived and searched too long. At night I only have the consolation of your face; I imagine that it is my own, that I have never really had another.

Who was Joe Gillis? White knight or gigolo? I saw the young woman on that final night; it was clear she was manipulative and uncertain of her emotions. He was bluffing when he considered running away with her; he was bluffing when he walked away from the house towards the pool. He would have turned right round, then or later on the road; at heart, he distrusted happiness. He was afraid of it: we all were – him, me, you, the girl – because, at heart, we hated ourselves.

Life, I have heard, can be strangely merciful. Yet tell me now, I must know now: did any of us all those years ago deserve mercy?

. . . we started out big, and we just got smaller and smaller . . .

Some Things to Watch out for and Consider

- Consider the themes and issues surrounding relationships and the characters' image of themselves. In particular, ask yourself:
  - Do you agree with Max's view of his relationship with Norma? How are stardom and love connected in this film?
  - Max in his testament is unclear about what Joe wanted. What do you think he did want? Did he get it?
  - How does the power game between Joe and Norma operate in this film? Max made a comment on this. Judging from the evidence of the film, is he right?
  - By the end of the story, how have the characters changed, and what inner journey have they completed?
  - Is Max correct when he says all the characters hate themselves?
  - Do you agree with the last line of Max's analysis?

Further Viewing

Queen Kelly (Von Stroheim, USA, 1929)
A Star is Born (Wellman, USA, 1937)
The Bad and the Beautiful (Minnelli, USA, 1952)
A Star is Born (Cukor, USA, 1954)
Fedora (Wilder, France/West Germany, 1978)

Further Reading

T. Curtiss, *Von Stroheim* (London, 1971)
G. Swanson, *Swanson on Swanson* (London, 1980)
A. Walker, *Stardom* (London, 1970)
M. Zolotow, *Billy Wilder in Hollywood* (London, 1977)

15 SINGIN' IN THE RAIN

Kelly and Donen, USA, 1952

Awards

Academy Awards: Nomination – Best Supporting Actress (Jean Hagen) and Best Score

Production Details

Production company/studio	MGM
Producer	Arthur Freed
Directors	Gene Kelly and Stanley Donen
Cinematographer	Harold Rosson
Editor	Adrienne Fazan
Music	Herb Brown

Cast Includes

Gene Kelly	*Dan Lockwood*
Donald O'Connor	*Cosmo Brown*
Debbie Reynolds	*Kathy Seldon*
Jean Hagen	*Lina Lamont*
Millard Mitchell	*R.F.*
Rita Moreno	*Zelda Zanders*

FOCUS: Genre

On the face of it, *Singin' in the Rain*, like the genre of which it is one of the outstanding examples, is daft beyond words. The absurdities are worthy of Lewis Carroll's *Alice through the Looking Glass*: orchestras coming out of nowhere, as if the Los Angeles

Philharmonic had been hanging round a street corner just waiting for Gene Kelly or Debbie Reynolds; sappy boy and girl romances strung together by songs that warble of lucky stars and smiles on the face; in fact, it is not going too far to say that the world can be divided into two distinct camps: those who think the musical is one of the great art forms of popular American cinema, and those who think that, at best, it is harmless entertainment and, at worst, an insult to the intelligence.

To a certain extent, the party-poopers are right: judged by the naturalistic conventions of, say, a television soap opera, musicals are trivial and ridiculous. The question, though, is whether that ridiculousness is a sign of defective vision, or whether it is a consequence of a different, but equally valid, way of seeing, like X-ray vision, for example. Keep that thought in mind as you watch this film, for it is interested not in everyday reality as such, but in heightened reality, in feeling rather than fact; it aims to lift us out of the Here and Now and up into the clouds of Otherwhere, a land of miraculous transformations within both individuals and their relationships.

To see this Cinderella principle in action, take a closer look at the famous 'Singin' in the Rain' sequence itself.

As a unit of meaning, the true beginning of this scene occurs a minute or so before the dance, in the everyday, intimate farewell of a man and a woman (Gene and Debbie), who kiss goodnight and realise as they do so that the love bells are ringing. After the two have parted, the man walks down the ordinary street in an ordinary suit and goes 'dum-de-dum-dum' to himself in an ordinary way. So far, so naturalistic.

Then there is the big moment, the X-ray beam. In musicals, transitions in sound are as significant as transitions in vision – a device that the radio-trained Orson Welles used to different, but equally eloquent, effect in *Citizen Kane* (see chapter 10). Here, the orchestra bursts into full life, acting like an aural rather than a visual dissolve, creating a transition, not between two different pictures, but between two different worlds. Once the big number is in full swing, then, Gene should be seen as existing in the musical Other Street, a magical place where his emotions take on physical and vocal life, and even awnings, rain troughs and people synchronise themselves to his own rhythm and emotional pitch. As you enjoy this great piece of Hollywood movie-making, think about the music and movement being meanings in themselves, both indicating that our hero has discovered the full wonder of his love.

In time, the song ends and the appearance of the policeman signals the drift down to traditional reality. Notice, however, that back in the mundane world Kelly gives his umbrella to a passer-by. This is significant in general structural terms: the gesture indicates that, though the miraculous moment is over, something of the miracle lives on inside Gene, in his awakened lover's heart that is impervious to the rain. In other words, the solitary life has been transformed, and this knowledge carries the character, and us, through the remainder of the story. The musical sequence, then, like so many of its sisters and brothers in this genre, is not a corny or 'harmless' bit of showbiz bunged into the plot to give it a boost; it is part of a carefully conceived narrative strategy, developing character and deepening meaning, though not according to the by-laws as laid down by our television-jaded expectations.

It has to be said that this convention (which can also reveal emotion between two potential lovers – see 'You Are my Lucky Star' on the empty studio floor) requires a readjusting of the sensibilities that some viewers are reluctant to make. Still, this is the price of admission to the magic of *Singin' in the Rain*. If you feel the ticket is a bit on the dear side, then think about your own life.

Reflect on Gene Kelly strutting his stuff in that downpour. You are unlikely to follow his example and go scouring the streets for a rain trough to leap into, but you may find that the experience has an 'I-want-to-leap-into-a-rain-trough-I'm-so-happy' kind of feeling to it. That is the central narrative intent of the musical genre: to take our most dreamlike inner states and give them outward form in song and dance and expressions of perfect joy. You probably know from experience that any kind of joy can look as daft as a brush from the outside.

Some Things to Watch out for and Consider

- Think about transformations:
  - In the 'Good Morning, Good Morning' sequence, how does the magic of the musicals transform the objects in Gene Kelly's house?
  - In the same sequence, what is the significance of the rain and how does it have an impact on the meaning of the 'Singin' in the Rain' number itself?
  - What is the nature of the transformation in the movie-within-a-movie towards the end of the film?

- Think about characters and values:
  - What is the major obstacle to Gene and Debbie getting it together?
  - How does the film depict gender roles?
  - How does Jean Hagen, who plays Gene's dreadful movie partner, help to define the Kelly–Reynolds relationship?
- Try writing an outline story for *The Dancing Cavalier*, based on evidence from the film.
- Watch the 'Moses Supposes' sequence with the diction coach and write a non-musical scene that would have exactly the same meaning and role within the story's structure.

Further Viewing

On the Town (Kelly and Donen, USA, 1949)
Take Me Out to the Ball Game (Berkeley, USA, 1949)
An American in Paris (Minnelli, USA, 1951)
The Band Wagon (Minnelli, USA, 1953)
Funny Face (Donen, USA, 1957)

Further Reading

J. Kobal, *Gotta Sing, Gotta Dance* (Feltham, 1970)
V. Minnelli (with Hector Arce), *I Remember it Well* (Garden City, NY, 1974)
S. Morley, *Gene Kelly* (London, 1999)

16 *REAR WINDOW*

Hitchcock, USA, 1954

Awards

Academy Awards: Nomination – Best Director, Best Screenplay and Best Cinematography

Production Details

Production company/studio	Paramount
Producer	Alfred Hitchcock
Director	Alfred Hitchcock
Cinematographer	Robert Burks
Editor	George Tomasini
Screenwriter	John Michael Hayes

Cast Includes

James Stewart	*'Jeff' Jeffries*
Grace Kelly	*Lisa Fremont*
Wendell Corey	*Detective Doyle*
Thelma Ritter	*Stella*
Raymond Burr	*Lars Thorwald*

FOCUS: Film Production and Consumption

Rear Window is not Alfred Hitchcock's solid gold masterpiece; that honour belongs to *Vertigo* (see chapter 19). It is, however, his gold-plated masterpiece, an unsettling insight into the very nature of movie viewing itself. 'Hitch' is interested in why we watch, in the feelings and moral assumptions that inform the act,

Rear Window. Paramount (courtesy Kobal)

and also in the language of film, its limitations and processes. As you watch this remarkable thriller, be aware of how its techniques are channelling your reactions, encouraging you to become an observer of your own observing. Hitchcock is like Jiminy Cricket in *Pinocchio* – your own mini-conscience whispering about the complexities that surround the relationship between the seer and the seen.

All the difficult questions are embodied in the troubled psyche of the film's main character. 'Jeff' (James Stewart) is physically and symbolically marooned, a man whose plaster cast prevents him from leaving his wheelchair and his room, and whose anxieties about Lisa (Grace Kelly) are blocking the development of their relationship. The main issue is the impact he suspects her fashion-plate femininity may have on his roustabout lad's life; he fears being trapped by the grace of Grace, yet at the same time he is strongly attracted to her. This 'Gordian knot' is only one aspect of the film's complex attitude towards women and is worthy of an analysis in its own right. What matters here, though, is that Jeff is haunted by conflicting emotions, and the characters he observes from his rear window are like ghosts wandering in the landscape of his inner dilemma.

'Miss Lonely-Hearts', for instance, hints at his fear of isolation; the composer and his unfinished song dramatise a possible spiritual sterility. Above all, Thorwald (Raymond Burr), the man who may have murdered his invalid wife, is a shadow-Jeff, caught in the kind of emotional prison that our protagonist/ photographer most dreads; the salesman displays reactions that mirror what the photographer's own might be. Viewed in this light, Jeff's determination to establish his neighbour's guilt can be seen as an attempt to purge himself of the fearful, even aggressive, feelings he harbours towards the young woman. To hunt down Thorwald is somehow to hunt down, and hence to absolve, himself.

Motives for watching, then, are contaminated in this movie, and by implication so are ours. The world through the window is like a film, a collection of fragmented sights, sounds and gestures; the only elements binding them together are our own moral perception and instinct for meaning, both of which can be questionable, to say the least. In Jeff's case, he reads his 'film' as a clear case of murder because he wants to see a brutal crime. His act of watching is an act of self-projection, of looking falsely outward rather than truly inward.

To complicate matters further, the nature of Jeff's visual evidence is unreliable, as the director's camera continually reminds us. Throughout this film, Hitchcock denies us the full scope of cinema, particularly its magic-carpet ability to traverse time and space and present multiple points of view. Instead, he chains us firmly to Jeff's wheelchair and to his restricted field of vision, making us aware that movie language, like any language, has its limits and is also susceptible to the constructions human beings place upon it. The camera lies, because people want it to support their lies. A 'peeping Tom', as the sneakiness of the name suggests, is a form of moral criminal.

Rear Window is such a gripping movie because it continually tests us with these issues of truth, appearance and participation. Unfortunately, when it enters the area of crime, the chrome starts to peep through the gold plate. Although Jeff's dramatic confrontation with Thorwald clearly demonstrates the murderer's vulnerability and the photographer's qualification for the Nasty Neighbour of the Year Award, the salesman is still established as a genuine murderer; his guilt guides the story into a relatively safe harbour where some of the deeper waters are avoided. By contrast, if he had turned out to be innocent, and Jeff and Co. had been left culpable among the ruins, then the film would have been nastier; it would have shown more strongly how wrong seeing is an aspect of wrong being and how both can actively lead to wrongdoing.

Still, these criticisms are a matter of personal judgement: watch, thrill and make up your own mind. *Rear Window* is indisputably a key text; it maps out a central movie territory that directors are frequently keen to explore. Long before the closing credits have rolled, your personal Jiminy Cricket is crooning a revised version of his famous song from *Pinocchio* (Luske and Sharpsteen, USA, 1940): 'When you get in trouble and you don't know right from wrong – spy on someone.'

Some Things to Watch out for and Consider

- Think about the representation of women in this film. Ask yourself:
  - In the sequence that introduces Grace Kelly, how do we know there is something threatening in her beauty?
  - What are the images and motifs that tell us there is a fundamental incompatibility between Jeff and Lisa?
  - How do the roles of 'Miss Torso' and 'Miss Lonely-Hearts' contribute to this film's construction of women?
- Think about the camera's point of view. Ask yourself:
  - What specific device does Hitchcock use to tie our interpretation of events to that of the wheelchair-bound protagonist?
  - What is the significance of the sequence in which the audience sees an event that Jeff misses because he is asleep?
  - When does the camera break away from Jeff's point of view and why is this significant?
- Try:
  - Writing Thorwald's statement to the police, revealing the events that led up to the murder of his wife.
  - Telling the story from the point of view of the policeman, played by Wendell Corey (as Hitchcock could well have done).

Further Viewing

Vertigo (Hitchcock, USA, 1958)
Peeping Tom (Powell, UK, 1960)
The Conversation (Coppola, USA, 1974)
Sliver (Noyce, USA, 1993)

Further Reading

J. Belton (ed.), *Alfred Hitchcock's Rear Window* (Cambridge, 2000)

T. Modleski, *The Women who Knew Too Much: Hitchcock and Feminist Theory* (London, 1988)

R. Wood, *Hitchcock's Films* (London, 1969)

17 THE SEVEN SAMURAI

(Shichinin no samurai)

Kurosawa, Japan, 1954

Awards

Academy Awards: Nomination – Best Art Direction, Set Decoration and Best Costume Design (B/W)
British Academy Awards: Nomination – Best Film from any Source and Best Foreign Actor (Toshirô Mifune)
Venice Film Festival: Winner – Silver Lion

Production Details

Production company/studio	Toho
Producer	Sojiro Motoki
Director	Akira Kurosawa
Cinematographer	Asakazu Nakai
Editor	Akira Kurosawa
Screenwriters	Shinobu Hashimoto, Akira Kurosawa and Hideo Oguni
Music	Fumio Hayasaka

Cast Includes

Toshirô Mifune	*Kikuchiyo*
Takashi Shimura	*Kambei Shimada*
Yoshio Inaba	*Gorobei Katayama*
Seiji Miyaguchi	*Kyuzo*
Minoru Chiaki	*Heihachi Hayashida*
Daisuke Katô	*Shichiroji*
Isao Kimura	*Katsushiro*
Kamatari Fujiwara	*Manzo, Father of Shino*

Kokuten Kodo	*Gisaku, the Old Man*
Bokuzen Hidari	*Yohei*
Yoshio Kosugi	*Mosuke*
Yoshio Tsuchiya	*Rikichi*
Keiji Sakakida	*Gasaku*

FOCUS: The Auteur and International Art Cinema

Akira Kurosawa was born 3 March 1910 in Tokyo, Japan, and died 6 September 1998 in Tokyo. *The Seven Samurai* was made at the height of the great director's creative powers. It is impressive, influential and an example of film as both high art and popular entertainment.

After training as a painter, Kurosawa became engaged in cinema as a way of portraying movement. He began directing with *Horse* (*Uma*, Japan, 1941) and got his first director credit with *Judo Saga* (*Sugata sanshiro*, Japan, 1943). He had spent five years learning his craft since a third assistant job on *Tokyo Rhapsody* (*Fushimizu*, Japan, 1936).

As well as directing, Kurosawa had produced most of his films since *Throne of Blood* (*Kumonosu jo*, Japan, 1957), edited many of them and wrote (or co-wrote) almost all of the scripts. Kurosawa's directorial reputation is based on a decade of outstanding creativity, which produced a series of masterpieces. His golden age began with *Scandal* (*Shubun*, Japan, 1950) and *Rashomon* (Japan, 1950). *Rashomon* was the director's breakthrough film in international terms, as it won the top prize at the Venice Film Festival. The film was also a breakthrough for Japanese cinema, being the first Japanese film seen widely in Europe.

The Seven Samurai followed in 1954 and *Throne of Blood* – Kurosawa's reading of Macbeth – in 1957. *Donzoko* (Japan, 1957) was released in the West as *The Lower Depths* in 1962. *Kakushi toride no san akunin* (Japan, 1958) was released in the USA in 1962 as *The Hidden Fortress* (and has latterly gained a reputation as the model for *Star Wars* (Lucas, USA, 1977) (see chapter 28). *The Bad Sleep Well* (*Warui yatsu hodo yoku nemuru*, Japan, 1960) was followed by two more Samurai films, *Yojimbo* (Japan, 1961) and *Sanjuro* (Japan, 1962).

Kurosawa experienced ill health, critical misunderstanding at home and a lack of attention abroad during a lean period in the

1960s and early 1970s. He returned to form with a Russian co-production *Dersu Uzala* (1974). With the support of admirers Francis Ford Coppola and George Lucas, he returned to a favourite genre to make the Samurai epic *Kagemusha* (Japan, 1980) and followed up with the richer and even more visually sumptuous *Ran* (Japan, 1985).

Kurosawa the film-maker is worthy of a place in our pantheon via his influence. Kurosawa's later films were certainly more popular in the West than at home. In Japan, critics have viewed his repeated dalliances with Western genres (including the Western) and authors such as Shakespeare and Dostoyevsky with some suspicion. Nonetheless, Kurosawa remains a revered artist by American and European film-makers – as evidenced by the remakes of e.g. *The Seven Samurai* itself as *The Magnificent Seven* (Sturges, USA, 1960), *Yojimbo* as *A Fistful of Dollars* (*Per un pugno di dollari*, Leone, Italy/Spain/West Germany, 1964) and *Last Man Standing* (Hill, USA, 1996) and – possibly – *Kakushi toride no san akunin* as *Star Wars* (1977) (not least for the wholesale borrowing of 'the wipe' as an editing technique).

Kurosawa has a strong claim to auteur status via a discernible 'authorial voice' (acclaim supported by his role as producer and through his writing credits). The director shaped the narrative (more often than not taken from 'art' literary sources) to highlight his concerns. His recurrent themes include fate as a driving force as well as nobility, dignity and personal honour (in Kurosawa the focus is on the personal – codes of honour may be broken as and when a character has to do so to remain true to themselves or because of force of circumstance).

There is also a visual signature. The *mise en scène* is often that of the feudal Japanese setting. The actor Toshirô Mifune (a leading player in *The Seven Samurai*) became Kurosawa's icon. Kurosawa's cinematography is characterised by extremely high contrast black and white photography and the use of highly mobile camerawork via tracking and panning.

The director also acted as his own editor and Kurosawa's films frequently employ stylised editing techniques, including jarring changes of pace, long shots (usually of crowds) cut directly to extreme close-ups and in particular the frequent use of 'the wipe' (one image pushing the previous one from the screen space) to fade from one scene to another.

The Seven Samurai is a quintessentially simple tale. A veteran samurai, who has fallen on hard times, answers a village's request for help. He seeks out samurai to help him. A desperate bunch of characters, they learn about themselves and each other as they teach the peasants how to defend themselves. The film culminates in a giant battle when 40 bandits attack the village. Nonetheless, the film lasts over three hours and has a reputation as one of the greatest films ever made. The reason for both points is simple. There is a real sense of depth in Kurosawa's masterpiece. The fight scenes are important and exciting (Kurosawa is a magnificent choreographer of action), but their power comes from our privileged position of having got to know the characters and their motivations.

As with *Citizen Kane* (Welles, USA, 1941) (see chapter 10), technique and craft are utilised to tell a compelling story and explore interesting characters. *The Seven Samurai* is proof that film is a great humanist art form – and also first-class entertainment.

Some Things to Watch out for and Consider

The material for the film, like many of Kurosawa's, is historical. It is set in a particular place: Japan, at a particular time: the sixteenth century. This was a period when a rigid social system was coming under increasing strain after decades of civil war. The peasants in the film break with tradition (a) by refusing to accept their lot and (b) by approaching the Samurai. The Samurai are of a particular kind – *ronin* (masterless) – who behave in often very un-samurai ways (including working for peasants). Kurosawa was from Samurai stock and obviously attracted to *bushido* (the way of the warrior). When watching the film, we must consider how movies portray and mythologise historical events and periods. After all, this film was influenced by, and greatly influenced, a *lot* of Westerns.

This film is also – obviously – Japanese. What is it trying to tell us about Japan? How does a Western audience read its messages? Remember, when *The Seven Samurai* (a film about a warrior's code of honour) was released, the Second World War was very recent history. A recent book on Kurosawa (by Mitsuhiro Yoshimoto) suggests that Kurosawa's films arouse anxiety because they foreground and explore Japan's self-image and the West's image of Japan.

On a more cinema-specific level, notice the combination and juxtaposition of energy and gracefulness (watch how Kurosawa employs the sudden change of pace from rapid movement to absolute stillness or vice versa). Consider how pictures are used to tell the story.

Notice the contribution made by the austere musical score (by Fumio Hayasaka) and by the soundtrack in general.

Look out for Kurosawa's use of *all* the elements and thrill to that final battle scene that every Hollywood great wants to better – but never quite does.

In what ways does this Japanese film differ from the American and European films that have been influenced (or copied) it?

How different does the Hollywood version of *The Seven Samurai* look? Would it be possible to make a 'neo-realist' Samurai movie (see *The Bicycle Thieves*, chapter 13)?

Further Viewing

Rashoman (Kurosawa, Japan, 1950)
The Hidden Fortress (Kurosawa, Japan, 1958)
Yojimbo (Kurosawa, Japan, 1962)
Tokyo Story (Ozu, Japan, 1953)
Citizen Kane (Welles, USA, 1942)
Eight and a Half (Fellini, Italy, 1965)
The Magnificent Seven (John Sturges, USA, 1960)
Once upon a Time in the West (Leone, Italy, 1968)
Star Wars (Lucas, USA, 1977)
The Killer (John Woo, HK, 1989)

Further Reading

M. Yoshimoto, *Kurosawa: Film Studies and Japanese Cinema* (New York, 2000)

18 THE SEARCHERS

Ford, USA, 1956

Production Details

Production company/studio	Warner Brothers
Producer	Merian C. Cooper
Director	John Ford
Cinematographer	Winton C. Hoch
Editor	Jack Murphy
Screenwriter	Frank S. Nugent from a novel by Alan Le May
Music	Max Steiner

Cast Includes

John Wayne	*Ethan Edwards*
Jeffrey Hunter	*Martin Pawley*
Vera Miles	*Laurie Jorgenson*
Ward Bond	*Samuel Clayton*
Natalie Wood	*Debbie Edwards*
Henry Brandon	*Scar*

FOCUS: Genre and Narrative

The Searchers presents us with the apex of John Ford's career; he went on to make many more films but none so dark, mature and provocative as this. As well as occupying an important point in Ford's career, the film also represents an interesting turning point for the Western genre, moving it away from the classic perfection of *Stagecoach* (Ford, USA, 1939) (see chapter 9) to much darker more ambiguous territory. Perhaps the most significant feature of this film now is the extent of its influence on contemporary directors through which it has earned its place in cinema history. We can find references to *The Searchers* in films as diverse as *Taxi Driver* (Scorsese, USA, 1976) (see chapter 26), *Star Wars* (Lucas, USA, 1977) (see chapter 28), *Crouching Tiger, Hidden Dragon* (Lee, USA, 2000) and even Disney's *The Lion King* (Allers, USA, 1994), which, like *The Searchers*, has a villain called Scar and concerns itself with the hero's alienation from his society. In viewing this film, then, we need to ask ourselves what is it about this 1950s Western that has had such a profound impact on some of the best and most success-ful directors of our time.

The narrative of *The Searchers* conforms in many respects to the conventions of both the Western and the classic Hollywood narrative. Although made in 1956 and therefore post-Paramount Decision and the break-up of 'the studio system', *The Searchers* was made by a team used to working within that system. In common with many Westerns, including John Ford's own *Stagecoach*, the narrative is structured around a staple device of the genre – the hero's quest for revenge. Ethan Edwards, the hero of *The Searchers*, like the Ringo Kid in *Stagecoach* (and a host of other Western heroes), seeks to avenge the deaths of members of his family. It is the way in which this revenge quest is presented that makes the films so strikingly different and *The Searchers* so disturbingly dark and ambiguous. In *Stagecoach* the film starts after the deaths of Ringo's father and brother. We do not see them being killed. The fact of their murder simply serves to highlight and explain Ringo's code of honour. As a Western hero, he must take the law into his own hands and seek justice for his family. The sympathetic way in which the other charac-ters respond to Ringo and the many positive qualities he exhibits encourage the audience to view his pursuit of revenge in clear moral terms; we are on his side. In contrast to this, Ethan's character and situation in *The Searchers* present us with a more complex and ambiguous situation, where it becomes difficult to take sides – both hero and villain in this film are presented to us in morally ambiguous terms. Both are capable of atrocities, racism and obsessive hatred and yet both are given motivation (the murder of their loved ones) that helps us to understand, if not condone, their actions. The very existence of such obvious parallels between hero and villain blurs the boundaries, making it difficult to decide who belongs in which category – in essence these men are the same.

The opening and closing scenes of the film indicate with classic

Hollywood economy of storytelling the problematic nature and status of Ethan's character. The film starts with the camera positioned inside a homestead. The doorway frames the wild landscape and the central figure is a mother. These images site the audience within the family, which is representative of white civilisation, vulnerable and isolated in the vast landscape of the wilderness. The camera moves us out of the house and into the wilderness and we have our first sight of the hero. His arrival brings uncertainty and discord to the family unit, whose reactions to him indicate a deep sense of unease. Thus, although he is the hero of the film, he is also the initial source of disequilibrium and disruption. Ethan's character is problematic in that he does not seem to belong either in the domestic, civilised world of the homestead or in the wilderness from which he first comes (and finally returns to), although it is here that he displays the competence and skill that identify him as the hero. His pursuit of revenge is motivated by the desire to venerate and protect the civilised world of the white settler, but the enactment of this revenge appears to taint and poison his character to the point where he can no longer fit into the very world he has tried to protect.

Ethan is driven by a racial hatred so dark and obsessive that his rescue mission becomes a murder quest. He is driven by the desire to kill Debbie because she has been tainted by the Indians. It is only at the last moment that he is able to overcome the inner demons tormenting him. As he lifts Debbie up in his arms (a graphic scene echoing the earlier one that occurred when she was still a child), his love for her overcomes his obsession and he is able to take her home. The final scenes of the film poignantly encapsulate the conflicts expressed within Ethan's character and the film as a whole. Ethan's inability to belong to the civilised family group that he has struggled so hard to restore is expressed in a single shot. In an echo of the opening images of the film, we again see him doubly framed at the centre of the screen and through the door of the homestead. He hovers awkwardly for a moment and then turns and walks away from the family group, once more outside in the wilderness, a lonely figure who does not seem to belong anywhere. Is this closure in the tradition of the classic Hollywood narrative? Order is certainly restored and the central driving quest of the narrative is over and yet the hero is poised awkwardly and left to an uncertain future.

In the darkly ambiguous character of Ethan, Ford pushes the

boundaries of the genre, creating a protagonist who is both savage and tender, monstrous and murderous, but also vulnerable, isolated and tormented. We recoil from, and sympathise with, Ethan, by turns – possibly an uncomfortable experience for viewers expecting staple genre fare, but one indicative of Ford's (auteurist?) ability to work within the construct of generic and classic narrative conventions whilst simultaneously creating something unique, disturbing and profound.

Some Things to Watch out for and Consider

- What cinematic techniques does Ford employ to introduce Ethan's character?
- What is the nature of the relationship between Ethan and Martha (his sister-in-law)? How are their feelings conveyed?
- How is Ethan's status as hero constructed?
- Do you feel comfortable with Ethan's beliefs and attitudes? Why / why not?
- Do you sympathise with Ethan? Why / why not? Does this change over the course of the film?
- Compare *The Searchers* to an earlier and a later Western – e.g. *Stagecoach* and *Dances with Wolves* (Costner, USA, 1990). Consider the similarities and / or differences in the way these films represent the hero, the role of women, white Americans, non-white Americans. What do your results tell you about the development of the genre? Each film's relationship with the time in which it was made? The Western as a reflection of America?
- Compare *The Searchers* to *Taxi Driver* (directed and written by huge admirers of the earlier film). What similarities / differences can you find in themes and characterisation?

Further Viewing

Stagecoach (Ford, USA, 1939)
The Man who Shot Liberty Valance (Ford, USA, 1962)
Dances with Wolves (Costner, USA, 1990)
Unforgiven (Eastwood, USA, 1992)
Taxi Driver (Scorsese, USA, 1976)

Further Reading

E. Buscombe, *Back in the Saddle Again* (London, 1998)
A. Tudor (ed.), *The Genre Reader* (London, 1990)
A. Tudor (ed.), *The Genre Reader II* (London, 1997)

19 *VERTIGO*
Hitchcock, USA, 1958

Awards

Academy Awards: Nomination – Best Art Direction and Best Sound

Production Details

Production company/studio	Paramount
Producer	Alfred Hitchcock
Director	Alfred Hitchcock
Cinematographer	Robert Burke
Editor	George Tomasin
Screenwriter	Alec Coppel (from a novel by Pierre Boileau and Thomas Narcejac)
Music	Bernard Hermann
Art director	Hal Pereira

Cast Includes

James Stewart	*John 'Scottie' Fergusson*
Kim Novak	*Madeline/Judy*
Barbara Bel Geddes	*Midge*
Tom Helmore	*Gavin Elster*

FOCUS: Auteur

Alfred Hitchcock is well known as the 'Master of Suspense'; he is also well known for being fat, and, as that great, if rotund, literary critic Cyril Connolly once wrote: 'Imprisoned in every fat man a thin one is wildly signalling to be let out.' The fat/thin struggle is a symbolic dichotomy in many Hitchcock movies. For example, in *North by Northwest* (USA, 1959), he speaks to us as our chubby Uncle Alfred, offering up outlandish situations and dazzling narrative twists, all at the service of a story that is (as told to Truffaut and Bogdanovich) 'just a game in the end, my dear children, just a jolly wizard wheeze'. Meanwhile, a more haunted figure, 'Thin Alf', is signalling from the story's inner core: 'Don't listen! He's obscuring the truth! There are darker shadows here than the old butterball cares to admit! Let me out!' Viewed in these terms, *Vertigo* is Hitchcock's great 'skinny-flick'; for once, he unbuttons his cardigan and gives 'Thin Alf' total freedom. It is arguably the director's only solid gold masterpiece because it goes all the way, right to the heart of darkness, into the centre of some very unsettling things indeed.

The movie is concerned with, and gripped by, obsession: love obsession, control obsession, white-knight-to-the-rescue obsession, obsession obsession. In modern jargon, James Stewart's character 'Scottie' is a 'love addict' – that is, he cannot conceive of a relationship as a mature matter between equals, but only as a game of power and pursuit revolving ultimately round himself. He is an empty soul, and this film possesses some of the paranoid chase qualities that mark much of Hitchcock's best work: *The Thirty-Nine Steps* (UK, 1935), both versions of *The Man who Knew Too Much* (UK, 1934; USA, 1956), even the wheelchair-bound *Rear Window* (USA, 1954) (see chapter 16). The 'vertigo' of the title is not just a nifty plot device, but an emblem of deep and debilitating fears. Intimacy and tenderness, along with all their emotional and sexual connotations, are the true villains crouching at the centre of this narrative maze, so much so that Scottie never dares enter its heart; instead, he pursues the nothingness inside himself and ends up as dead in his own way as poor Madeline (Kim Novak).

At the core of this film, too, is an unsettling failure to grasp the nature of love itself. No one here – not Scottie, Madeline, or the lovelorn Midge (Barbara Bel Geddes) – can quite work out what it means to live freely and healthily with others. Notice how the camera makes the characters seem so alone in their sterile rooms, how the microphone captures them muttering in flat tones, as though to speak openly were to set off a trail of emotional dynamite. This must be one of the most erotic films ever produced by Fifties Hollywood, yet the sexuality seems to be squeezed out under a terrible pressure. Moreover, once these passions are exposed, the experience is not one of release, but of pain. The viewer senses that everyone would be happier if they could be turned into stone.

At least stone does not feel. Despite the technical showmanship and surface bravado that tells us only Alfred Hitchcock could be in the director's chair, this movie is grappling with a horror more chilling than Norman Bates wandering around at the motel in *Psycho* (see chapter 24); it is the horror of having to live and love at all.

For example, pay attention, particularly in the early sections of the film, to the electric charge generated by the act of embracing (Bel Geddes and Stewart in their first scene), or of touching (Stewart and Novak, when he has hauled her from the Bay and taken her back to his flat). These are not the usual 'steamy' moments so loved by Hitch's many imitators (including even De Palma); they are the revelation of the nitroglycerine that is constantly being jarred in this story, of the experience the characters most want, hate and fear. No wonder, then, that they are haunted by ghosts; they are really dead themselves, or, at least, yearning for death. By the time we get to the final act, when Stewart tries to remake Judy / Madeleine, humanity itself seems to have been swallowed up; in the tower, the man has fossilised into hatred and the woman has disappeared inside the negative identity of 'The Love Object that Never Was.' The film's almost hysterical power is rooted in the depth of its despair.

Claustrophobia, discreet fetishism, coiled misery: the elements in this movie cast disturbing shadows. Watch and shudder, then, but, as you do, consider how Hitchcock's trademark techniques contribute to the impact of the story: the way in which we are often shown a character's reaction before we see what he or she is reacting to; the showy trick shots that make this narrative of the interior even more inward looking and tense; the camera's fascination with the emptiness of streets and open spaces, as though they were deserted arenas just waiting to be occupied by our own anxieties. 'Listen,' whispers Thin Alf, 'is this really all there is? Why bother to live at all? Children, my dear children, how do we find a way out of this hell?'

Some Things to Watch out for and Consider

- Think about Hitchcock's use of the camera. Ask yourself:
  - In the early scene in the restaurant, when Scottie first sees Madeline, how does the camera link them together?
  - How does the green lighting in Judy's hotel room convey meanings about her relationship with Scottie?

- In the scene where Scottie follows Madeline to the grave of Carlotta, how do editing and shot selection build up a sense of tension and mystery?
- Think about metaphors and meanings. Ask yourself:
  - What is the significance of the film's frequent references to 'Old' San Francisco?
  - What is the significance of the tree rings?
  - What is the significance of Scottie's relationship with Midge?

Further Viewing

The Man who Knew Too Much (Hitchcock, UK, 1934)
The Thirty-Nine Steps (Hitchcock, UK, 1935)
Rear Window (Hitchcock, USA, 1954)
The Man who Knew Too Much (Hitchcock, USA, 1956)
Psycho (Hitchcock, USA, 1960)
High Anxiety (Brooks, USA, 1977)
Dressed to Kill (De Palma, USA, 1980)

Further Reading

S. Gottlieb (ed.), *Hitchcock on Hitchcock* (London, 1995)
D. Spoto, *The Dark Side of Genius: The Life of Alfred Hitchcock* (London, 1994)
F. Truffaut, *Hitchcock* (London, 1968)

20 THE 400 BLOWS
(Les Quatre Cent Coups)
Truffaut, France, 1959

Awards

Academy Awards: Nomination – Best Original Story and Screenplay
Cannes – Winner: Golden Palm

Production Details

Production company/studio	Carosse
Producer	François Truffaut
Director	François Truffaut
Cinematographer	Henri Decas
Editor	Marie-Josephine Yoyotte
Screenwriters	François Truffaut and Marcel Moussy (from a story by Truffaut)
Production designer	Bernard Evein

Cast Includes

Jean-Pierre Leaud	*Antoine Doinel*
Claire Maurier	*Madame Doinel*
Albert Rémy	*Monsieur Doinel*
Guy Decombie	*The Teacher*
Patrick Auffay	*Rene Bigley*

FOCUS: The Politics of Authorship

Along with Jean-Luc Godard (with whom he collaborated on a number of projects, most notably as screenwriter for *A bout de souffle*, see chapter 21), François Truffaut is the best known and most influential of the French 'New Wave' directors. In an industry that has inspired many devoted practitioners, Truffaut's relationship with the cinema was obsessive. Both his wife and daughter have testified that Truffaut lived, ate and breathed cinema. Later in his career he admitted that his obsession with the movies was probably not healthy and certainly not one that he could, or would, change.

His appearance in Steven Spielberg's *Close Encounters of the Third Kind* (USA, 1977) illustrates the way in which Truffaut was both fêted by, and enamoured of, American cinema. Which other radical French director would turn up in an American blockbuster? Certainly not Godard. For Truffaut, cinema was, quite simply, life. Unlike Godard, he was not really interested in experimentation for its own sake. What appealed to him was creating strong narratives out of the material of his own life. Thus five of his best films feature a character called Antoine Doinel (a thinly disguised version of Truffaut). *Les Quatre Cent Coups* is the first and arguably the best of these. What makes it an outstanding piece of film-making is Truffaut's masterly ability to convey emotion. *Les Quatre Cent Coups* is absorbing, funny and painful at the same time – but above all it is emotionally convincing. This is a portrait of early adolescence that captures the angst and trauma of family conflict with a rawness of feeling that both shocks and captivates the viewer.

Truffaut's relationship with cinema started when he was a boy. Like Antoine Doinel, the central character of *Les Quatre Cent Coups*, Truffaut slept in the hall of his parents' cramped Paris flat and was expelled from a series of schools. He has said of his life that to compensate for being unwanted at home he made cinema his family. Living in Pigalle (a bohemian area near the centre of Paris) during and after the war, he was certainly well placed to do so. From 1946 France was increasingly flooded with 'American cinema'. The vast back-catalogue of studio production was being exported to France in 1946 and 1947. The Boulevard du Fichu, near where Truffaut lived, had 25 cinemas in it. Every week there were 25 new films to see – many of which were Hollywood products. Thus, as a teenager, Truffaut was saturated in American cinema (which he evidently liked much more than the French product).

As his tastes developed, he sought out films by the likes of Hawks, Ford and, most of all, Hitchcock. These epitomes of craftsmanship were to have a profound effect initially on his opinions about cinema and finally on his work as a film-maker.

Truffaut's initial impact was as a writer, most memorably in his January 1954 article for *Cahiers du cinéma*, 'A Certain Tendency in French Cinema', in which he attacks the 'Tradition of Quality' in French cinema and sets out the basis for what became 'auteur theory' (*politiques des auteurs*). In the development of auteur theory, Truffaut is responsible for changing the nature of cinema studies. It is arguable that his auteurist approach has profoundly affected (for better or worse) the course of French, even world, cinema.

One of the darkest points of *Les Quatre Cent Coups* is the moment when Antoine's father has him arrested for stealing the typewriter. Here, as in much of the film, Antoine's fictional life is a reflection of Truffaut's real experience, except that Truffaut's crime was not the stealing of a typewriter but, true to his passion for cinema, running a cinema club with stolen funds. Truffaut's crime (misguided rather than malicious) was also the source of his escape to another life. He had met and impressed the renowned film theorist André Bazin. After his arrest he wrote to Bazin from reform school pleading for his help. Bazin helped him on this occasion and again in 1951 when Truffaut was once more imprisoned, this time for going AWOL from the French army.

It was thanks to Bazin's influence that Truffaut was appointed in 1952 as a film critic for the French cultural magazine *Arts* and also began to write regularly for the *Cahiers du cinéma* (edited by Bazin and Langlois).

As a film critic Truffaut was blisteringly vitriolic in his attacks of the 'Tradition of Quality' of post-war French cinema, which he abhorred for its literary (rather than visual) style. In 1958 Doniol-Valcroze said of him: 'What many muttered he dared to say out loud . . . He has firmly kicked the conformist backside of French cinema.' Examples from his reviews illustrate this – for example, 'In not seeing *Cheri-Bibi* you will doubtless spend an excellent evening' and 'French Cinema will produce many more films of this non-quality until the public learns to choose and eventually to smash the seats.'

In such writing about film we can see the themes and ideas that would later inform his work as a film-maker, namely an abhorrence of the 'Tradition of Quality' and an admiration for the popular culture cinema of the American studios, two very different contexts that form the major influences on the French New Wave.

Like his first short film *Les Mistons* (*The Brats*) (1958), *Les Quatre Cent Coups* focuses on youth and delinquency. It is very different from Godard's *A bout de souffle* in its subject matter and style (as you would expect from two directors interested in the personal nature of auteurism). Of the two, Truffaut is less interested in experimenting with the conventions of cinema, and yet *Les Quatre Cent Coups* is still quintessentially 'New Wave'. It has a quality of freshness still apparent, not least in the subject matter: the story of Antoine's neglect at the hands of his parents and the French authorities. The film can hardly be described as either literary or designed to reflect well on France and French institutions. What this story was at the time was contemporary and original, fittingly in keeping with the 'youthful spirit' described by Françoise Giraud in her characterisation of the *Nouvelle Vague*. The structure of the film is also essentially New Wave. Less fractured than *A bout de souffle*, it still presents us with a total contrast to the tightly structured glamour of Hollywood. The resultant effect is that the film looks and feels like a glimpse into the real life of Antoine Doinel. We are presented with a series of loosely linked events where Antoine struggles to escape the confinements of his life. A claustrophobic sense of imprisonment created by the static camera in the indoor scenes (flat, school, prison, Borstal) is contrasted dramatically with the glorious bursts of feeling in the outdoor scenes, which are filmed with a fluid mobile camera as Antoine frequently runs in search of escape.

Perhaps the most famous and characteristic feature of the film is its ending, where Truffaut abandons the classic narrative convention of closure. The camera pursues Antoine in a long tracking shot as he runs away from Borstal towards the sea. In the final seconds of film Antoine turns to face the camera, which then freezes on his face, leaving the character suspended in mid-dilemma. The viewer is left to ponder the possible outcomes. In effect we are denied closure and left with questions – a stunning ending to a brilliant debut.

Some Things to Watch out for and Consider

- How does the film compare and contrast 'indoors' and 'out of doors'?
- What does this film ask us to consider about outsiders (and particularly delinquents)?
- What are we to make of Doinel's (and by extension Truffaut's) relationship with women?
- Consider the film's approach to cause and effect (and, in particular, endings).

Further Viewing

Shoot the Pianist (Truffaut, France, 1960)
Day for Night (Truffaut, France, 1973)
Love on the Run (Truffaut, France, 1984)
Breathless (Godard, France, 1959)
Rear Window (Hitchcock, USA, 1954)
Psycho (Hitchcock, USA, 1960)
Close Encounters of the Third Kind (Spielberg, USA, 1977)

Further Reading

J. Douchet, *French New Wave* (New York, 1999)
S. Hayward, *French National Cinema* (London, 1993)

21 BREATHLESS
(A bout de souffle)
Godard, France, 1959

Awards

British Academy Awards: Nomination – Best Foreign Actress (Jean Seberg)
Berlin Film Festival: Winner – Silver Bear

Production Details

Production company/studio	Société Nouvelle de Cinématographie, Productions Georges de Beauregard, Imperia Films
Producer	George de Beauregard
Director	Jean-Luc Godard
Cinematographer	Raoul Coutard
Editor	Cécile Decugis
Screenwriter	Jean-Luc Godard (based upon an idea by François Truffaut)

Cast Includes

Jean-Paul Belmondo	*Michel Poiccard*
Jean Seberg	*Patricia Franchini*
Daniel Boulanger	*The Inspector*
Jean-Pierre Melville	*Parvelescu*

FOCUS: Institutional Context of the French New Wave

A bout de souffle or *Breathless* (its American release title) is probably the best-known and certainly the most influential film to emerge

Breathless. Courtesy of BFI Stills, Posters and Designs

from the French 'New Wave' – a movement in French film-making from 1958 to 1968. The 'New Wave' or *Nouvelle Vague* consisted of a group of – initially like-minded – critics who became film-makers. They were aware of the history of their art and interested in the nature and form of that art. In direct contrast to the conventions of Hollywood, they delighted in making the audience aware of the artifice of film by referencing/playing with icons, forms, and so on, and questioning the nature and value of film-making. All were restless artists constantly moving on and changing their responses to issues. Thus the 'movement', however brilliant, was short-lived.

The New Wave was a reaction to, in Truffaut's phrase, the *cinéma du papa* (grandad's cinema) of post-war France. More politely termed the 'tradition of quality', this approach to film-making was a direct result of the French government's policy to foster a French cinema and protect the industry from the twin demons of post-war economic depravation and the backlog of American product (denied to audiences for six years by the war), which flooded into France in 1946. The government set up the CNC (the National Cinema Centre) to introduce some element of financial security and therefore confidence in the French film industry. As a result, they wanted to see the money on the screen. The bureaucrats required lavish, cultural product. Thus the films drip with high production values and opulent studio sets – e.g. *The*

Gates of Night (Carné and Prevert, France, 1946). Literary adaptations and historical epics prevailed. In short, mainstream French cinema of the 1950s is expensive but dull. Thus Truffaut in a *Cahiers du cinéma* article of 1954 ('A Certain Tendency in French Cinema') railed against the *cinéma du papa* as too literary. Godard called it overblown and ugly, accusing it of not being 'cinema' at all. Godard believed in cinema as cinema – not a vehicle for transmitting something else (literature) but an art in its own right with its own language/systems and aesthetics.

Beyond the youthful desire to react against *cinéma du papa*, there was a technological impetus to the *Nouvelle Vague* 'style'. In addition to the lighter cameras (developed initially for documentary work), European film-makers could also benefit from the availability of faster emulsions on film stock. There was no longer a need for powerful lights. Film-makers could go into the streets, thus creating a new look to their films and avoiding the expense of constructing sets. Films became cheaper to make and film-makers became more independent.

In viewing *Breathless* we need to keep in mind two powerful but different contexts – American genre films from the classic Hollywood period and the French Tradition of Quality – and consider the ways in which Godard reacts to them.

Breathless begins with a dedication to 'Monogram', a US B-movie studio. This is the first of a series of gestures deliberately inviting us to make a connection to Hollywood. The homage to Hollywood continues via the central character's parody of Bogart in both dress and gesture. Further parallels may be found in the narrative, which is loosely based around the conventions of *film noir*, following the pursuit and final capture of Michel for the shooting of a policeman and the hero's female nemesis embodied in the character of Patricia. Here the similarities to classic Hollywood narrative end. Indeed, the two defining characteristics of classic Hollywood films – conventional narrative structure and the smoothness achieved by continuity editing – are not present in *Breathless*. The opening of the film illustrates this. Godard eschews the usual establishing shot at the start of the film in favour of a close-up of a newspaper depicting a scantily clad girl. An accompanying voice-over states, 'I am a scumbag', but the relationship between image and words is not made clear. In the scene that follows the relationship between shots is confusing: it is not clear whether the characters are in the same scene as each other, or whether they are looking at each other or at something else. This is the result of Godard's deliberate abandonment of the conventions of continuity editing, with the result that the viewer has to work much harder to make sense of what he or she is seeing. Such jarringly obvious editing is a startling contrast to the conventions of both classic Hollywood and the Tradition of Quality. Godard demonstrates in these opening seconds of film that he knows what the rules are but is not afraid to break them. This iconoclastic approach is demonstrated on many other occasions. Having escaped the city for the open road, Michel looks at and speaks directly to camera, entirely dispensing with the conventions of verisimilitude. Similarly, when Michel drives Patricia through the streets of Paris, the scene is composed almost entirely of jump cuts. In 1959 such departures from the norm made the film shockingly original.

Godard's experimental style is not restricted to the way in which he constructs his scenes but is present in every aspect of the narrative. His characters – even his 'hero' – are dysfunctional. Relationships between characters are not well drawn or even explained and contextualised, creating a sense of separation that is underlined by the use of discontinuous editing. There is certainly plenty of action in *Breathless*, but events occur seemingly for their own sake, and actions (including the final betrayal) have little or no motivation. The chain of cause and effect and clear motivation that binds the classic narrative together is only loosely adhered to, with many scenes appearing to meander in an inconsequential fashion. In the final scene the spectator is left contemplating yet another misunderstanding (mis-readings, misunderstandings and even grammatical errors have been a key motif through the film) as Patricia (Jean Seburg) contemplates her dead lover and asks directly to camera 'what is a "bummer"?'

The New Wave is not simply an interesting footnote in cinema history. Its influence lives on, not least because of its impact on the 'new' cinema of the USA in the 1960s and beyond to Tarantino *et al*.

Some Things to Watch out for and Consider

- How does *Breathless* reveal Godard's awareness of and fascination with the dominance of American popular culture?
- In what ways does *Breathless* present us with a radical and original departure from the conventions of American genre films? You could consider
    - *The role of the protagonist.* Through the iconography Godard invites us to consider parallels between Michel and Humphrey Bogart. Compare Michel to Bogart's

character Sam Spade in *The Maltese Falcon* (Huston, USA, 1941). How far is Michel in control of events? Does the narrative of *Breathless* consistently present us with Michel's point of view?

- *The narrative structure*. Consider the long scene between Michel and Patricia in her bedroom. What is the purpose of this scene? Does it fit into a cause-and-effect chain of events? What is the impact of the dialogue, which appears to be improvised and is certainly meandering/inconsequential?

• Look carefully at the ending of the film. Does it have closure? What kind of closure could it claim?

• Pick any scene and look at the way the shots are composed and organised. In what ways does this present us with a departure from the conventions of continuity? How does this affect the spectator?

• Look at the long scene between Michel and Patricia when they are walking down the Champs-Élysées. Look at where Godard positions the camera to film this scene and consider the effect on the spectator of such camera placement. What changes would you have to make in the cinematography and editing if this scene were to be filmed in the classic Hollywood manner?

Further Viewing

The Maltese Falcon (Huston, USA, 1941)
Les Quatre Cent Coups (Truffaut, France, 1959)
Breathless (McBride, USA, 1983)

Further Reading

J. Orr, *Cinema and Modernity* (Manchester, 1995)
G. Roberts and H. Wallis, *Introducing Film* (London, 2001)

22 EIGHT AND A HALF
(Otto e mezzo)
Fellini, Italy, 1963

Awards

Academy Awards: Winner – Best Costume Design, Cinematography (B/W) and Best Foreign Language Film; Nomination – Best Director
Italian National Syndicate of Film Journalists: Winner – Silver Ribbon, Best Cinematography (B/W), Best Director, Best Original Story, Best Producer, Best Score and Best Screenplay
Moscow International Film Festival: Winner – Grand Prix (Federico Fellini)
New York Film Critics Circle Awards: Winner – Best Foreign Language Film

Production Details

Production company/studio	Cineriz (Italy), Francinex (France)
Producer	Angelo Rizzoli
Director	Federico Fellini
Cinematographer	Gianni Di Venanzo
Editor	Leo Catozzo
Screenwriters	Federio Fellini and Ennio Flaiano
Art director	Luciano Ricceri
Music	Nino Rota

Cast Includes

Marcello Mastroianni	*Guido Anselmi*
Claudia Cardinale	*Claudia*
Anouk Aimée	*Luisa Anselmi*
Sandra Milo	*Carla*

Rossella Falk	*Rossella*
Barbara Steele	*Gloria Morin*
Mario Pisu	*Mezzabotta*
Guido Alberti	*The Producer*
Madeleine Le Beau	*The French Actress*
Jean Rougeul	*The Writer*
Eddra Gale	*La Saraghina*
Annie Gorassini	*The Producer's Girlfriend*
Tito Masini	*The Cardinal*
Eugene Walter	*The Journalist*

FOCUS: 'Art' Cinema and Cinema as Art

Fellini's 1963 film *Eight and a Half* is centred on the character of Guido Anselmi, an Italian director. The director is struggling to prepare another movie project. He cannot find the peace and space he needs to think. Most of the interruptions are caused (not always deliberately or maliciously) by the people who have worked with him in the past constantly looking for more work. Seeking both solace and inspiration, he retreats into his unreliable memories and surreal fantasies.

The film, occasionally rather lugubrious in pace and often (deliberately) disjointed, contains some marvellous set pieces that have entered the iconography of art cinema.

The opening scene is a striking metaphor for the frustrations of day-to-day life. The director sits trapped in his car in a traffic-jammed underpass. This visual metaphor has been revisited or revised in films such as *Weekend* (Godard, France, 1967), *Wings of Desire* (Wenders, Germany, 1987) (see chapter 33) and countless music videos. Eventually Guida escapes by literally climbing out of the frame and floating off into the sky. It is a breath-taking moment of pure cinema. Fellini transmits to his audience the central themes of his film and the dreamlike nature of his presentation in a directly visual manner. A central problem of the film is that there does not seem to be much else to say – but the striking images continue.

Guido's tribulations continue at a Spa resort. The scene where Guido queues for water is a prime example of Fellini's ability to frame and choreograph crowd scenes. Fellini's sense of scene composition is all the more impressive as the stiff formality of the scene is broken by the vision of Claudia – a symbol of fresh hope

– from the woods. Saraghina's dance on the beach – part of a flash-back to the comforts of childhood – is beautiful and haunting *as an image*. Whether it has much value beyond looking interesting is open to question. The same might be said of the fabled 'spaceship' finish to the film.

Fellini – along with Ingmar Bergman and Jean-Luc Godard – personifies the European auteur. He has an easily identified visual signature, a set of themes (even obsessions) and a desire to be seen as a creative artist. As a European auteur's rumina-tion on the trials and tribulations of film-making, *Eight and a Half* is both self-indulgent and insightful. In a sense, the self-indulgence is the most insightful element of the film. Guido struggles to come up with a new idea not least because of the milieu he exists within. To some extent this situation is of his own making. The circus around him is his responsibility. Fellini is clearly exploring his own troubles. The shot of Guido staring into the bathroom mirror is clearly a personal statement of anxi-ety from 'the director' and the director. The title refers to the number of movies Fellini himself had directed up until that point: eight features and one short. Much of the material in this film (for example, Guido recalling major happenings in his life, especially the women he has loved and left) is autobiographical for Fellini.

Eight and a Half is – if nothing else – a chance to wander within the mind of a great European 'auteur'. As such it is also a valuable insight into the nature of European 'art cinema'. By extension, the film can serve as a study in how European art cinema sees cinema itself – this is particularly true if compared to Hollywood's portrayal of itself. The 1930s musicals of Busby Berkeley *et al.* through to *Singin' in the Rain* (Kelly and Donen, USA, 1952) (see chapter 15) relished the power of the movies to change people's lives. In the post-war period from *Sunset Boulevard* (Wilder, USA, 1950) (see chapter 14) to *The Player* (Altman, USA, 1992), however jaded and cynical Hollywood may have chosen to portray itself, the audience was never left in any doubt of the glamour of the industry. In *Eight and a Half* and other European films – e.g. Truffaut's *Day for Night* (*La Nuit américaine*) (France, 1973) the film-making process is portrayed as pain. In particular the pain is felt by the director. The director is the central, tragic creative figure stuck within a soul-destroying process. Thus European cinema – indeed great European cinema – can take on the characteristics of auteur theory gone mad.

Some Things to Watch out for and Consider

* 'If you are moved by it, you don't need it explained to you. If not, no explanation can make you moved by it' (Fellini on *Eight and a Half*). Where does film analysis/criticism go after that?
* 'Remember this is a comic film' (Fellini's note attached to the camera during filming). What kind of comedy is *Eight and a Half*?
* 'His films degenerated into rambling, mostly inconsequential rag-bags made up of comic anecdote, facile metaphor, nostalgic reminiscence and flamboyant set-pieces ... He evidently saw himself as a great artist, whereas a more accurate assessment might describe him as a magnificent showman' (G. Andrew, *Directors A–Z* (London, 1999)). How could you defend Fellini against such criticism? Is Fellini a great artist or a magnificent showman? Is it possible to be both?
* Has the (mainland) European tendency to treat film as 'art' and directors as auteurs been a help or a hindrance (to what)?

Further Viewing

La Strada (Fellini, 1954)
La Dolce Vita (Fellini, 1960)
Singin' in the Rain (Kelly and Donen, USA, 1952)
The Bad and the Beautiful (Minnelli, USA, 1952)
Day for Night (Truffaut, France, 1973)
The Player (Altman, USA, 1992)

23 PERFORMANCE
Roeg and Cammell, UK, 1968

Production Details

Production company/studio	Goodtimes Enterprises / Warner Brothers (US Distributors)
Producers	Sanford Lieberson and David Cammell
Directors	Donald Cammell and Nicolas Roeg
Cinematographer	Nicolas Roeg
Editors	Antony Gibbs and Brian Smedley Aston
Screenwriter	Donald Cammell

Cast Includes

James Fox	*Chas*
Mick Jagger	*Turner*
Anita Pallenberg	*Pherber*
Michèle Breton	*Lucy*
Ann Sidney	*Dana*
Johnny Shannon	*Harry Flowers*

FOCUS: 'New' British Cinema, Cultural Forms, Montage and Narrative

Performance was widely loved, loathed and dismissed on its late release in 1970, but holds an important place in film history. Whether truly visionary and innovative, or the unmatured promise of a future master, it remains nevertheless unique, provocative and intensely *cinematic* to the extreme: drama that could only be cinema. Additionally, its subversive narrative is powerfully laced with the contemporary ideas, ideals and challenges of narcissistic pop music counter-culture. Despite the glaringly obvious (and undisputed) fact that directing tasks were *shared* by Cammell and Roeg, speculation about authorship has dragged on. It is fair to say that *Performance* shows little similarity to Cammell's later work, whilst, in the cinematic elements of camera zoom lens use, lighting and the provocative style of editing montage, it bears Roeg's unmistakable creative signature. Regardless of its own merits, the film heralded the arrival proper of one of Britain's greatest film-makers. Roeg's next films consistently displayed his great fascination with (and handling of) time, fantasy, reality, memory and meaning and he made some of the most important British films to date, including his next feature *Walkabout* (1971), *Don't Look Now* (1973), *The Man who Fell to Earth* (1976) and *Bad Timing* (1980). Even when less successful, Roeg's films quite literally make most other Western directors' work look *conventional*.

Roeg belongs to those post-war British directors who were inevitably marginalised whenever cinema became fashionably judged in terms of socio-political content by 'serious' critics – a critical approach still common in popular film reviews. He belongs in a group of visually and cinematically literate directors that would have to include Michael Powell, whose *Peeping Tom* (UK, 1960) led to the most extreme example of virtuoso film-making being utterly ignored, following critical rejection of content. *Performance*, as disturbing as Powell's study of voyeurism, can now be appreciated as an authentic reflection of a period of social upheaval that would, among other changes, bring down the most rabidly prudish and conservative powers of the critical establishment.

Performance is still admired as much for its precious vision of England in 1968 as for its innovative handling of narrative structure. Its rediscovery and re-evaluation could be expected to enjoy a welcome in 1990s postmodernist, pseudo-culture, but the film offers far more than simply images, sounds and atmosphere of late 1960s 'swinging London'. They are all there; however, they exist not as celebration but as part of a formally dazzling violence between characters and places, beliefs and coda, that were in shocking contrast. We are in a city / universe where Chas, a small-time, violent East End gangster (James Fox), becomes pulled into personality-disorientating mind games with the occupants of a house belonging to jaded, faded rock star Turner (Mick Jagger), having gone there to escape the brutal troubles of his own milieu. The film's second half is dominated by scenes depicting the mind / sexuality / identity-bending exchanges and liaisons between Chas, the teasing, taunting women in Turner's

Performance. Courtesy of
BFI Stills, Posters and
Designs

flat (especially Pherber played by Anita Pallenberg), as well as woman, devil-incarnate Turner–Jagger).

It is not possible to 'explain' *Performance* with some well coordinated global interpretation. It is deliberately disturbing on so
many levels, not least in form. Centrally, it contemplates and
expresses feelings about the astounding gulf between its utterly
opposed cultures, both of which had to an extent been experienced
by Donald Cammell in particular. There is little point in using the
milestones of plot for a sense of the film, and, without the usual
comforts of those goals and resolutions relied on by Hollywood,
expanding on the film poster's verbal (and visual) conflict is more
useful. In addition to the 'madness' and 'sanity', 'fantasy' and
'reality', 'death' and 'life', 'vice' and 'versa', *Performance* is about
Britain and social class, the British establishment, class identity,
culture, counter-culture, violence, sex, sexual violence, hatred,
fear, shame, repression, liberation, love, class, observation,
involvement, manipulation, sexual identity, heterosexuality,
homosexuality, gender role subversion, mirrors and reflections.
Among all this, taking in a wealth of textual and subtextual references from literature, poetry, drama and cinema, *Performance* is
also about the Rolling Stones or, more specifically, their visual icon
– Mick Jagger.

The production of *Performance*, on location in and around

London, has been surrounded by so many myths that it has become difficult to know which stories to believe ever since, but enough has always been known to raise the question as to how Warner Brothers could ever have funded such a wild creation, shaped by novice directors, exerting so little studio control until it was too late. Any studio executives' blindness is explained partly by just how 'hot' the very idea of film starring arch-Stone Jagger was. In purely commercial terms, the Rolling Stones were second only to the Beatles. As an embodiment of the dangerous tide of youth rebellion against the establishment on both sides of the Atlantic, Jagger himself was 'His Satanic Majesty', Emperor of all that was abhorrent to the protectorates of 'common decency'. Cammell and Roeg knew exactly what Jagger represented and at one level Turner was simply Jagger in close up. In this respect, a reading of *Performance* demands reading of the headlines and newsreels of the mid–late 1960s. The film's narrative structure upset Warner Brothers, but its depiction of sex and violence, unprecedented in a Hollywood project, appalled them. *Performance* was almost closed down during shooting, but its 'final' cut was the limit, and Warner Brothers forced a re-cut. The impression was that Warner Brothers were still deeply disturbed and embarrassed by *Performance* when it was finally released in 1970. The critical reaction in America was extremely negative, although considerably better in Britain in 1971, where the critical establishment was now considerably more liberal than the one that had condemned *Peeping Tom* in 1960 (when condemnation had gone beyond 'this is a bad film' and into the realms of 'this is evil and should be destroyed').

Cinema audiences have a long-standing appetite for being frightened, but there is little evidence of a willingness to be profoundly disturbed in mainstream theatres. Part of *Performan*ce is a straightforward gangster-thriller plot, but its cinematic 'persona' had everything to do with its skilful, complex, unques-tionably powerful use of image and sound overlapping and juxta-position. Violence screams familiar anger and blood, but also stuns in the abstract, with the visual conflict between motion and stillness/stills, continuity and fragmented non-verbal connec-tions. Censorship is part of the film, as unwelcome necessity, but equally as part of the film's own territory and interest in voyeurism. Roeg and Cammell's success in sheer visual impact seems like a precursor to later directors who may be less revolu-tionary, but still greatly accomplished in taking British film out of the theatrical/verbal and towards the visual. Neil Jordan's films, from the outset, are good examples. What Alan Parker tried to do non-verbally with his Pink Floyd music vehicle *The Wall* also has similarities. *Performance* has to be celebrated as a landmark British film, one that showed there were ideas and talent around that promised the possibility of surprise, even liberation from the constraints of conventionality shown by even 'revolutionary' forms, including the post-neo-realist British 'working-class' films of the late 1950s and 1960s. The mirrors and echoes of its free-style construct makes it one of a very few works in mainstream cinema about which the word 'explores' might be used with justification – a regular critics' phrase that is, in the vast majority of applications, utterly groundless. There can be only one satisfactory way to grasp why *Performance* has to be a key film text: sit and observe the film, in the light of any and every film you have seen before or since.

Some Things to Watch out for and Consider

- Would you describe *Performance* as 'dated'? What *precisely* does this mean?
- Were you aware of any documentary style of presentation while watching it?
- Why did Roeg and Cammell shoot/edit the scene of Chas's violent beating in the fractured way that they did?
- What are the main themes/ideas/concerns about sex expressed in the film?
- Can aspects of *Performance* be compared with music videos?
- In what sense was/is *Performance* disturbing?

Further Viewing

Walkabout (Roeg, UK, 1971)
Don't Look Now (Roeg, UK, 1973)
The Man who Fell to Earth (Roeg, UK, 1976)
Bad Timing (Roeg, UK, 1980)
Two Deaths (Roeg, UK, 1995)
White of the Eye (Cammell, UK, 1987)
Black Narcissus (Powell, UK, 1946)

Peeping Tom (Powell, UK, 1960)
The Company of Wolves (Jordan, UK, 1984)
Mona Lisa (Jordan, UK, 1986)
Gimme Shelter (Maysles and Maysles, UK, 1970)
The Wall (Parker, UK, 1982)

24 **PSYCHO**

Hitchcock, USA, 1960

Awards

Academy Award: Nomination – Best Director, Best Supporting Actress (Janet Leigh) and Best Cinematography (B/W)

Production Details

Production company/studio	Universal
Producer	Alfred Hitchcock
Director	Alfred Hitchcock
Cinematographer	John L. Russell
Editor	George Tomasini
Screenwriter	Joseph Stefano (from the novel by Robert Bloch)
Production designer	Joseph Hurley
Music	Bernard Hermann

Cast Includes

Anthony Perkins	*Norman Bates*
Janet Leigh	*Marion Crane*
Vera Miles	*Lila Crane*
John Gavin	*Sam Loomis*

FOCUS: Genre and Auteur

Psycho is, of course, a 'horror film' – but it is one made by Alfred Hitchcock. Hitchcock was the 'master of suspense', a genre related to, but not necessarily coupled with, horror. It is important to note that Hitchcock was a studio director working within genre, but horror was not his usual medium. At the time of making *Psycho*,

'Hitch' had already made his great American films: *Rear Window* (1954*)*, *Vertigo* (1958) and *North by Northwest* (1959) – all thrillers.

The pleasures of horror include the thrill of the forbidden and all the joys of scopophilia at their darkest. Hitchcock as a film-maker was always interested in the motivations of his audience (i.e. why do we watch?) as well as manipulating us into how and what we watch. Thus *Psycho* is constantly questioning the viewer's motives before it ever reveals the motive of the monster. Once again – as in *Rear Window* (see chapter 16) – Hitchcock is acting as the viewer's own conscience 'whispering of the complexities that surround the relationship between the seer and the seen'.

Hitchcock is often described as 'the master' of suspense because so many of his films are brilliantly crafted and constructed. He achieves his control of the level of suspense by deliberately with-holding knowledge. What we do not see arouses our curiosity.

There is more to Hitchcock's genius than a rather misanthropic view of popular psychology. Included in an overarching building of information and tension are masterstrokes of film construction – for example, the shock factor of killing the 'star' early in the film, not to mention the brutal violence of the shower scene.

One of Hitchcock's contributions to the 'language' of the horror genre was the staccato editing of that shower scene. It could not have escaped his dark sense of humour that the power of this godfather of all 'slasher' sequences was predicated on a host of 'cuts'. The action takes place in the interior of Marion's cabin and we see a mid-shot of her sitting at a desk in her dressing gown, writing in a notebook. The scene develops following the rules of continuity, so that the narrative is clear and easy to follow. The pace is measured, with lengthy shots being used to suggest that the character is thinking.

As Marion starts her shower, the pace accelerates and remains measured, with each shot lasting 4–5 seconds. The audience is allowed the privileged position of observing Marion showering. Through the curtain we see the bathroom door open and a shad-owy figure appears. Marion remains oblivious. Hitchcock refrains from cutting to focus on the figure entering the bathroom. Instead, the camera tracks slowly closer to the curtain until Marion disap-pears from view and the shadowy threat is centre frame. At this point the curtain is pulled back to the accompaniment of the sudden dramatic violin sounds and we see a figure in darkness raising a knife into the air. This one shot lasts for 17 seconds and takes us from the peaceful solitude of Marion's shower through rising tension to the moment of crisis.

The abrupt and dramatic action of pulling back the curtain signals the moment of change – in action, in pace, in technique and in sound. The next 29 shots take place in just 20 seconds. Many of the shots obviously last for less than a second. This tremendously dramatic change in pace effectively conveys the frenzy of the attack and Marion's panic as she tries to protect herself from the assault. The brutality is made more vivid by the way that the speed of the edits matches the speed of the knife strokes raining down on her. Or so it seems. What do we actually see? Shots of Marion's screaming face, shots of a silhouetted figure raising a knife, shots of the arm and knife plunging downwards, a shot of her belly with the blade of the knife approaching, a shot of her feet with water and blood beginning to splash round them. We do not see her being stabbed (unlike in the remake (Van Sant, USA, 1998), which is more graphic in its portrayal). Hitchcock has moved from the continuity technique to associative montage. A series of images is sequenced in such a way that we infer something that has not been shown.

Sound is particularly effective in this scene. The shrieking staccato sound of the violins emulates the stabbing motion, dramatically enhancing the sense and horror of what is taking place. The change of tonality in the music to much slower deeper notes indicates the next change in pace. After the murderer's exit we see a slow detail shot of Marion's hand beginning to slide down the tiled wall of the shower. The next eight shots, which take us to the end of the shower scene with Marion lying static and staring on the floor, take over 80 seconds. Hitchcock has calmed the pace down sufficiently to continue the narrative: a slow build to the final bizarre denouement.

Hitchcock was a (surely *the*) master of suspense. His approach to horror is one of building tension. The key to Hitchcock successfully raising the level of the genre's quality is in the careful control of pace. He also revels in and understands our enjoyment of the thrill of uncertainty. The lack of knowledge preys on our fears and is heightened by the *mise en scène* constructed of overpowering shadows redolent of threat and possibility. Constantly 'kept in the dark', we as spectators are also offered a privileged view – for example, we see a character's reaction before we see what he or she is reacting to.

In many ways *Psycho* shifted the horror genre in a new direction. The grotesque and yet pathetic figure of Norman Bates spawned a host of similarly grotesque individuals. His (and Hitch's) shadow is cast over the crazed family of *The Texas Chainsaw Massacre* (Hooper, 1974) and Hannibal Lecter in *The Silence of the Lambs* (Demme, 1991) and *Hannibal* (Scott, 2001), as well as the host of dysfunctional monsters who stalk their prey in the 'teen slasher' movies of the 1980s and 1990s. These later 'post'-horrors – e.g. *Scream* (Craven, 1996) – are also characterised by their use of intensely black humour. Hitch described *Psycho* as his 'little joke'.

Some Things to Watch out for and Consider

- What is it that makes *Psycho* a Hitchcock movie? What makes it a horror movie? Can we separate these two classifications?
- Consider the character of Norman Bates and how he is presented. What moral position are we expected to take?
- With Norman Bates, Hitchcock created a new kind of horror 'hero', not a creature of darkness like 'Nosferatu', not other-worldly, but something scarier – an ordinary person gone wrong. If our sympathies are aroused by Norman, what are we to make of Marion? What do we make of Hitchcock's sexual politics?
- Should we contextualise this film's politics or require it to stand up to current standards and mores?
- If *Psycho* is Hitchcock's 'little joke', should we be laughing?
- Could/should the same question be asked of *Pulp Fiction* (Tarantino, 1994)?
- Is Hitchcock really 'the viewer's own conscience', or is *Psycho* just an entertaining, cheap thrill in the dark?

Further Viewing

Nosferatu (Murnau, Germany, 1922)
Rear Window (Hitchcock, USA, 1954)
Frenzy (Hitchcock, USA, 1972)
The Silence of the Lambs (Demme, USA, 1991)
Scream (Craven, USA, 1996)
I Know What You Did Last Summer (Gillespie, USA, 1997)
Psycho (Van Sant, USA, 1998)
Hannibal (Scott, USA, 2001)

Further Reading

C. Clover, *Men, Women and Chainsaws* (London, 1992)

S. Gottlieb (ed.), *Hitchcock on Hitchcock* (London, 1995)

D. Spoto, *The Dark Side of Genius: The Life of Alfred Hitchcock* (London, 1994)

F. Truffaut, *Hitchcock* (London, 1968)

25 *THE GODFATHER*

Coppola, USA, 1972

Awards

Academy Awards: Winner – Best Picture, Best Actor (Marlon Brando)
and Best Adapted Screenplay

Production Details

Production company/studio	Paramount
Producer	Albert S. Ruddy
Director	Francis Ford Coppola
Cinematographer	Gordon Willis
Editor	William Reynolds
Screenwriters	Mario Puzo and Francis Ford Coppola
Production designer	Dean Tavoularis
Music	Nino Rota

Cast Includes

Marlon Brando	*Vito Corleone*
Al Pacino	*Michael Corleone*
James Caan	*Sonny Corleone*
Richard Castellano	*Clemenza*
Robert Duvall	*Tom Hagen*
Sterling Hayden	*McCluskey*
Diane Keaton	*Kay Adams*

(This entry focuses on *The Godfather* but it is worthwhile viewing all three
parts of the trilogy – see Further Viewing.)

FOCUS: Genre

The gangster genre had its first major wave of popularity in the
1930s with films like *Little Caesar* (LeRoy, USA, 1931), *The Public*

Enemy (Wellman, USA, 1931) and *Scarface* (Hawks, USA, 1932). These films were a hugely popular response to the public notoriety of Al Capone in the late 1920s, upon whom the heroes of both *Scarface* and *Little Caesar* were based. Whilst earlier films of the genre developed the background of the criminal placing the blame for his anti-social activities on his environment, *Scarface* in particular depicts the gangster as a brutal monster thriving on murder and power in the most violent and bloody film the genre had seen. We can compare this to *The Godfather*.

Coppola's film is not short of blood and violence, but in both its representation of violence and the gangster heroes Vito and Michael Corleone we find something both complex and interesting. The violence is both repellent and beautiful in its choreography and cinematographic execution. Marlon Brando and Al Pacino present us with characters with whom we can sympathise almost to the point that compromises our response to the nature of their activities. Coppola brings to the genre an operatic, epic quality, making a film that succeeded both as popular entertainment and as high art. A central concern, therefore, for viewers of this film has to be the consideration of the film's moral impact. Does it glamorise the violence it depicts?

The Godfather opens with a black screen and an Italian accented voice stating 'I believe in America'. A slow fade from black reveals Buona Serra speaking almost directly to camera. The way the shot is framed and the pleading voice of this wheedling funeral director create an uneasy sense of intimidation. The scene hints both at the confessional and at interrogation. This sense is created by the fact that we do not see to whom he is speaking. Coppola has deliberately chosen not to use a two-shot or shot/reverse shot where both characters would be revealed. The identity and therefore the character of the Godfather remain in darkness, and, for the moment, suspense. The suspense is held as the camera pulls back revealing a desk and then a hand. The discussion between them, which is about Buona Serra's desire for justice for his daughter, foregrounds the two driving themes of the film(s): the nature of America and the nature/role of the Mafia within American society both as crime organisation and as family. These early scenes of the film also introduce us to Michael Corleone, in whose character we see these themes and the inevitable conflicts between them played out.

Of all his family Michael is marked out as separate. He is the most American of the Corleones. He stumbles speaking Italian, he fought for his country in the Second World War, he has an American girlfriend and he is the only one who is free from the family business and its adherence to tribal violence. As he states at the wedding party that opens the film, 'That's my family Kay. That's not me.' One of the interesting things about this film is that Michael's rise to power is presented ambiguously. Is it a tragedy? Is it a fall from grace and loss of freedom or a return to the fold? Does he want to be Godfather? Does he have a choice? If so, where does it come and what is his motivation? His rise to worldly power is certainly paralleled by his fall into sin. Coppola explicitly illustrates these themes of good and evil, grace and sin, through the elaborate Catholic ceremonies (the film contains two weddings, a funeral and a christening) and through the cinematography with its extreme contrasts and the frequent use of a very dark screen with patches of illumination (look, for example, at Michael's shadowed demonic face in the christening scene).

One of the aspects that makes *The Godfather* such a powerful film is the way Coppola takes us inside the Corleone family. We see their beliefs, traditions, rituals, births, deaths, and marriages (across the trilogy of films). We sympathise with the motivations and dilemmas of these very charismatic and powerful individuals. Does this have an impact on our judgement of their actions? Does the film-maker condemn their moral code? In the scene where Michael becomes Godfather to Connie's baby, Coppola juxtaposes images of the christening with images of violent murder. Thus he makes explicit the evil nature of Michael's actions as he simultaneously takes on the Mafia role of Godfather as well as the religious one. Is it enough? We see so clearly into his motivation, and his enemies are so negatively represented, that ultimately perhaps his charisma wins the day.

Some Things to Watch out for and Consider

- How does the film-maker use costume/make-up and changes in costume/make-up to illuminate character and status? Look at:
    - Michael's costume in the early scenes of the film. What does it tell you about him? How is it/he different from the rest of his family?

- Don Vito's costume in the early scenes of the film. How does this change once he relinquishes power?
  - Michael's costume in the final sequences of the film.
- How does the film-maker engage our sympathy with the character of Michael? Look at:
  - His education.
  - His occupation at the start of the film.
  - The way the rest of the family speak to him before and after his rise to power.
  - The motivation for his first murders. (Look at the scene with his father in the hospital. What does Michael say to him? Is this a turning point?)
  - Michael's actions and reactions as juxtaposed with those of his brothers, especially Sonny.
  - The violent murders of both Michael's brother and his first wife. (How does this effect his actions/our responses to them?)
- What impact does the christening scene have on our responses to/understanding of Michael. Look carefully at the way the film-maker has chosen to juxtapose shots here. What effects are created?
- What aspects of characterisation encourage us to sympathise with Don Vito? Look at:
  - His belief in the importance of family.
  - His dignity when Sonny dies.
  - His refusal to engage in narcotics. (Look at how he is presented during the 'heads of families' meeting in comparison to the heads of the other families.)
  - The representation of his enemies.
  - His death scene.
  - The star image of Brando.
- In the context of the film what different meanings does the title Godfather have? What does this choice of title tell you about the values and beliefs of the family? Do you find it sinister?

Further Viewing

The Godfather Part II (Coppola, USA, 1974)
The Godfather Part III (Coppola, USA, 1990)

The Public Enemy (Wellman, USA, 1931)
Scarface (Hawks, USA, 1932)
Goodfellas (Scorsese, USA, 1990)
Casino (Scorsese, USA, 1995)
Apocalypse Now (Coppola, USA, 1979)
One from the Heart (Coppola, USA, 1982)

26 TAXI DRIVER

Scorsese, USA, 1976

Awards

British Academy Awards: Winner – Best Film Music (Bernard Herrmann)
Cannes: Winner – Golden Palm
National Society of Film Critics USA: Winner – Best Director (Martin Scorsese)
New York Film Critics Circle: Winner – Best Actor (Robert De Niro)

Production Details

Production company/studio	Columbia Pictures/Bill-Phillips/Italo-Judeo
Producers	Julia Phillips and Michael Phillips
Director	Martin Scorsese
Cinematographer	Michael Chapman
Supervising editor	Marcia Lucas
Screenwriter	Paul Schrader

Cast Includes

Robert De Niro	*Travis Bickle*
Jodie Foster	*Iris*
Cybill Shepherd	*Betsy*
Harvey Keitel	*Sport*
Peter Boyle	*Wizard*
Leonard Harris	*Charles Palantine*

FOCUS: Character, Performance and Film Expression

Taxi Driver brought a character whose lone stance against evil makes him a direct descendent of classic 'American Dream' heroes such as James Stewart and Gregory Peck, but the hero cabby Travis Bickle was a post-Vietnam, alienated, psychologically tortured version of these 'good men', capable of unspeakable violence during his own 'last stand'. Crucially, Scorsese makes Robert De Niro's incarnation of the insomniac, psychotically introspective cab driver the absolute centre of his intense psychological drama. Expressionistic, impressionistic, hallucinatory – cinematography, sound, music and editing are primarily shaped to express the disintegrating psyche and experience of a persona that dominates almost every scene.

Taxi Driver established Scorsese firmly as a major new creative talent who now delivered real box-office success in a personal work, following the promise and critical acclaim of his *Mean Streets* (1973), and the respectable success of *Alice Doesn't Live Here Anymore* (1974). De Niro's Johnny Boy in *Mean Streets* had made a great impression on critics, and Travis Bickle was the major role that sealed a new famous director–actor collaboration. *New York, New York* (1977), *Raging Bull* (1980), *The King of Comedy* (1982), *Good Fellas* (1990), *Cape Fear* (1991) and *Casino* (1995) followed. *Mean Streets* had marked Scorsese as a striking newcomer: a cinema-immersed Italian-American with a deep personal and religious vision of the culture that he knew and understood. *Taxi Driver* clearly showcased rapidly developing creative skills that would eventually set him on the cinematic world stage as one of a few truly virtuoso film-makers with an extraordinary grasp of the craft.

Taxi Driver opens with a nightmarish threat that never leaves the film. Blood-red titles on black screen: 'Columbia Pictures ... Robert De Niro ...'. A drum rises and rises then crashes outwards with brass and woodwind. Fade up to billowing steam that rises from the bowels of New York through a drain vent. Taxi emerges slowly from vapour and glides malevolently across the screen, trailing the film title in its wake. Music sprawls across the entire opening, drifting into dreamy jazz clarinet, drugging us into false rest, to be disturbed again with fear delivered by strings and percussion as the montage flows: garish coloured street lights pulsating over the cabby's staring, scanning eyes; surreally colour-saturated wet windscreen clears; travelling view of New York at night dissolving into bleeding lights and harsh contrast; people staring into the stopped cab as they cross the street in slow motion, ambiguously (threatening or viewed with threat?); driver's eyes, reddened by the stop light, following them. Music drags the sense

Taxi Driver. Columbia (courtesy
Kobal)

of danger into cold daylight 'reality', where we meet Travis applying for the job. We discover that he is a man who cannot sleep at
night, wants to work long hours, does not seem educated or well
read, served in the marines in Vietnam and does not seem able to
communicate well.

In *Taxi Driver* we see Travis working at night and filling his days
by going to seedy porno-flick cinemas, watching TV and writing
his diary. Travis is appalled by the sexual squalor that he sees
around him and inside his cab as he drives around areas of New
York that other cabbies shun. His contempt eats away at his
perception like a cancerous obsession ('Some day a real rain'll
come and wash the scum off the streets'). The narrative exposes
him slipping from reality and failing to find a place in society.
Travis becomes fixated on Betsy, angel-like campaign-worker for a
presidential candidate, and secures a date with her, but fails to
keep her owing to sheer naivety, after taking her to a porn film just
because he saw other couples do it. Finally realising that Betsy has
spurned him completely, he becomes obsessed with child prostitute Iris, who tried to get into his cab one night to escape her pimp,
only to be dragged away. He stalks Palantine, half-tries to talk his
way into the secret service with one of his security guards, then
spends his savings on an arsenal of handguns, ammunition,

knives and target practice sessions. His first 'kill' happens when he shoots a youth holding up a late-night grocers. After nearly hitting Iris with his cab another night, he seeks her out and tries to persuade her to leave Sport, her pimp, but she refuses. Seeing no way of finding peace and a place in a world that he despises, he leaves his money and a note to Iris and goes to assassinate Palantine. When his attempt is thwarted, he runs home, loads himself up with weapons and drives to the tenement brothel, intending to save Iris and kill himself.

The narrative constantly swings from day to night and back again, and the transition is never smooth but comes as a shock, like being blinded when stepping out of a dark room into sunlight. The night shots are never over-lit, but dark with clashing electric colours, while the day shots are sometimes deliberately over-bright and washed out. The pallid sleeplessness showing on Travis's face is regularly reinforced by jarring removal from the fluid motion and languid music of driving scenes to the stark daylight of his existence in his shabby apartment, executed with sudden changes of music or hard sounds. Bernard Herrmann's film score plays an integral part in creating the film's all-pervading sense of disturbance, provoking and fracturing itself with harsh changes that verge on the chaotic. Its illusionary melodies and lurching chords reflect Travis's upset psychological state, and recurring devices like the thumping drum that intrudes on Travis's diary voice-overs intensify the sense that he is losing control of his thoughts, like his helpless confession to his veteran cabby guru Wizard, 'I've got some bad ideas in my head'. That same admission sets off a blaring car horn nearby as the emotion of the statement shows on his face, as if his own world is turning against him, or providing another warning, like the wailing siren that accompanies his first visit to Iris's brothel, which screams and screams, hinting at the carnage that will follow. Travis's dream existence and his spiritual detachment from the city and its inhabitants are also reflected by distorted sound – like the isolated fizz-hiss of an indigestion tablet and broken voices of colleagues whom he is not listening to, as he disappears into his own head, pushed there by the sight of a man who looks like a rich pimp – sounds heightened and isolated as in a state of semi-consciousness.

Taxi Driver is a kind of horror film, with no single 'beast' to fear, but an entire city. Terror arrives at night, suddenly, from anywhere, outside or inside the cab. To the increasingly paranoid Travis, the New York that he is cocooned from by his metal crate is the 'thing' to fear and hate. Fear grows out of his isolation, and the loneliness in *Taxi Driver* is suffocating, explicit in his first-person narration, but equally created by Scorsese's framing of his exclusion from society and desperate desire for friendship, as he gazes at couples walking holding hands. In the end, Travis sees no hope of finding peace and happiness, so seeks redemption by becoming Iris's unsolicited avenging angel, embarking on a suicidal mission to slaughter her exploiters. Scorsese was pushed into having Travis acclaimed as a hero in the ending, and photographically toning down the violence of the ending. The final carnage was originally scripted as surreally bloody, to the extent that it was unclear whether it was 'real' or Travis's fantasy. What Scorsese retains in the end is a darkly poetic depiction of isolation leading to madness.

Some Things to Watch out for and Consider

- How do the elements express Travis's physical and inner state, rather than simply his viewpoint of the world? Look for and consider examples throughout the film of:
    - cinematographic colour;
    - camera movement;
    - editing (picture/sound);
    - music;
    - 'natural' sound.
- Is *Taxi Driver* a serious, analytical, psychological study of alienation? If not, what is the film meant to convey?
- Travis is completely out of touch with reality, racist, insane – but is he still likeable? Are we meant to admire him for what he did?
- Is the extreme violence justified in this film? Why/why not?
- Why is there no music during the brothel carnage?
- What do the film's many occurrences of slow motion suggest/convey?
- What is the importance of the last shot we see of Travis?

Further Viewing

The King of Comedy (Scorsese, USA, 1982)
Bringing out the Dead (Scorsese, USA, 1999)

Metropolis (Lang, Germany, 1927)
The Crowd (Vidor, USA, 1931)
The Searchers (Ford, USA, 1956)
Hardcore (Schrader, USA, 1979)
Mona Lisa (Jordan, UK, 1986)

Further Reading

I. Christie (ed.), *Scorsese on Scorsese* (London, 1999)

G. Roberts and H. Wallis, *On Directors: Martin Scorsese* (London, forthcoming)

27 **1900**
(Novocento)
Bertolucci, Italy, 1976

Production Details

Production company/studio	TCF / FEA / Artemis
Producer	Alberto Grimaldi
Director	Bernardo Bertolucci
Cinematographer	Vittorio Storaro
Editor	Franco Arcalli
Screenwriters	Franco Arcalli, Bernardo Bertolucci and Giuseppe Bertolucci
Production designer	Ezio Frigerio
Music	Ennio Morricone

Cast Includes

Burt Lancaster	*Alfredo Berlingheri*
Robert De Niro	*Alfredo Berlingheri*
Paolo Pavesi	*Young Alfredo*
Sterling Hayden	*Leo Dalco*
Gerard Depardieu	*Olmo Dalco*
Roberto Maccanti	*Young Olmo*
Donald Sutherland	*Atilla*
Romoto Valli	*Giovanni*
Anna-Maria Gherandi	*Eleonora*
Laura Betti	*Regina*

FOCUS: European 'Art Cinema'; Film as Political Art – the Epic

1900 is undoubtedly 'epic' – it celebrates a century, it displays generations in conflict and (in its original version) lasted five and a half hours. The film's $6 million budget was supplied by three different sources: $2 million from United Artists, $2 million from Paramount and $2 million from 20th Century Fox. Thus *1900* can be seen as an impressive example of the Hollywood/Europe synergy – as usual the relationship was not unproblematic. The production went $3 million over budget, which might seem slight in this day and age until we consider the brutal fact that the film went *50 per cent* over budget.

Bertolucci was already a famed European auteur owing to *Before the Revolution* (1964), *The Spider's Stratagem* (1969) and *The Conformist* (1970) as well as the *succès de scandale* of *Last Tango in Paris* (1972). Bertolucci ('European', with all that involves, including possibly 'difficult') had proved himself capable not only of making very stylish films but also of attracting great attention to himself and his movies. Thus he found himself fêted by Hollywood at a time when the studios were going through a decade where they attempted forays into financing original talent (before the blockbusters soaked up all the finance). Bertolucci collected a large amount of studio money, his favoured cinematographer Vitorrio Storaro and an international cast around him to begin filming on location in the countryside of Parma and Lazio (Rome). He aimed to make a film about collective memory – specifically the collective memory of working people rarely explored in cinema and certainly not in epic terms (see, for example, the work of the Italian neo-realists or more recently Ken Loach and Mike Leigh in the UK). If anything, *1900* is closer in visual style to *Days of Heaven* (Malick, USA, 1978) or in sentiment to John Sayles' s *Matewan* (USA, 1987), but as an expression of epic sensibilities *1900* is closer to Coppola's *The Godfather Part II* (USA, 1974).

Set in Italy from the birth of the century to the end of the Second World War, the film follows the lives and interactions of two boys/men, one born a bastard of peasant stock (Depardieu), the other born to a landowner (De Niro). The drama spans from 1900 to 1944 and focuses largely on the fortunes of the two contrasting families, set firmly in the decadent/threatening atmosphere of the rise of Fascism, which threatens any hope of peace between the classes. Finally the peasants seize the opportunity to rise up and assert their communist faith. Espousing Stalin, their socialism is really rather more a form of rural anarchism. Their victory reasserts the moral strength of the peasant patriarch Leo (Sterling Hayden).

The politics of the film are clearly displayed in the opening shot, when the agenda of the film is set by the image of workers as classical heroes. The style of presentation – i.e. painterly – (and the musical accompaniment) give to the working man a sense of dignity that he will hold throughout the film. The opening text, thanking the peasants for their spirit, songs and culture, hammers the didactic points home (in a way reminiscent of the silent films of Sergei M. Eisenstein).

The opening moving images of the film show us the fall of Fascism. Even as the Fascists retreat, they engage in senseless savagery (a continuing theme of the film). The workers are now armed and dangerous. A young boy shouts 'I want to kill too, Long Live Stalin!' This same boy 'arrests' Alfredo, the landowner, telling him: 'There are no bosses any more.' The rest of the film deals – in elongated detail – with how this situation has come about.

In 1976 this rather romantic left-ism was still fashionable enough (rather than the exclusive territory of Warren Beatty and Tim Robbins) to give the film counter-culture cachet. Hollywood thrived (and continues to thrive) by packaging the semi-danger-ous – e.g. *Bonnie and Clyde* (Penn, 1967) and *Easy Rider* (Hopper, 1969) – rather than the genuine radicalism of, for example, Jean-Luc Godard – e.g. *Weekend* (France, 1967) or *Sympathy for the Devil* (France, 1968). *1900* went rather too far for its paymasters. Financed by Hollywood, Bertolucci still managed to produce material that was way beyond their ability (or nerve) to distribute – not least because of its length. Bertolucci's version of the film included a scene of sexual activity featuring Alfredo, Olmo, and an epileptic prostitute, which European distributors could handle but that would never have been certified by the MPAA.

In the original version of the still surviving scene of Olmo and Alfredo in the fields, the pubescent boys go beyond 'screwing' the ground and examine each other's erections. Not only would this have removed any possibility of a certificate in the United States: it would probably have qualified as child pornography, thus lead-ing to charges against United Artists, Paramount and Fox – as well as Bertolucci never being allowed into the USA. Most of all, *1900* is (for commercial and to be fair formal purposes) too long and too political – and just too foreign for American audiences. By the time of *The Last Emperor* (1987), Bertolucci had got the length and the opulence under control and the politics was more 'palatable' (being about personal tragedy and arguably *anti*-communist), added to which English-speaking audiences did not have to strug-gle with tricky subtitles all through the film. The result was a cart-load of Academy Awards and a major international success. By the time of *The Sheltering Sky* (1996) and *Stealing Beauty* (1996), only the opulence was left.

Some Things to Watch out for and Consider

- Bertolucci begins the film with a number of graphic images of violence by the peasants against the Fascists. How does this fit with or develop in the flashback narrative that follows?
- Notice how the personal often unites as well as separates characters in this film, particularly the two central male characters. Bertolucci is thus able to make what could be rather dry polemic into engaging cinema.
- Consider the effect of music in this film – both diegetic (the songs and classical pieces) and non-diegetic (the swelling romantic orchestral score).
- The relationship between Hollywood and Europe goes back to the 1920s (see *Nosferatu*, chapter 2). Notice the ways in which European films and film-makers (including Hitchcock) influenced, for example, De Palma, Malik, Schrader, Scorsese and Tarantino.
- Has cinema ever been a successful medium for political messages? When? On what terms would we define success?
- Is Hollywood the most successful ideological machine of all?

Further Viewing

Intolerance (Griffith, USA, 1917)
Battleship Potemkin (Eisenstein, USA, 1925)
Gone with the Wind (Fleming, USA, 1939)
The Conformist (Bertolucci, Italy/France/West Germany, 1970)
The Last Emperor (Bertolucci, Italy/USA/China, 1987)
Reds (Beatty, USA, 1977)
Days of Heaven (Malik, USA, 1978)
Land and Freedom (Loach, UK, 1996)

28 ***STAR WARS***
Lucas, USA, 1977

Awards

Academy Awards: Winner – Best Editing, Best Musical Score, Best Art Direction, Best Special Effects and Best Costume Design; Nomination – Best Picture, Best Director and Best Supporting Actor (Alec Guinness)

Production Details

Production company/studio	Twentieth Century Fox
Producer	Gary Kurz
Director	George Lucas
Cinematographer	Gilbert Taylor
Editors	Richard Chew, Paul Hirsch and Marcia Lucas
Screenwriter	George Lucas
Music	John Williams
Costume designer	John Mollo
Special effects	Industrial Light and Magic

Cast Includes

Mark Hamill	*Luke Skywalker*
Harrison Ford	*Han Solo*
Carrie Fisher	*Princess Leia*
Peter Cushing	*Grand Moff Tarkin*
Alec Guinness	*Obi-wan Kenobi*
David Prowse	*Darth Vader* (voiced by James Earl Jones)

FOCUS: Institutional Context/Narrative

At the time of its release *Star Wars* was the biggest box office hit of all time. On its re-release in 1997 (with the sound remixed and some additional scenes) it took $46 million in its first week and became the first film to gross more than $400 million at the US box office. The distributor's press book for the special edition (1997) proclaimed: 'While *Star Wars* was a defining event for one generation, it has been embraced by new generations assuring its place as a timeless epic of grand design and boundless fun.' This claim was confirmed by articles in *Time*, *Newsweek*, the *New Yorker* and the *New York Times*, which said that the film was 'part of the culture' and its 'lessons' about good and evil, humanity and technology, pride and redemption were a 'very powerful force indeed'. These publications commented that contemporary mass media are full of references to the film and that many words and phrases from it have entered into everyday life. The most striking example of this must surely be the appropriation of the film's title to describe Ronald Reagan's missile defence programme in the mid-1980s. In other words, it is a film of enormous impact, in terms of its effect both on the film industry and on the American culture/sense of national identity.

Star Wars is a prime example of bricolage (the combining of elements from different film genres), drawing as it does on the Western, the war film and the science-fiction film. It changed the course of the science-fiction genre away from films that questioned the nature of human society – e.g. *Planet of the Apes* (Schaffner, USA, 1968) and *Rollerball* (Jewison, USA, 1975) – towards films that celebrate escapism and daredevil heroics – e.g. *Superman* (Donner, USA, 1978) and *Star Trek – The Motion Picture* (Wise, USA, 1979). For the film historian, one of the interesting features of *Star Wars* is the degree to which it is derivative. There are specific allusions to a number of films. The bombing raids and dogfights have their origins in films like *The Dam Busters* (Anderson, UK, 1955) and *633 Squadron* (Grauman, UK, 1964). The victory celebration at the end is based on sequences in *Triumph of the Will* (Riefenstahl, Germany, 1936) and the scene where Luke Skywalker returns to his aunt and uncle's burn-out homestead is similar to a scene in *The Searchers* (Ford, USA, 1956) (see chapter 18).

The impact of *Star Wars* is undisputed; the important question for the contemporary viewer is to consider how the film achieved such an effect. Part of the answer has to lie in the film's pioneering use of special effects, in particular 'motion control' (the computerised control of the camera movements used in filming models) and the use of Dolby stereo and multi-track sound recording. This certainly had an impact on films and audience expectations, so that the desire for bigger and better spectacles became the rage for years afterwards. The other part of the answer lies in the way *Star Wars* manages to combine so many different elements. In its narrative, characterisation and genre characteristics, it is satisfyingly familiar, drawing on many old films, and yet all this was relocated in space with dazzling special effects and *mise en scène* that at the time of release was stunning in its unique other-worldliness. For example, Luke Skywalker, the quintessential American farmboy longing for some excitement in a landscape as flat, rolling and unadventurous as the American prairie, gazes off into the sunset – but this is a world with two suns. It is this kind of detail, combining the familiar and the strange, that gives *Star Wars* its impact.

The narrative structure of *Star Wars* departs from the classic Hollywood pattern in favour of an episodic structure based on the B-movie serials of the 1930s. This allows the film to move back and forth between parallel spheres of action, characteristically cutting between scenes with the horizontal or vertical wipe. The advantage of this structure is that it allows for the frequent excitement and tension of last-minute escapes and rescues. Criticism has been levelled at *Star Wars* and subsequent New Hollywood blockbusters (with a similar focus on spectacular stunt sequences) for dispensing with the virtues of the classic Hollywood narrative (character-driven psychologically motivated storytelling) in favour of loosely linked action sequences with little character depth. It is certainly true that the characters lack depth, falling into simple but recognisable types. The film, which is entitled 'Episode 4', starts with a series of titles telling the story so far and then leaps straight into the action – the pursuit and capture of Princess Leia by Darth Vader. The subsequent episodes are linked by a good old-fashioned (but updated) struggle between good and evil, the fairytale elements of magic, knights and a princess, with the added thrills of impossible odds and daredevil heroics from the small band of heroes.

The virtues of the classic narrative may have been dispensed with. Nonetheless, this approach has proved to be a staggeringly successful formula with audiences. Thus *Star Wars* had, and continues to have, an enormous impact on the narrative structure of the new Hollywood blockbuster (see *Raiders of the Lost Ark*, chapter 31).

Some Things to Watch out for and Consider

- Although ostensibly set a long time ago in a galaxy far, far away, *Star Wars* is, of course, an American film, with American actors taking the lead roles. In many respects it follows the characteristics of the Western genre (a genre that has traditionally presented us with America's reflections upon itself) – the main difference being that the frontier has changed from the Wild West to space. Given the worldwide impact of the film, it is particularly important to look at the underlying messages and values the film presents about gender, race and nation. In order to do this, compare the 'good' characters with the 'bad' characters. Look at:
  - costumes (note the symbolic use of colours);
  - behaviour, beliefs and attitudes of the characters;
  - accents.
- Which characters appear to be most American? What values does the film associate with them? Does the film endorse these values? If so, how?
- What is the role of women in this film? Compare Luke's aunt with Princess Leia. What is their role/sphere of action? How do the male characters respond to them?

Further Viewing

Flash Gordon (Raymond, USA, 1936)
Flash Gordon (Hodges, UK, 1978)
Triumph of The Will (Riefenstahl, Germany, 1936)
The Hidden Fortress (Kurosawa, Japan, 1954)
The Searchers (Ford, USA, 1956)
2001 (Kubrick, UK, 1968)
Raiders of the Lost Ark (Spielberg, USA, 1981)
The Empire Strikes Back (Kershner, USA, 1980)
Return of the Jedi (Marquand, USA, 1983)
The Phantom Menace (Lucas, USA, 2000)

Further Reading

G. Roberts and H. Wallis, *Introducing Film* (London, 2001)
S. Neale and M. Smith (eds.), *Contemporary Hollywood Cinema* (London, 1998)

29 ***ANNIE HALL***
Allen, USA, 1977

Awards

Academy Awards: Winner – Best Picture, Best Director and Best Original
  Screenplay; Nomination – Best Actor (Woody Allen) and Best Actress
  (Diane Keaton)

Production Details

Production company/studio	United Artists
Producer	Charles H. Joffe
Director	Woody Allen
Cinematographer	Gordon Willis
Editor	Ralph Rosenblum
Screenwriters	Woody Allen and Marshall Brickman

Cast Includes

Woody Allen	*Alvie Singer*
Diane Keaton	*Annie Hall*
Tony Roberts	*Rob*
Shelley Duvall	*Pam*
Colleen Dewhurst	*Mrs Hall*
Donald Symington	*Dad Hall*

FOCUS: Auteur

Classical 'auteur' theory ascribes the chief creative force of a film
to the director. Thus the director is auteur (author) of the film. He
'writes' in pictures. To be described as an auteur, a director must
present his or her world view. In terms of narrative, Allen
appears to fit the criteria for auteurship to the point where the
films can become a blur, with the angst-ridden, New York,

Jewish, intellectual central character from one film blending almost seamlessly with the angst-ridden, New York, Jewish, intellectual central character from the next. Allen's themes, indeed his films, centre around himself and his neurotic obsessions with sex, death and psychoanalysis amongst the intellectual elite of New York. *Annie Hall* is no exception to this, but this does not detract from the qualities of the film and its director. In tackling the problems and frustrations of adult relationships he addresses adult anxieties with wit, insight and imagination as well as humour.

The obvious argument against auteur theory is that film is a collaborative art form requiring the creative input of a team of people other than the director. Thus we might wish to consider the creative input of writer, actors and cinematographer, to name but a few. Here Allen sidesteps the issue by taking on these roles too. He is the writer of most of his films. He usually plays the central character and the subject matter is based on himself and his relationships. Taken together these roles make him a very strong candidate for auteurship; as writer, performer and director, he appears to have overall creative control over the themes and content as well as the look of his films.

Perhaps the fact that Allen seems to be the quintessential auteur tells us more about the flaw in the theory than anything else. The idea of authorship is borrowed from literature. Thus applying it to film is always problematic; it can be a useful analytical tool but only if we recognise that pure auteur theory is nonsense. Films are not like novels – they do not have a single author. In Allen's case we come as close as possible to an author and this perhaps reflects his literate and literary background. He began his career writing jokes for Sid Caesar before moving into stand-up and going on to write plays and screenplays – e.g. *What's New Pussycat?* (Donner, USA/France, 1965). This theatrical training is ever present in his work, so that the films still rely on character and dialogue for their effect. The humour lies in the words. Perhaps we should best describe him as an 'author' rather than an 'auteur', filming his words rather than writing in pictures. But in this film we are watching the work of a master cinematographer (Gordon Willis). Herein lies the problem. Classic auteur theory requires a visual signature as well as a unifying set of themes. Does Allen have one?

Annie Hall centres around the relationship between Alvie Singer (Allen) and Annie Hall (Diane Keaton). A key to its creator is the fact that the film is titled *Annie Hall* but starts in documentary style (a strategy utilised earlier with *Take the Money and Run*, 1969) with Alvie (Allen) talking to camera about his feelings on life, 'full of loneliness and misery and suffering', childhood, relationships and psychoanalysis. Already the boundaries between Allen, the man, and Alvie, his character, seem tenuous, and it is clear that this is only a film about Annie Hall in so far as it deals with *his* feelings for, perception of and relationship with her.

The most striking aspect of the opening sequences of the film and one of the keys to the film's success is the imaginative and comic way in which Allen constructs character and explores identity and repression. For example, the adult Alvie tells us with an absolutely deadpan face, 'I had a reasonably happy childhood in Brooklyn'; the film then cuts to a flashback where the child Alvie is with his mother seeing a psychiatrist. His mother tells us, 'He's been depressed.' This kind of comic irony abounds throughout the film. In a further flashback to childhood we see the young Alvie in school. In a technique borrowed from Bergman's *Wild Strawberries* (*Smultonstallet*) (Sweden, 1957), the adult Alvie then appears in the classroom, sits at one of the desks and attempts to defend his youthful self from the criticisms of the teacher. This kind of imaginative narrative device is both comic and illustrative of character, suggesting as it does the forces that influence development. Further examples continue to break the diegesis of the film – for example, when Alvie produces Marshall McLuhan to uphold his argument (about McLuhan's work) in the cinema queue or when Alvie and Annie observe and comment on Annie with her previous lover. It is this kind of (European?) freewheeling through the Hollywood convention of verisimilitude that gives *Annie Hall* its particular, sophisticated and ironic brand of comedy.

Annie Hall provides us with a funny, touching, accomplished and original examination of relationships. It is an adult film about adult life that succeeds in making the issues facing real people (although from a particular and sophisticated milieu) cinematically interesting. The strengths of *Annie Hall* without doubt lie in the writing as well as the performances. It is worth noting that Allen's visual style has become more polished with time. Some of the later films – e.g. *Manhattan* (1979) and *Everyone Says I Love You* (1996) – are as distinctive in their visual style as their writing.

Some Things to Watch out for and Consider

- Consider the symbiotic (?) relationship between Allen the man – his life and times – and Allen the director and character actor.
- Within his work and within individual films Allen seems uncertain whether to go for broad comedy or psychological complexity. Consider how *Annie Hall* deals with this dichotomy. Consider if (and if so why) *Annie Hall* is seen as one of his most successful films.
- Compare the ways in which Allen breaks the diegesis of *Annie Hall* with those used in *The Purple Rose of Cairo* (1985) (including 'The Purple Rose of Cairo'!).
- In some of the later films – e.g. *Bullets over Broadway* (1994) – Allen has attempted to 'move away' from himself, both as subject and star. How effective has this strategy been?

Further Viewing

Manhattan (Allen, USA, 1979)
The Purple Rose of Cairo (Allen, USA, 1985)
Hannah and her Sisters (Allen, USA, 1986)
Manhattan Murder Mystery (Allen, USA, 1993)
Bringing up Baby (Hawks, USA, 1938)
It's a Wonderful Life (Capra, USA, 1946)
Wild Strawberries (Bergman, Sweden, 1957)

30 APOCALYPSE NOW

Coppola, USA, 1979

Awards

Academy Awards: Winner – Best Cinematography and Best Sound
British Academy Awards: Winner – Best Direction and Best Supporting
   Actor (Robert Duvall)
Cannes: Winner – Golden Palm
Golden Globes: Winner – Best Director

Production Details

Production company/studio	Omni Zoetrope
Producers	Francis Ford Coppola, Fred Roos, Gray Frederickson and Tom Sternberg
Director	Francis Ford Coppola
Cinematographer	Vittorio Storaro
Editors	Lisa Fruchtman, Gerald B. Greenberg, Richard Marks and Walter Murch
Screenwriters	John Milius and Francis Ford Coppola
Narration	Michael Herr

(NB Running time varies depending on different versions'
exclusion/inclusion treatment of a final 'air-strike' sequence with the
film's end credits. Coppola has recently released an even longer version,
Apocalypse Now Redux.)

Cast Includes

Martin Sheen	*Captain Benjamin Willard*
Robert Duvall	*Lieutenant Colonel Kilgore*
Frederic Forrest	*Chef (Hicks)*
Albert Hall	*Chief Phillips*
Marlon Brando	*Colonel Walter E. Kurtz*
Dennis Hopper	*The Photo-Journalist*

FOCUS: Genre – the War Film; Cinema Spectacular

When *Apocalypse Now* was shown at Cannes, the risk was taken to screen it as a near complete work-in-progress: a film print with soundtrack that had not been properly married, with the danger of problems in picture/sound synchronisation. The gamble worked: *Apocalypse Now* shared the coveted Golden Palm award with *The Tin Drum* (Schlondorff, France/Yugoslavia/Polland/West Germany, 1979). Hollywood was approaching the close of a period of much bigger risk-taking, where young, talented directors from the LA and New York film schools, such as Coppola, George Lucas and Steven Spielberg (the 'movie brats'), were handed great opportunity and large budgets early in their careers. Like Martin Scorsese and Brian De Palma, they arrived from nowhere and rose rapidly on the strength of real promise shown in early works, plus an exploding enthusiasm for the medium, and the legacy of their ancestors, both American and European. Stakes were raised with the promise of huge returns such as those generated by surprise, enormous successes such as *The Godfather* (Coppola, 1971) and *Jaws* (Spielberg, 1975). The swelling bubble had to burst. Industry fingers were badly burned with expensive flops like *New York, New York* (Scorsese, 1977), then the disastrous Second World War comedy epic *1941* (Spielberg, 1979). The crash finally hit in 1980. On the strength of *The Deer Hunter* (1978), Michael Cimino was handed a $17 million budget to make *Heaven's Gate*, but even that was not enough. It spiralled up to $44 million as Cimino's exacting, grandiose demands were pandered to. The studio had committed so much that cutting losses was too hard to contemplate, so 'double-or-quits' prevailed. On completion, the film was so dismally received that its losses nearly sank United Artists forever.

Insanity, madness – at Cannes, Coppola compared the shooting of *Apocalypse Now* to the lunacy of the American involvement in the Vietnam War itself, referring that they were in the jungle with too much money, too much equipment, and that 'little by little we went insane'. *Apocalypse Now* ran as far out of control as *Heaven's Gate* would do, bringing Coppola himself close to total bankruptcy, but in the end it did touch a chord with huge audiences around the globe and made large profits. Coppola's production company Zoetrope stayed afloat, allowing him to go on and make a visually stunning, spectacularly expensive romantic studio fantasy *One from the Heart* (1982), which flopped, losing Zoetrope a fortune.

A legend of the madness surrounding the making of *Apocalypse Now* started long before even shooting had been completed, and the experience was well documented in *Hearts of Darkness: A Filmmaker's Apocalypse* (Eleanor Coppola, USA, 1991). Coppola's wife's film, based on her own taped diaries and 16mm filming, has become essential viewing to accompany the epic drama that it covered. Madness is the central theme of *Apocalypse Now*, whether in the shape of Colonel Kurtz, whom the main protagonist Captain Willard is sent to 'terminate with extreme prejudice', or the collective madness that bursts forth over a Vietnamese village, carried in by a phalanx of helicopter gunships rushing in at low level over breaking surf waves, spurred on by Wagner's 'Ride of the Valkyries' blasting from speakers attached to Colonel Kilgore's leading chopper that has 'Death from Above' painted on the nose. The helicopter assault scene that follows, designed to leave an audience open-mouthed, is stunning – shocking, obscene and exciting. The scene precedes Kilgore's obviously wistful disappointment as he casually comments 'Some day this war's gonna end . . .', just after his endlessly quoted 'I love the smell of napalm in the morning' speech.

The film is saturated with such emblematic words and images: Kilgore's cavalry stetson; an aborted Playmates show in the middle of the jungle; a lamb being raised high into the air by a helicopter; a television crew directing the soldiers' movements as they land on the beach; young soldiers sunbathing, water-skiing, smoking dope and firing machine guns to the army radio broadcasts of the Doors and the Rolling Stones; Willard emerging from the waters of the Mekong river, like a demon who may prove to be Kurtz's nemesis or just his heir-in-waiting.

Apocalypse Now is notable at the very least because it had, and still has, no equal. It concentrates precious little on either the bravery or the camaraderie that forms the core of so many heroic war films before it. Nor does it use characters to convey intellectual arguments that are either polemically anti-war or anti-militaristic. It is a sensual vision of a particular conflict – the Vietnam War, conducted by people incapable of understanding it; the first war fought on television. As a cinematic symphony of human obscenity, the film itself is inevitably capable of being obscene, never more so than when offering up the sight of hundreds of yards of Philippine forest line erupting into a napalm inferno – all for our great entertainment. Following one man's quest to confront a military genius who has gone insane, creating carnage while surrounded by a tribe who 'worship the man like a God', we are constantly faced with the results of a film-maker who was allowed to go over the edge. *Apocalypse Now* is extreme, and its level of crazed commitment is perhaps best reflected in Martin Sheen's face in one scene near the start of the film, where he ends up covered in blood then crying in shocking anguish, having performed the scene in a genuine drunken near-stupor, and smashed a large mirror by punching it. Sheen's serious heart attack during production was just one of a series of disasters, which included a massive set being completely destroyed by a hurricane, and set-piece shooting being postponed when the helicopter gunships and pilots leased from Marcos's Philippine army were called away at zero notice to fight a real war against rebels to his regime. The production's excesses are never very far removed from the frame itself. *Apocalypse Now* seems either the masterpiece of an artist, or a disgusting commercial exploitation of a not-so-distant human tragedy, or both.

Coppola recognises the sense of dislocation from reality that seems to have been part of the process of his directing *Apocalypse Now*. The impression is he was sucked into a project that had developed a terrifying momentum of its own, driven by a genuine personal desire to make a truly great film – and it was never destined to be a small-scale drama. Certainly, he did make a great film in terms of its epic scale. In the documentary of its making, he talks of the ultimate artist's fear: to be seen 'to be pretentious'. Whether or not 'pretentiousness' is visible in *Apocalypse Now* can be discussed. But in contemplating the mesmerising power of its images and narrative, it is equally debatable whether or not any identifiable pretentiousness would have affected its chances of success anyway.

Some Things to Watch out for and Consider

- What are the moments/images/lines that linger in the memory most strongly after seeing *Apocalypse Now*?
- Can you identify the main elements that set it apart from other war films that you have seen?
- Do you find the film's attitude to war clear? What is it trying to convey?
- As a mainstream American film, does Coppola's film surprise you? Yes/no? Why/why not?
- What message does the film's ending leave you with?

Further Viewing

All Quiet on the Western Front (Milestone, UK, 1930)
La Grande Illusion (Renoir, France, 1937)
Gone with the Wind (Fleming, USA, 1939)
The Treasure of the Sierra Madre (Huston, USA, 1948)
Deliverance (Boorman, USA, 1972)
Cross of Iron (Sam Peckinpah, USA, 1977)
The Deer Hunter (Cimino, USA, 1978)
The Big Red One (Fuller, USA, 1980)
Southern Comfort (Hill, USA, 1981)
Platoon (Stone, USA, 1986)
Full Metal Jacket (Kubrick, UK 1987)
Casualties of War (De Palma, 1989)
Saving Private Ryan (Spielberg, 1998)
The Thin Red Line (Malick, 1998)
The Godfather (Coppola, USA, 1971)
The Godfather II (Coppola, USA, 1974)
One from the Heart (Coppola, USA, 1982)
Hearts of Darkness: A Filmmaker's Apocalypse (Eleanor Coppola, USA, 1991)

31 RAIDERS OF THE LOST ARK

Spielberg, USA, 1981

Awards

Academy Awards: Winner – Best Film Editing, Best Art Direction, Best Sound and Best Visual Effects; Nomination – Best Picture, Best Director, Best Original Score and Best Cinematography

Production Details

Production company/studio	Lucasfilm / Paramount
Producer	George Lucas
Director	Steven Spielberg
Cinematographer	Douglas Slocombe
Editor	Michael Kahn
Music	John Williams

Cast Includes

Harrison Ford	*Indiana Jones*
Karen Allen	*Marion Ravenwood*
Paul Freeman	*Belloq*
John Rhys-Davies	*Sallah*
Denholm Elliot	*Brody*

FOCUS: Film Form and Narrative

Raiders of the Lost Ark is an early example of the New Hollywood blockbuster that can be identified with the success of the *Star Wars* franchise. There is no question as to the high production values and entertainment content of these films. However, criticism has been levelled at the (lack of) narrative and character development. Some critics (e.g. S. Neale and M. Smith (eds), *Contemporary Hollywood Cinema* (1998)) have expressed the opinion that the qualities associated with the classic Hollywood film of psychologically driven, clearly motivated narrative linked by cause and effect has been replaced by loosely linked action sequences built around stunts and special effects.

Spielberg, however, has emphasised the importance of narrative, not least for its commercial value:

> You need good storytelling to offset the amount of . . . spectacle the audiences demand before they will leave their television sets. And I think people will leave their television sets for a good story before anything else. Before fire and skyscrapers and floods, plane crashes, laser fire and spaceships, they want good stories. (quoted in P. Biskind, 'Blockbuster: The Last Crusade', in M. Miller (ed.), *Seeing through Movies* (1990), 145–6)

It is clear then that, whatever the critics might say, Spielberg has a commitment to narrative, and audiences flock to see his films. Their enduring appeal is illustrated by the number of them that appear in genuinely popular polls such as *Empire* magazine's top 100 films and so on.

Raiders of the Lost Ark, like many Spielberg and/or Lucas vehicles, has an episodic narrative structure that is based on the B-movie serials of the 1930s rather than the 'beginning–middle–end' structure of the classic Hollywood film. This is illustrated if we look at the opening sequence of the film, which acts as a mini narrative in itself, plunging us into an ongoing storyline with its own goals (the retrieval of the golden icon), conflict (between hero and villain) and closure (with the dramatic escape of the hero in a biplane). In a sense, the story of the icon and the trials engendered by the escape from the temple are perfect examples of the type of criticism described above. The icon is not relevant to the rest of the film but a device around which the daredevil stunts and last-minute escape sequence can be structured – that is, a means of overwhelming the audience with the thrills and spills of adventure for its own sake.

The film then goes on to provide us with a further five episodes that also provide us with the excitement of the last-minute rescue/escape scenario. These episodes are linked by the overarching themes of the struggle between good (Dr Jones and the

American government) and evil (Belloq, the Nazis) and the relationship between Indiana and Marion. Whilst there is no doubt that the film is structured in this episodic way and that this allows for the frequent insertion of cliffhangers, stunts, escapes and rescues all presented in a visually spectacular way, it is possible to argue that this is not at the expense of the virtues of the classic Hollywood narrative and that we need to look carefully at how Spielberg uses his episodes to delineate character and keep the action firmly based within the story. It is our contention that Spielberg's enormous popularity comes from his ability to tell stories visually. This can be illustrated if we return to the opening sequence of the film.

As has already been stated, the golden icon is irrelevant to the story. The film is centred round a different archaeological treasure: the Ark of the Covenant. But, whilst the quest for the icon is not central to the narrative in itself, the sequence does more than provide us with spectacular action. Spielberg uses the whole of this mini-narrative as a means of introducing his central character, Indiana Jones. His skill as a film-maker is evident in the fact that he does this almost entirely through careful choices in the *mise en scène*, cinematography, music and sound effects. Dialogue is kept to a bare minimum and is a method of reinforcing narrative information already communicated by the visuals. Like Hitchcock and other great craftsmen before him, Spielberg uses careful placement of the camera and positioning of objects and characters within the frame, as well as setting, costume and lighting, to tell his story.

The opening shot presents us with the image of a mountain, a graphic match of the Paramount logo that precedes the moving images. The hero walks into the frame and is positioned so that we see him from behind, silhouetted against the skyline and looking at the mountain, which is obviously his destination. His importance is signalled by the fact that he is in the centre of the frame, but his identity is withheld from us; we do not see his face. This kind of positioning continues for the first few minutes of the film, creating a mystery, a curiosity in the audience to know who he is. Withholding his face from us forces us to concentrate on the actions we do see and much of his character is established in this way.

We see that he is a leader, knowledgeable and decisive in this jungle terrain, able to interpret signs like the poisoned dart in the tree and weigh up the risks. He is separated from the group, through his position (isolated in the lead), his actions (which instigate the actions of the whole group) and his costume, the leather jacket and battered hat (redolent of Bogart in *Casablanca*, see chapter 11), suggesting he is American in contrast with the bare heads or tattered straw or knitted hats of his followers. His status as leader is further marked out by the fact that he carries no pack of equipment and is not leading a mule like the others. The reluctance with which these others follow him, the apprehension expressed in their faces (which we do see, a further contrast), highlight his determination and lack of fear. He pauses to consult the torn pieces of an ancient-looking map (again our view is restricted to a detail shot showing the hands) and this is the first clear indication that this expedition is some kind of treasure hunt. We have already seen him fearlessly take the lead, undaunted by whatever dangers may be lurking in the jungle. Now in his reading of the map he demonstrates skill and then further proves his bravery/heroic status.

One of his followers, bent on treachery, takes out and cocks his gun behind the hero's back. A shot of Jones's ear indicates super alert hearing and then he moves swiftly and decisively, spinning round as he cracks his whip with perfect aim to disarm his assailant. His face remains briefly in darkness and then he steps forward into the half-light finally revealed to us (note the way music and type of shot work in conjunction with the *mise en scène* to create the powerful impact of our first sight of Indiana Jones). Sun-tanned, unshaven, sweat-stained and frowning, he looks mean, tough and competent. We already associate him with bravery and leadership. It is a tremendously dramatic and powerful introduction of character.

All the elements of *mise en scène* – setting, costume, lighting, position and movement within the frame – have been utilised to establish Jones's heroic credentials. So far he has not said a word. Once inside the temple he faces a new series of trials that demonstrate further heroic qualities. It is not just bravery that enables him successfully to navigate the temple, but knowledge. Both these qualities are highlighted by their absence in his sidekick, played by Alfred Molina, whose face and voice express his fear, selfishness and greed.

As this sequence illustrates, *Raiders of the Lost Ark* is not a film that is concerned with character depth; Indiana Jones is a comic book hero with the accompanying superhuman skills. What the film does do, however, is delineate character clearly by grounding it within the action of the film, so that the adventure sequences are not simply tacked on to the narrative but arise out of the characters' motivations and conflicts, providing the audience with all the excitement of a series of adventures along the way.

Some Things to Watch out for and Consider

- *Raiders of the Lost Ark* presents us with a number of different settings from the jungles of South America to the sand dunes of Egypt. Consider how the film represents different nationalities and races. With whom are we encouraged to sympathise? How?
- Consider the representation of gender within this film
- Take any sequence from the film and analyse the film language considering how the different aspects of *mise en scène*, cinematography, editing and sound communicate narrative information.

Further Viewing

Flash Gordon (Raymond, USA, 1936)
Flash Gordon's Trip to Mars (Raymond, USA, 1938)
Flash Gordon Conquers the Universe (Raymond, USA, 1949)
Casablanca (Curtiz, USA, 1942)
Star Wars (Lucas, USA, 1977)
Pulp Fiction (Tarantino, USA, 1994)

Further Reading

M. Miller (ed.), *Seeing through Movies* (New York, 1990)
S. Neale and M. Smith (eds.), *Contemporary Hollywood Cinema* (London, 1998)
Philip M. Taylor, *Steven Spielberg: The Man, his Movies and their Meaning* (London 1995)

32 BLADE RUNNER

Scott, USA, 1982

Awards

British Academy Awards: Winner – Best Production Design/Art Direction and Best Costume Design
Los Angeles Film Critics Association Awards: Winner – Best Cinematography

Production Details

Production company/studio	Blade Runner Partnership/The Ladd Company
Producers	Michael Deeley, Brian Kelly, Hampton Fancher, Jerry Perenchio and Bud Yorkin
Director	Ridley Scott
Cinematographer	Jordan Cronenweth
Editor	Marsha Nakashima
Screenwriters	Hampton Fancher and David Peoples

Cast Includes

Harrison Ford	*Deckard*
Rutger Hauer	*Roy Batty*
Sean Young	*Rachael*
Darryl Hannah	*Pris*
Joanna Cassidy	*Zhora*
Brion James	*Leon*
M. Emmet Walsh	*Bryant*
Joseph Turkel	*Eldon Tyrell*
William Sanderson	*J. F. Sebastian*

FOCUS: Auteurship; Genre

Blade Runner belongs to a small number of films of the early 1980s that seemed to herald a new era where talented young British directors could once again shine out, following Britain's lowest point in the 1970s, at least in terms of empty cinemas. After the critical success of *The Duellists* (1977) and the popular success of the *Alien* (1979), Ridley Scott seemed poised to follow Alan Parker. He brought a strong and economical visual style learned in telling stories in television commercials, and was apparently less concerned with a notion of 'auteurship' than with making films that would find audiences, building on the spectacular success of the David Puttnam–Hugh Hudson partnership's *Chariots of Fire* (1979). Soon after Scott, other names appeared who can still be recognised as directors with an eye on the audience reception that ensures they continue in work: Stephen Frears, Mike Newell and Tony Scott (Ridley's brother), and then in the 1990s names like Michael Caton-Jones, Mike Figgis and Guy Ritchie. Like them, Scott has rarely been hailed as an 'auteur' director, although partly because enthusiasm for the very concept has since waned. Reasons for this may include the very repopularisation of film itself, with its later fashion for 'making-of' promotion documentaries that let large audiences in on the 'auteur's secrets, exploding some fanciful notions regarding the nature and realities of film directing.

Another later development, growing largely during the 1990s, was the film studios' willingness to support a re-edited 'director's-cut' version of earlier releases as a way of increasing each film's income. Whilst the trend should encourage audiences and academics to be cautious about attributing the details of content and structure to 'auteur signature', the 'director's cut' of *Blade Runner* shows the original release to be one of the most blunt examples of directorial vision altered radically to meet the commercial interests represented by the producer/production company. The plot centres around Deckard, a retired 'detective' who specialises in tracking down and killing rogue 'replicants', synthesised humanoids whose programming is so sophisticated that they are hard to detect from humans. He is coerced into coming out of retirement to hunt down a group of killer replicants, 'Nexus 6' series, who have even been programmed with memories and emotions. In the film, he assassinates three of them, and a fourth is killed by the fifth replicant, Rachael. Deckard refuses to kill Rachael himself, affected by her emotional communication with him to the extent that he desires, maybe loves, her. *Film noir* aspects were apparent in the original release, including comparison with Deckard and the cynical whisky-drinking characters played by Humphrey Bogart in the 1940s, and Rachael's classic *femme fatale* visual style. But the most emblematic noir element, Deckard's voice-over, was forced on Ridley Scott by the studio, which insisted that the film was confusing without it.

The most fundamental change forced on Scott was to create an upbeat ending, achieved with Deckard's final voice-over as he (presumably) flies off with Rachael, not into the sunset, but over beautiful landscapes grabbed from out-takes of the opening sequence to *The Shining* (Kubrick, USA, 1980). The director's cut is almost the same length, but, as well as deleting the pointless voice-over, the reinsertion of Deckard's brief vision/dream of a unicorn recovered the single most crucial plot point: Deckard himself is a replicant. Another studio rehash of a major mainstream work (even more extreme) was *Once upon a Time in America* (Leone, 1984). Not content with cutting the film down by minutes for its original US release, the studio insisted that the film's temporal criss-crossing plot be reordered chronologically in an utter travesty of Leone's intention. In relation to the notion of film 'authorship', conflict between producer/studio and directors' favoured versions does offer interesting debate – certainly more provocative than discussion of the 'deleted scenes' included in DVD special features (often scenes about which the need for removal was never seriously questioned or fought over). The DVD-released 'alternative ending' for another Ridley Scott film, *Thelma and Louise* (1991), gives another example of that more substantial dilemma, the choice having real impact on emotional effect, rather than simply a question of pace.

Although well received critically, the studio-doctored *Blade Runner* was not successful in America on its first-run release – despite Harrison Ford's association with the blockbuster *Star Wars* (Lucas, USA, 1977). Its reputation seems to have grown since, especially since the 'director's cut' was offered, justifying regular global re-release in domestic video formats. The film may have survived long enough to benefit from a renewed taste for darker, more violent sci-fi cinema, but its appeal has less to do with a fascination for outer space (which does not feature beyond reference in a few lines of dialogue) than with a vision of earth and humankind in the near future. *Blade Runner* takes place in the imagined Los Angeles of 2019, and Deckard's character is wearied more by life in a human-created urban nightmare than by any fear of the unknown universe. *Blade Runner*'s LA depicts a city that has grown technologically, with small-craft vertical take-off flight and the proliferation of sophisticated computer technology, but that has also slid in terms of infrastructural decay. The city where massive aerial video-screen adverts (representing Japanese manufacturers that seem to have flourished) reside against a corporate backdrop of congestion and pollution is claustrophobic and vastly overcrowded. There are no brightly lit scenes in the film, suggesting a world that is choked with an atmosphere of dark smog and that has to conserve power everywhere owing to the density of the population and its high consumption. In a world where it is a crime to own real animals (as though extreme rarity is the norm), the film clearly depicts a society where consumerism continues to reign and increase. As its inhabitants intoxicate themselves in overcrowded bars seeking ersatz 'exotic' entertainment, their rooms, buildings and streets crumble around them, grubby, neglected, vacated and above all dark and leaking with water from rainfall that never stops – climate change has hit LA. 'Replicants' are just one more dangerous example of a need to synthesise 'life' in a society where the real is close to extinction.

Blade Runner's great strength is in the way its valedictory vision of the future pervades every image and scene, but without resorting to heavy explanatory dialogue. The richness of the designs and art direction depicting a decadent society showing a clearly faltering modernism are arguably more important in their dramatic weight than the core thriller plot, when tied to the film's existential interest in life, humanity and reality. The thrill and violence that mark the death of the first three replicants are less central to the film's emotion than the reflective sadness of the most malevolent replicant (Rutger Hauer's Roy Batty) when he confides his own (synthesised) anxiety to Deckard after their life-and-death struggle. Sensing his own end (programmed termination of his four-year life span), Batty seems to seek some kind of vicarious sense of 'immortality' by allowing Deckard to live. *Blade Runner* has also proved frighteningly visionary – there now seems surprisingly little that is wildly fantastical about its bankrupt society investing so much hope in genetics.

Some Things to Watch out for and Consider

- People who direct films are sometimes referred to as 'director', sometimes as 'film-maker'. It this only / partly a question of fashion?
- Is it right to think of the labels as different and apply them carefully?
- Do you regard Ridley Scott as an 'auteur' director – the author of his films? How can you justify your answer with reference to his body of work?
- In an analysis of *Blade Runner*, how crucial is the plot, the basic story? Can the film's visual and aural background be considered more important in overall assessment of its quality?
- With no first-person voice-over from Deckard, how justified is any *film noir* comparison?

Further Viewing

The Duellists (Scott, UK, 1977)
Alien (Scott, UK/USA, 1979)
Black Rain (Scott, USA, 1989)
Thelma and Louise (Scott, USA, 1991)
Gladiator (Scott, USA, 2000)
Metropolis (Lang, USA, 1927)
Brazil (Gilliam, USA, 1985)
Twelve Monkeys (Gilliam, USA, 1995)
The Fifth Element (Besson, USA, 1997)
AI: Artificial Intelligence (Spielberg, USA, 2001)

33 WINGS OF DESIRE
(Der Himmel über Berlin)
Wenders, Germany, 1987

Awards

Cannes: Winner – Best Director; Nomination – Golden Palm

Production Details

Production company/studio	Argos Films / Road Movies
Producers	Anatole Dauman and Wim Wenders
Director	Wim Wenders
Cinematographer	Henri Alekan
Editor	Peter Przygodda
Screenwriters	Peter Handke and Wim Wenders
Production designer	Heidi Lüdi
Music	Jürgen Knieper

Cast Includes

Bruno Ganz	*Damiel*
Solveig Dommartin	*Marion*
Otto Sander	*Cassiel*
Curt Bois	*Homer*
Peter Falk	*Himself*
Lajos Kovács	*Marion's Coach*
Bruno Rosaz	*The Clown*
Jerry Barrish	*The Director*
Nick Cave	*Himself (with the Bad Seeds)*

FOCUS: New Waves; the New German Cinema (Europe/Hollywood)

As the poster for *Wings of Desire* put it: 'There are angels on the streets of Berlin.'

The first 'New Waves' that enlivened cinema across Europe (particularly Britain, France and parts of the Soviet bloc) were a phenomenon of the late 1950s. The national results, like the reasons, were many and complicated (for example, in Eastern Europe the death of Stalin was a factor). What was consistent and exciting was that young film-makers stepped forward.

Why was there an injection of youthful enthusiasm in Europe at such a time?

- TV had not taken off yet in the way it had in post-war USA (although Britain was fast catching up).
- Consumption patterns were affected by the rise of a clearly targeted 'youth market' of teenagers. This phenomenon had already been utilised as a highly successful marketing ploy in the USA.
- Post-war Europe was itself entering its teenage years (1957 was 13 years since the 'liberation').
- Western Europe was experiencing a long-term and steady economic expansion, not least because of US 'Marshall Aid' in 1948–58.

In film-making terms:

- The availability of new technology – i.e. lighter equipment and faster film stock – allowed for 'freer' film-making away from studio restrictions and lower production costs.
- The increased availability of access to film clubs created a growing awareness of film history – including early/non-Hollywood film, which was looser in style (and entertained more visual possibilities).

As the baby-boomers became consumers in the early 1960s, popular culture catered more and more for the 'me' generation. So, whilst the cinema could be more direct and 'real', it could leave documentary realism to the TV and essay a more visually exciting 'subjective realism'.

Thus the British film industry benefited from the talents of Richardson, Anderson and so on. In France the *Cahiers du cinéma* critics became original and exciting film-makers. The Italian industry recovered creatively from the early demise of neo-realism with such individual talents as Fellini and Pasolini. Yet, into the 1960s the Germans – who before the Nazi takeover had dominated European cinema both artistically and economically – remained in the doldrums.

A key figure in the revitalisation of German film-making was Alexander Kluge, the head of the Institut für Filmgestaltung in Ulm, Germany. In 1962 at the Oberhausen film festival Kluge, who had already made two features, led 26 young film-makers who signed a manifesto declaring old film dead and offering to revitalise the industry. They organised themselves to lobby the government. West German governments – whether left or right – were always of a part with the (mainland) European tradition of being highly interventionist in cultural matters. This approach is centred upon a belief that national culture is important and that it is important to keep a watchful eye on the types who are engaged in cultural production. Thus in 1965 the Federal government set up the Commission of Young German Film. First-time film-makers were invited to make a short film as proof of competence and to submit a script for a (cheap) feature movie. The Commission provided loans for these 'rucksack films'. This low-level funding was a form of 'pump-priming' for a new German cinema. It was a training ground for a host of technicians and artists, including the director Volker Schlondorff, who made films such as *Young Torless* (*Der Junge Torless*) (Germany, 1966) and *Degree of Murder* (*Mord und Totschlag*) (Germany, 1967), before going on to international success in the 1970s and 1980s.

It was a strong and literally rejuvenated industry that faced the political challenges that followed the radical upheavals of 1968. Artistically pre-eminent amongst the 'new' new German film-makers was Rainer Werner Fassbinder, whose provocative and audience-challenging stance made him the German Godard. Born in 1946 (dying tragically young in 1982), Fassbinder emerged in 1969 with *Katzelmacher*, going on to produce masterpieces such as *Fear Eats the Soul* (*Angst Essen Seele Auf*) (Germany, 1973) and *The Marriage of Maria Braun* (*Die Ehre der Maria Braun*) (Germany, 1978).

Fassbinder, like Godard and indeed Wim Wenders, played with the conventions and visual style of American cinema to create challenging films. The 'new' post-1968 German cinema confronted Nazi guilt (which had been totally taboo in the post-war period). The younger film-makers also began to question the value of the US 'occupation' (asking serous questions about when 'liberation' ceases to be a good thing). Of central importance in the new German film-making was the relationship between Germany/Europe (including the 'film-as-art' tradition) and the USA, Hollywood and the power of American popular culture.

Wenders was born in August 1945 just months after 'victory in Europe' (i.e German surrender). He was supposed to train as a doctor – dropped out, went to Paris and tried to be an artist. He watched lots of films at the *Cinémathèque* (thus becoming submerged in cinema history). He even went to film school – where he claims he learnt nothing. In the tradition of Godard and co., Wenders worked as a critic from 1968 to 1971. His feature-directing debut was *Summer in the City* (Germany, 1970), followed by the quirky (i.e. 'European') *Goalkeeper's Fear of the Penalty* (*Die Angst des Tormanns bein Elfmeter*) (Germany, 1972). By 1976 he was exploring overtly the US–Europe relationship in his first 'road movie' *Kings of the Road* (*Im Lauf der Zeit*, Germany) ('The yanks have colonised our subconscious'). In 1977's *The American Friend* (*Der Amerikanische Freund*, Germany) Dennis Hopper plays the American crook/corrupter (the film contains bit parts for American directors Sam Fuller and Nicholas Ray). Wenders was lured to the USA himself, making the visionary *Hammett* (USA, 1982) and *Paris Texas* (USA, 1984).

Wings of Desire was Wenders's homecoming. It has obvious links to Frank Capra's *It's a Wonderful Life* (USA, 1946) (the film of the 'American Dream'). Although continuing to work in Hollywood, he has held onto a distanced (and distancing) approach to America, which has allowed him to make the intriguing and fresh films of an 'outsider.'

(E)motion Pictures (1989), Wenders's collection of film criticism/journalism, is all about American culture. The book ends with a long prose poem, 'The American Dream', which ends 'the dream is over'. (Wenders points out that Kafka's novel *America* was first entitled 'The Lost One'.) The book is also a celebration of the beauty of motion pictures: 'I felt that films were extraordinary, necessary, they were about life, they gave me life and life had given them to me, I gave them life too, I passed them on . . .'.

Wings of Desire is a film about life. It is a celebration – not of the teenage hedonism so beloved of Hollywood, but of adult emotions and responses. Peter Falk – famous as TV cop Columbo, who plays himself – comments on the simple pleasure of human existence as preferable even to being an angel: 'To smoke, and have coffee . . . and if you do it together, it's fantastic.'

Some Things to Watch out for and Consider

- What does this film tell us about our approach to American culture (including Columbo!)?
- Film is often discussed as a form of dream state. Is Wenders attempting to lull us to sleep or wake us up?
- What is Nick Cave's role in the film?
- Consider the driver's speech from *Wings of Desire*:

Are there still borders? More than ever! Every street has its borderline. Between each plot, there's a strip of no-man's-land disguised as a hedge or a ditch. Whoever dares, will fall into booby traps or be hit by laser rays. The trout are really torpedoes. Every home owner, or even every tenant nails his name plate on the door, like a coat of arms and studies the morning paper as if he were a world leader. Germany has crumbled into as many small states as there are individuals. And these small states are mobile. Everyone carries his own state with him, and demands a toll when another wants to enter. A fly caught in amber, or a leather bottle. So much for the border. But one can only enter each state with a password. The German soul of today can only be conquered and governed by one who arrives at each small state with the password. Fortunately, no one is currently in a position to do this.

So . . . everyone migrates, and waves his one-man-state flag in all earthly directions. Their children already shake their rattles and drag their filth around them in circles.

Is this speech about Germany or Europe or the human condition?

- In terms of Germany/Europe, has this situation changed since the fall of the Berlin Wall and the 'end' of the cold war?
- In terms of the human condition, can film make any difference?
- Is cinema essentially an escapist medium? Is escapism a good or a bad thing?

- Can 'international cinema' contribute to reconciling this situation?
- Can cinema be 'national' any more?
- What exactly is the 'star image' that Peter Falk brings to *Wings of Desire*?
- Which movement is more engaging: the German or French 'New Wave' (or German cinema of the 1920s as opposed to that of the 1970s/1980s)?

Further Viewing

It's a Wonderful Life (Capra, USA, 1946)
Paris Texas (Wenders, USA, 1984)
End of Violence (Wenders, USA, 1999)

Further Reading

D. Bordwell and N. Carroll (eds.), *Post-Theory* (Wisconsin, 1996)
J. Orr, *Cinema and Modernity* (Oxford, 1993)
P. Sorlin, *European Cinemas, European Societies* (London, 1991)

34 DO THE RIGHT THING

Lee, USA, 1989

Awards

Los Angeles Film Critics Association Awards: Winner – Best Director, Best Music and Best Supporting Actor (Danny Aieollo)
New York Film Critics Circle Awards: Winner – Best Cinematography

Production Details

Production company/studio	40 Acres and a Mule/Filmworks
Producers	Spike Lee and Monty Ross
Director	Spike Lee
Cinematographer	Ernest R. Dickerson
Editor	Barry Alexander Brown
Screenwriter	Spike Lee

Cast Includes

Spike Lee	*Mookie*
Danny Aiello	*Sal*
John Turturro	*Pino*
Ruby Dee	*Mother Sister*
Bill Nunn	*Radio Raheem*
Giancarlo Esposito	*Buggin' Out*
Richard Edson	*Vito*
Ossie Davis	*'The Mayor'*
Rosie	*Perez Tina*

FOCUS: Black American Cinema/Political Cinema/Race

Do the Right Thing prompts study from many perspectives, not least its extremely striking visual style imposed by the cinematographic handling of lenses, camera angles and colour film stock printing. Still, it demands consideration within the racial context that reflects the thrust of its own political engagement, particularly since Lee's film seeks so consciously to provoke thoughts about the subject of race and society. This factor fuels its most overt visual stylisations, and the subject of racial tension is rarely far from the surface, right from the opening credits, which feature Rosie Perez dancing/boxing, sometimes face into the lens (audience), to the chant of a rap song (by Public Enemy) that incites its own audience to 'fight the powers that be'.

Do the Right Thing leads us towards a grim denouement, where a large group of (mainly) black citizens of the deprived Bedford–Styvesent area of Brooklyn, New York, respond to the killing of a young black man, Radio Raheem (asphyxiated by two white policemen during arrest), by rioting in their own neighbourhood. The crowd wreck and burn down 'Sal's Famous Pizzeria', owned by a local Italian-American family, although it caters almost exclusively for the young African-Americans, who use it as a hang-out, ordering 'Sal's Famous' by the slice. The scenario is of itself remarkable in the context of American cinema history. Questionable representations of black Americans are found throughout the first cinema century, from the singing, dancing simpletons of *The Birth of a Nation* (Griffith, 1915) (where the Ku Klux Klan are portrayed as heroes), to the Oscar given to Hattie McDaniels for her cotton-pickin' caricatured maid in *Gone with the Wind* (Fleming, 1939) (see chapter 12), to the casting tendencies of the 1980s, which seemed to portray black men most often as violent, out-of-control drug dealers. Sidney Poitier's status as a black Hollywood star and director is notable for its very exception to the rule, and even so his career following *In the Heat of the Night* (Jewison, 1967) was limited by the lack of black protagonists' roles in the films that Hollywood developed. Liberal Hollywood has produced many films with a sympathetic view of black Americans, attacking the segregation era, Ku Klux Klan and Deep Southern racism, such as *To Kill a Mockingbird* (Mulligan, 1968), *Mississippi Burning* (Parker, 1988) and *Driving Miss Daisy* (Beresford, 1989). What makes *Do the Right Thing* stand out is that, instead of showing 'good', abused black Americans meekly defended by heroic whites, it portrays ordinary black citizens rising up at injustice and reacting violently towards the most convenient symbol of the establishment, in the shape of Sal's little corner of the American Dream.

Spike Lee had already shown solid commitment to a (male) black perspective on American life with *She's Gotta Have It* (1986) and *School Daze* (1988). With *Do the Right Thing*, his intention to express black politics through directly polemical dramas was firmly established, and the film's frustration with black Americans' situation within a society loaded against them would be followed through with later films like *Jungle Fever* (1991), *Malcolm X* (1992), *Clockers* (1995) and *Get on the Bus* (1996). *Do the Right Thing* is concerned squarely with the street politics of racism that echo around most scenes in the film. From the very outset, the film bombards the audience with vignettes of petty racial conflict, the cumulative effect starting to create the sense that some kind of explosion will be inevitable: Sal's embittered son Pino insulting the old street 'Mayor' who seeks work sweeping the pavement in front of the shop for a dollar; NYPD police mouthing 'what a waste' towards a trio of unemployed black men sitting chatting in the street; the wilful stereotyping of blacks voiced by a man who complains to the police about the youths who deliberately drenched his convertible with a gushing fire hydrant; young Hispanics goading Radio Raheem in their fight for the street supremacy determined by the volume output of their 'ghetto-blasters'; constant needling between pizza delivery boy Mookie and Pino over everything from Mookie's monopolisation of the pizzeria telephone to resentful argument about the merits of black political leaders. It is one of Pino and Mookie's exchanges that prompts the pivotal scene of the film, where, one after another, a series of individuals simply hurl a tirade of insults towards some other racial group, directed to camera, until its ugly momentum is broken by Mr Love Daddy, the local DJ, who pleads with everybody to 'Chill out!'.

Do the Right Thing conveys the idea of simmering racial tension in danger of spilling over by placing the action against the dramatic background of New York's hottest day of the year so far, with constant reference to the unbearable heat, established from Mr Love Daddy's verbal introduction to the story, and reinforced by Sal, the Mayor and other characters throughout the film. Lee builds the film's stylistic appearance entirely around the heatwave metaphor that constantly pushes the dramatic line, where characters' petty niggling and bickering fester and grow into angry frustration. The film is full of both heavily drawn and casually planted images of people fighting to 'cool off' in the heat, which gets worse as the day wears on, from the Mayor's feverish mission to buy a cold beer, to Mookie's aggravated partner Tina cooling her face in a basin of water. But, beyond these pointed images, the entire film is saturated with the impression of unrelenting heat by the warm, glowing, sometimes bleached-out tones of Ernest Dickerson's highly luminous colour cinematography, its oppressive glow compounded by the very strong presence of the colour red in key scenes, and even further by frequent and striking use of low/wide-angle lenses when shooting people in verbal conflict. The lens effects are extreme, and *Do the Right Thing* does not aim for subtlety. The clean portrayal of neighbourhood shows little interest in documentary realism, and seems designed to enhance the sensual evocation of heat, while ensuring that location/social setting remains less important dramatically than human interaction and politics. These elements' consistency guaranteed *Do the Right Thing*'s singular dramatic look, where every visual aspect of the place reflects the dangers growing along the verbal development of the script. The structure does not always seem to maximise dramatic power, however, and Lee's own flat acting is certainly a real flaw, but it is a testament to the power of the film's evocative strengths that it can still transcend having a poorly delivered protagonist. Political as it is, Lee's film is perhaps most memorable as a powerfully sensual work, projecting intense impressions of a blisteringly hot day and the racial strife that it is meant to represent.

The film ends with a lengthy survey of the aftermath of the destruction of Sal's place, showing the characters whose intercut stories form the body of the narrative. The impression is that some things have changed (the Mayor now communicates with Mother Sister, who had previously done nothing but berate him), some things have not (Mookie's day begins as before with Tina cursing his absence and inattention as a father). The clearest statement (from Mookie) seems to be that the burning of Sal's place is no big deal – he can collect the insurance money – whereas Radio Raheem's murder cannot be undone. In contrast, Lee (as Mookie) seems to defuse his own plea for direct action. Alongside an end-quote from Malcolm X, he placed an opposing pacifist quotation from Martin Luther King. *Do the Right Thing* leaves one wondering whether Hollywood is still simply unable to accept the voice of black Americans who insist on 'being difficult'.

Some Things to Watch out for and Consider

- What are the clearest points Spike Lee makes in the closing scenes?
- Why do you think Spike Lee took the part of Mookie?
- Can you explain whether or not you think his decision is justified?
- What precise effects are created with wide-angle lens distortion?
- Do you notice anything interesting about the way argument scenes are edited?

Further Viewing

She's Gotta Have It (Lee, USA, 1986)
Jungle Fever (Lee, USA, 1991)
Malcolm X (Lee, USA, 1992)
Clockers (Lee, USA, 1995)
Get on the Bus (Lee, USA, 1996)
Summer of Sam (Lee, USA, 1999)
Shaft (Parks, USA, 1971)
Boyz N the Hood (Singleton, USA, 1991)
Waiting to Exhale (Whitaker, USA, 1995)
Hurricane (Jewison, USA, 1999)
Shaft (Singleton, USA, 2000)

RAGING BULL
Scorsese, USA, 1980

Awards

Academy Awards: Winner – Best Editing and Best Actor (Robert De Niro)
British Academy Awards: Winner – Best Editing
National Society of Film Critics USA: Winner – Best Director and Best
Cinematography

Production Details

Production company/studio	United Artists / Robert Chartoff-Irwin Winkler
Producers	Robert Chartoff and Irwin Winkler
Director	Martin Scorsese
Cinematographer	Michael Chapman
Editor	Thelma Schoonmaker
Screenwriters	Paul Schrader and Mardik Martin

Cast Includes

Robert De Niro	*Jake La Motta*
Joe Pesci	*Joey La Motta*
Cathy Moriarty	*Vickie La Motta*
Frank Vincent	*Salvy*
Nicholas Colasanto	*Tommy Como*

FOCUS: Editing and Film Form; Realism

With *Raging Bull*, Martin Scorsese was, as far as he was concerned,
directing his last film – throwing everything he had into a creative
swansong/suicide. He has since directed 11 feature-length
dramas, and many other projects. Thelma Schoonmaker's credit,
for which she won several major editing awards, appears over an

introductory scene that amounts to a single static shot lasting over two and three-quarter minutes with no cuts. These ironies fit well with a film that was an enigma. That *Raging Bull* was any kind of commercial success seemed against the odds. It was made in black and white – something considered to be a box-office 'kiss of death' by the time of release. Worse still, it was about a character (real-life former middleweight world champion Jake La Motta, the 'Bronx Bull') whose brutality towards everyone including his own wife and brother seemed to make him impossible to like.

In its favour was the presence of Robert De Niro, whose name alone had become a crowd-puller, following the enormous success of *The Deer Hunter* (Cimino, USA, 1978) two years earlier. His preparation for the role, particularly a spectacular weight gain for the older Jake, went straight into legend, sparking off the new interest in the 'star' as (method) actor, where it continues to be almost mandatory for publicity to boast about the depth of commitment demonstrated by actors' studied role preparation. Also, production duo Robert Chartoff and Irwin Winkler had been responsible for another boxing film that had been a gigantic hit just four years earlier: *Rocky* (Avildsen, USA, 1976), which had turned Sylvester Stallone into a star. *Raging Bull* looked nothing like *Rocky*, and, lacking the slightest feel-good element, it was much further from normally acceptable Hollywood fare than even *Taxi Driver* (Scorsese, USA, 1976; see chapter 26). But if *Raging Bull* risked being found depressing, its explosive drama was unlikely to be rejected as dull. If not Scorsese's masterpiece to date, it is his tour de force. In any event, *Raging Bull* is remarkable for its brutal moulding of cinematic form, particularly the visual and aural montage of the fight scenes, which seem so geared towards expression of feeling that they display a kind of self-destructive anti-continuity. Scorsese rejected having the narrative of the boxing sequences tied down by the simple shot–shot action continuity flow that dominates much of American mainstream cinema, which liberated him to present a stark montage of emblematic images that embody Jake's alternately enraged and penitential experiences inside the ring.

The redemption theme of *Raging Bull* is explicit, where Jake thinks in terms of his failures being a form of penance. 'I've done a lot of bad things Joey – maybe it's coming back to me.' He even seems to set out to make amends in the ring for his worst excesses – violence towards his own family – taking terrible punishment while 'playing possum' during a fight that he goes on to win confidently. Physical repression is another key part in the image

presented of the boxer, including pre-fight sexual abstinence (literally aborting foreplay with his second wife Vickie by pouring iced
water down his shorts), the constant battle with maintaining
weight and avoiding alcohol. Jake is barely capable of expressing
himself at all, other than expelling rage through violence, in his
own apartment as well as in the ring. It is his pathological jealousy
and mistrust of Vickie that leads him to batter opponent Janiro to
a pulp, after Vickie had angered him by referring to his up-and-
coming rival as 'young, good-looking'. The power of Jake's fury
drives images like one nauseating tilt-shot that follows Janiro right
down to the canvas, until his world is upended, ropes stretched
vertically up the screen. The static approach to scenes away from
the ring contrasts with the kinetics of the fights, which tend to stay
with Jake in the ring, but each fight is also shot and edited differently – emotionally or psychologically unique within the narrative. Each one shows a new point in Jake's downfall, filmed to
reflect his current state of existence. Where the Janiro fight focuses
on the harsh detail of Jake's devastating win, the first fight he loses
to Sugar Ray Robinson is characterised by disorientation and lack
of clarity, where images are unstable or their content obscured,
mirroring Jake's inability to grasp what is going on in a fight that
he thinks he should be winning.

Aspects of *Raging Bull* such as the performances and art direction give a strong sense of realism or naturalism, but also go far
beyond. Michael Chapman's black and white photography can be
taken as serving to evoke the boxing films of the period itself, but
its bright and stark contrast also becomes yet another externalisa-
tion of Jake's electric anger. The fights seem either like hyper-real-
ity or the opposite for Jake – either the time where he is most alive,
or just an intense experience that makes up for the failures in what
really is 'life'. Reflective sadness breaks through as an essential
aspect of *Raging Bull*, and the feeling that Jake could have had
happiness but threw it away is strongest in the post-fight scene
that carries us from his hand gently nursed in a bucket of ice, to
(colour) home-movie footage of family life with Jake, Vickie, Joey
and his wider family enjoying the idyllic lightness of existence that
is possible. The scratched but carefree images are intercut with a
series of black and white images of Jake's fights, either as stills or
as a dragging slow motion, which seem removed from life, their
value questioned, if not their destructive importance, clashing
with the undulating Italian classical music that serves as the film's
most wistful counterpoint. Jake's greatest achievement when he

takes the world title from Marcel Cerdan is strangely melancholy; following the adrenalin-charged pursuit of La Motta's entry to the arena, this fight is portrayed in a more fragmented manner than any other. Jake's glory eventually explodes with dazzling upward angles and an orchestra of flashbulbs, but on winning, when he walks to Cerdan to embrace him, the event feels overshadowed, as if suggesting its meaninglessness. Cerdan, Edith Piaf's lover, would be killed in a plane crash soon after. The final fight where Jake takes 'terrible punishment' from Sugar Ray is the most extreme, both in its bloody violence and in its distortion of time and reality, with sounds stripped away or slowed down, or used to evoke the fighters' dehumanisation through the sound of animals' exhausted breathing. This shock of Jake's apparent self-loathing/destruction is matched by the impact of a sudden leap to his bloated retirement from boxing, and his rapid demise that leads to incarceration for statutory rape. We end up with Jake where we met him – in the dressing room of his small-time club, with little apparent prospect of glory – but there is redemption, confirmed by the end titles' bible quote from John 9: 'Once I was blind, but now I can see.' Jake lost everything, and failed to win back fully the love of his closest ones, but he may have gained the ability to see himself and recognise his own humanity in all its flaws.

Schoonmaker's partnership with Scorsese goes back to his early days as a film-maker and she has edited all of his feature films since *Raging Bull*. She is overgenerous in suggesting that her Oscar was really his (because of his meticulous pre-designing of shots), but their creative fusion certainly provokes the most fascinating thoughts about film drama and the director–editor relationship. One could hardly offer a sharper illustration of the importance of marrying cinematic form and dramatic content than by contrasting a screening of *Raging Bull* with a screening of their subsequent collaboration, *The King of Comedy*.

Some Things to Watch out for and Consider

- Does the black and white cinematography enhance the dramatic impact of the film?
- In what way is the ideal of 'realism' important/not important?
- Are the fights exciting? (Yes? No? Some, but not all? Which?)

- How does their portrayal match the film's overall depiction of the sport/life?
- Can you select key scenes that seem to justify the awards for editing?
- Can you describe their contribution to the film?

Further Viewing

The Set-Up (Wise, USA, 1949)
Somebody up there Likes me (Wise, USA, 1956)
Rocky (Avildsen, USA, 1976)
The King of Comedy (Scorsese, USA, 1983)
The Color of Money (Scorsese, USA, 1986)

36 JURASSIC PARK

Spielberg, USA, 1993

Awards

Academy Awards: Winner – Best Sound, Best Sound Effects and Best Visual Effects

Production Details

Production company/studio	Amblin/Universal
Producer	Kathleen Kennedy
Director	Steven Spielberg
Cinematographer	Dean Cundey
Editor	Michael Kahn
Screenwriters	David Koepp and Michael Crichton (novel by Michael Crichton)
Visual effects	Stan Winston, Dennis Moren, Phil Tippett and Michael Lantern (Industrial Light and Magic)

Cast Includes

Richard Attenborough	*Dr John Hammond*
Sam Neill	*Dr Alan Grant*
Laura Dern	*Dr Ellie Sattler*
Jeff Goldblum	*Ian Malcolm*
Bob Peck	*Robert Muldoon*
Joseph Mazzello	*Tim*
Ariana Richards	*Lex*

FOCUS: The Event Movie; Cinema and Technology

Primarily and pre-eminently, *Jurassic Park* is a highly successful example of that most enduring phenomenon of the Hollywood cinema – the event movie. As such, as remarkable as it is in terms of technological and marketing advances, *Jurassic Park* can be seen as part of a lengthy tradition begun by Griffith and carried on by the moguls of the classical period.

The 'event movie' was not – as is commonly accepted – a result of the rise of television. Its resurgence in the 1960s was a response to that challenge – but it was not a new phenomenon. 'Hollywood' as a centre for film production had been kick-started when Griffith was sent there to film when the light and conditions were poor on the East Coast. Griffith was also responsible for the first genuine event movie – typified by epic scale, overarching production ambition and massive media campaign – with *Birth of a Nation* (1915).

Spielberg had already shown a masterly ability to plug into popular taste with films such as *Jaws* (1975), *Close Encounters of the Third Kind* (1977), *Raiders of the Lost Ark* (1981) (see chapter 31) and *ET – the Extra-Terrestrial* (1982). *Jurassic Park* shares some of their strengths – and all of their weaknesses. These highly entertaining films are not concerned with character depth. Heroes like 'Indiana Jones' and the kids in *ET* are more or less comic book. At their best, Spielberg's films (or at least the best bits of admittedly episodic films) are gloriously engaging – for example, in the case of Indy shooting the swordsman or the forest of fingers pointing to the sky in *ET*. Spielberg's work glories in high production values and entertainment content. The criticism levelled at the (lack of) narrative and character development is clearly missing the point. Spielberg's films – like those of the *Star Wars* franchise (see chapter 28) – do not have the qualities associated with the classic Hollywood film of psychologically driven clearly motivated narrative linked by cause and effect, which, for example, Scorsese and other craftsmen have kept alive and well.

Perhaps the key weakness of *Jurassic Park* is that Spielberg *is* striving for character and narrative development and largely – as with *ET* – failing. Put simply – and perhaps crudely – Spielberg (like Lucas) is at his best when he keeps to the 'whizz-bang' qualities of cinema and rarely succeeds with anything with more weight. It could well be argued that *Schindler's List* (1993) is a notable exception to this – but that film is so personal a project as to be by its nature exceptional.

Whatever its weaknesses, *Jurassic Park* as a film and franchise was and remains vastly successful. The film – shot during late 1992 – was produced (to budget) for $63 million. In its opening weekend in the USA (13–14 June 1993) it took $50.2 million. That a film could recoup its whole production budget in week one of release can only be the result of masterly marketing. The final gross income in the USA was $356.784 million (at the time second only to *ET*). The non-US theatrical gross was $556 million, including £47.14 million in the UK. The fact that the US gross was very much less than 50 per cent of the $913.1 million worldwide gross was most unusual. *Jurassic Park* was a global phenomenon – and remains so via video/DVD and the sequels (*The Lost World* (1997) and Part III (2001)).

It is a true monster.

Undoubtedly some of the film's success was a result of the most ubiquitous marketing campaign utilised in cinema history up to that point. But, whilst we should take stock of the commercial and marketing acumen of the (Hollywood) machinery behind *Jurassic Park*, it is important to consider what it was about the core product – i.e. the film itself – that attracted global audiences.

A simple plot summary for *Jurassic Park* holds part of the answer – it is a piece of hokum but packed with the thrills of a fairground ride. Scientists develop a means of bringing dinosaurs to life using prehistoric DNA taken from blood that has been preserved inside insects encased in amber. Hammond (Attenborough) shows off his dinosaur 'theme park' to a selected audience of stock characters: the lawyer Gerrano, the mathematician/chaos theoretician Malcolm, palaeontologist Grant, palaeobotanist Sattler and – in typical Spielberg style – Hammond's grandchildren (Tim and Lex).

Nedry – yes he really is called 'Nedry' – the disgruntled employee/computer expert, disables the security system so that he can make his escape with some stolen embryos. This enables all the dinosaurs to escape their enclosures – and the fun begins. The premise defies scientific logic: as Grant puts it: 'Oh my God. Do you know what this is? This is a dinosaur egg. The dinosaurs are breeding.' The plot clatters to its denouement via some very exciting special effects, some very hammy acting and heavy-handed swipes at 'science' and salutary lessons about the family unit. Even the dinosaurs teach us that the 'natural' is better than the technological. (Henry Wu: 'You are saying that a group of animals, entirely composed of females, will breed?' Ian Malcolm: 'No, I am merely stating that uhh . . . life finds a way.')

Malcolm – the chaos theorist – is the chorus who (constantly) points us to the moral. 'The complete lack of humility for nature that's being displayed here is staggering', and later: 'Your scientists were so preoccupied with whether or not they could, they didn't stop to think if they should.'

Jurassic Park can be positioned as an – admittedly spectacularly successful – example of cinema's response to technology, which is almost invariably as a quintessentially technological art form keen to utilise technological advantages and yet as a sophisticated and sensitive cultural product keen to express concern (indeed fear) about change.

Spielberg is a good enough storyteller to hammer home his message via some good old-fashioned sentiment. Ellie Sattler (the scientist so achingly maternal she is practically lactating) joins the chorus: 'I was overwhelmed by the power of this place; but I made a mistake, too. I didn't have enough respect for that power and it's out now. The only thing that matters now are the people we love: Alan and Lex and Tim. John, they're out there where people are dying.'

The plot device that allows the kids to be available as potential dinosaur fodder is that their parents are divorcing. When they are abandoned again – under dinosaur attack – the message of protection is clear: Lex: 'He left us! He left us!' Alan Grant: ' But that's not what I'm gonna do.' The film's world première took place in Bill Clinton's White House in aid of the Children's Defence League. By the end of the film we are left in no doubt that Lex and Tim's vulnerability has not only humbled their grandfather; it has also bought the palaeo-couple together in a new closer (and potentially procreational) relationship. That a film so global in its appeal could carry such a persuasive and all-pervading message of 'traditional' and 'natural' (i.e. North American) family value could well lead any reflective commentator if not back to Marx than at least to Antonio Gramsci's concept of cultural hegemony.

Some Things to Watch out for and Consider

- As already noted this film is packed with ironies:
  - It is deeply 'concerned' about science/technology and yet is in itself a showcase for 'computer graphics' (Spielberg saw an ILM demonstration animation of a T-Rex chasing a herd of galamides across a virtual recreation of his ranch and decided to shoot nearly all the dinosaur scenes using this method. The close-ups utilised computer-controlled 'animatronics' (note that the Academy Awards were for technological excellence)).
  - It is deeply cynical about 'marketing' – the audience thrills to the monsters destroying the merchandising paraphernalia of 'Jurassic Park'. Yet the film was a vehicle for a vast sales campaign – of the very artefacts seen in the film, which were on sale worldwide.
  - In a key moment of the film Ian Malcolm makes the following speech: 'I'll tell you the problem with the scientific power that you're using here: it didn't require any discipline to attain it. You read what others had done and you took the next step. We didn't earn the knowledge for ourselves, so you don't take any responsibility for it. You stood on the shoulders of geniuses to accomplish something as fast as you could and before you even knew what you had you patented it and packaged it and slapped it on a plastic lunchbox, and now you're selling it, you want to sell it!' Are you struck by an irony here? Is Spielberg deliberately questioning his own position as a film-maker? If not – can he be forgiven?
- In 1993 Spielberg made both *Jurassic Park* and *Schindler's List*. He has consistently made serious (if sentimental) films on very serious subjects, whilst being responsible (as producer or director) for the most vulgar of entertainment blockbusters. Is their any dichotomy between these two activities? Have the two areas of activity influenced each other? (For good or for ill?)

Further Viewing

Jaws (Spielberg, USA, 1975)
Close Encounters of the Third Kind (Spielberg, USA, 1977)
ET (Spielberg, USA, 1982)
Intolerance (Griffith, USA, 1917)
Metropolis (Lang, Germany, 1926)
Gone with the Wind (Fleming, USA, 1939)
Star Wars (Lucas, USA, 1977)
The Matrix (Warchowski Brothers, USA, 1999)

Further Reading

S. Neale and M. Smith (eds.), *Contemporary Hollywood Cinema* (London, 1998)
P. M. Taylor, *Steven Spielberg* (London, 1999)

37 **RESERVOIR DOGS**

Tarantino, USA, 1992

Production Details

Production company/studio	Dog Eat Dog Productions
Producer	Lawrence Bender
Director	Quentin Tarantino
Cinematographer	Andrzej Sekula
Editor	Sally Menke
Screenwriter	Quentin Tarantino

Cast Includes

Harvey Keitel	*Mr White/Larry*
Tim Roth	*Mr Orange/Freddy*
Michael Madsen	*Mr Blonde/Vic*
Chris Penn	*Nice Guy Eddie*
Steve Buscemi	*Mr Pink*
Lawrence Tierney	*Joe Cabot*
Randy Brooks	*Holdaway*
Kirk Baltz	*Marvin Nash*
Eddie Bunker	*Mr Blue*
Quentin Tarantino	*Mr Brown*
Steven Wright	*The Voice of K-Billy*

FOCUS: Popular Culture/Art Cinema; Violence and the New Hollywood

It is indicative of Tarantino's (highly popular) mix of popular culture and 'art cinema' sensibility that he named *Reservoir Dogs* as a tribute to *Au Revoir les enfants* (Malle, France, 1987), a film whose title he could not pronounce back in the days when he worked in a

Reservoir Dogs. Live Entertainment 1993 (courtesy Kobal)

video store. It is also indicative of Tarantino's quasi-mythical status in world cinema that such a story is central to the legend – and, as we learnt in Ford's *The Man who shot Liberty Valance* (USA, 1962), in film as well as newspapers you should always 'print the legend'.

Tarantino is the ultimate 'wannabee's wannabee' – the film nerd who worked his way up from the store to the studio set. He is Spielberg and Lucas for a new generation. Where their inspiration was the classic Hollywood text, Tarantino was the poet laureate for a mass movement of consumers (and later film-makers) who thrilled to the energy and surface style of Hong Kong action movies, thrilled to a trash ethic and were more than ready for a postmodern mix'n'match of bad taste. Added to which, Tarantino – derivative if not plain plagiarist as he might be – has been not only responsible for three very fine movies but a seminal inspiration for a new wave of independent American cinema.

The legend of *Reservoir Dogs* tells us that Tarantino was going to shoot the film in black and white, with his friends as actors. A friend of his was in an acting class given by Harvey Keitel's wife. Keitel saw the script, and was so impressed that he immediately signed on and helped raise funds. The rest is (the stuff of) history. *Reservoir Dogs* is the *Gone with the Wind* (see chapter 12) of independent cinema. The success of the film (financial and in terms of its cultural impact) is evidence that all things are possible if (*a*) you have the energy and (*b*) you get the breaks. America is still the land of opportunity – and Hollywood can still spot talent (eventually).

Reservoir Dogs is basically a classic 'heist' movie. Much as with Westerns, all truly great heist movies – e.g. Kubrick's *The Killing* (USA, 1956) and Peckinpah's *The Wild Bunch* (USA, 1969) – play with linear narrative and/or genre conventions. The joy of these genre pieces, particularly displayed in recent forays into horror (e.g. Wes Craven's *Scream* (USA, 1996)), is their sense of genre itself – including an ability to develop artful self-referentiality. *Reservoir Dogs* is almost painfully aware of its own milieu and willing to celebrate its forebears – for example, the criminals in *The Taking of Pelham One Two Three* (Sargent, USA, 1974) also used colours to identify each other anonymously. The (now) iconic 'dogs' walk across the car park is clearly a homage to the opening of Peckinpah's *The Wild Bunch*, and so on and so forth.

Tarantino brought more than the nerd's obsession with generic detail to his feature debut. In *Reservoir Dogs*, rather more than in the ostentatiously fragmented *Pulp Fiction* (1994), the narrative structure of flashback and forward is entirely of a piece with the desire of the thwarted criminals to 'piece together' their failed crime. The film also has a genuine sense of style – borrowed certainly – but borrowed from an eclectic mix of great films by great film-makers (including Godard, Woo and Scorsese). The film has a formal interest but, because of Tarantino's grasp of the intrinsic pleasure of popular culture (including the delights of old records on the radio and most of all the *sharing* of that pleasure), *Reservoir Dogs* had the power to enter the pantheon of popular culture itself. It can be no coincidence that the opening sequence revolves around a discussion of that most artful of postmodern pop-culture icons: Madonna.

Tarantino – beyond doubt a scriptwriter of real talent (even if, with a lengthening hiatus, the jury is out on his auteur status as a director) – has a genuine ability to capture the rhythm of language. That he can write dialogue that is both believable and wryly entertaining gives *Reservoir Dogs* a further claim to 'key' status. That a lot of people have tried since and failed to live up to his achievement (e.g. the raft of dreadful British crime movies – including those made by Mr Madonna) furthers the case for his achievement. He is quite simply (like Hitchcock or Scorsese before him) a hard act to follow.

The language that enriches the film is, of course, profane. It would be difficult to believe that a bunch of jewel thieves would not pepper their discourse with the f-word. The ubiquitousness of the profanity may or may not be open to charges of gratuitousness – as could the use of violence. As with the profanity, it would be equally difficult to argue that violent criminals should not be seen using and/or suffering from violence. Some of the violence creates creative leaps in cinematic composition – for example, the sheer shock, after the 'cool' ironic opening, of Mr Orange (Roth) lying in a lake of his own blood. If we find the machine-gun obscene repartee of the protagonists wearing (and faintly sad), if we find the 'ear-slicing' scene – including the use of humour in the set-up – disturbing, is that a bad thing?

The pleasures of *Reservoir Dogs* are many – if shallow and vicarious. Their very shallowness and vicariousness heighten those pleasures. We should not condemn films for flaunting some of the major virtues of the cinematic art.

Some Things to Watch out for and Consider

- There are no female speaking parts in the movie. What does this tell us about
  - the current state of American cinema;
  - the mind of Quentin Tarantino?
- It is undeniable that there is a high level of violence in *Reservoir Dogs*. Whilst the film is certainly an extreme example of this phenomenon in post-war cinema, there are a lot of violent films on our screens. The level of graphic violence is a question of concern for many people who either
  - would like to go to the cinema/hire a video and find it difficult to find a film they would like to see or
  - are concerned about the effect all this violence has on the people who do go to the movies.

Is it better to show the impact of violence (either as a method of catharsis or as a salutary warning) or to avoid such issues?

- Is Tarantino's clearly intelligent and entertaining use of humour in his presentation of violence worthy of our praise or opprobrium?
- Was it better when the killings in movies were many but the (physical) results never shown?
- Replace 'violence' with 'sex'. Does your opinion change?

Further Viewing

Pulp Fiction (Tarantino, USA, 1994)
Jackie Brown (Tarantino, USA, 1997)
The Wild Bunch (Peckinpah, USA, 1969)
Straw Dogs (Peckinpah, USA, 1970)
A Clockwork Orange (Kubrick, USA, 1971)
Bring me the Head of Alfredo Garcia (Peckinpah, USA, 1974)
Taxi Driver (Scorsese, USA, 1976)
The Killer (Woo, HK, 1989)
Goodfellas (Scorsese, USA, 1990)
Face/Off (Woo, USA, 1997)

38 UNFORGIVEN

Eastwood, USA, 1992

Awards

Academy Awards: Winner – Best Picture, Best Director, Best Supporting
Actor (Gene Hackman) and Best Editor (Joel Cox)

Production Details

Production company/studio	Malpaso / Warner Brothers
Producer	Clint Eastwood
Director	Clint Eastwood
Cinematographer	Jack N. Green
Editor	Joel Cox
Screenwriter	David Webb Peoples

Cast Includes

Clint Eastwood	*William Munny*
Gene Hackman	*Little Bill Daggett*
Morgan Freeman	*Ned Logan*
Jaimz Woolvett	*The Schofield Kid*
Richard Harris	*English Bob*

FOCUS: Genre

Unforgiven presents us with a return to a popular genre for
Eastwood, whose star image as a Western hero was constructed
initially in the television series *Rawhide* and later in a sequence of
films taking an ironic slant on the American Western. These are
known as Spaghetti Westerns; directed by Sergio Leone and shot
in Spain, they launched Eastwood as a star whilst reinventing and
reinvigorating the Western at a time when it was in decline in the

country of its birth. Eastwood first began directing with *Play Misty for Me* (1971) and has become known for directing films in which he takes the starring role. Other Westerns he has directed include *High Planes Drifter* (1973), *The Outlaw Josey Wales* (1976) and *Pale Rider* (1985).

Unforgiven conforms to the characteristics of the Western genre but presents us with some developments. One of the interesting things about this film is the way in which it takes the characteristics of a genre that reached its creative heights in the 1940s and 1950s and reinvents them for a 1990s audience. This discussion will focus on two examples, the setting of the homestead and the role of the Western hero, and consider how *Unforgiven* takes these staples of the genre and develops them.

The isolated homestead is one of the iconographic images of the Western. Typically it represents the values of pioneering white America. In films like *The Searchers* (Ford, USA, 1956) the homestead is an oasis of civilisation surrounded by the lawless wilderness that is the untamed West. A central concern of all Westerns is the tension/conflict between civilisation and the wilderness. The homestead is presented as an essentially female domain, thus encouraging us to associate civilising values with women. We can compare this to the homestead in *Unforgiven*. It looks ramshackle, almost derelict. There are no homely feminine touches. It is still the family home, but in this film the children are motherless and Eastwood is playing the role of William Munny, a single parent attempting to be both father and mother to his children. This representation of the family is one of the elements that locates the film in the 1990s. It makes it different from earlier Westerns; it is more appropriate to a modern audience, yet the basic idea of the homestead has not changed. We are constantly reminded that it is the influence (if not the presence) of a woman that has transformed and civilised the hero. Munny's dead wife is ever present – in the written text that opens and closes the film; in the scene where Munny prays over her grave; in his instructions to his children and his constant comments that she changed him. Thus the homestead is still associated with the character of the good woman (the wife, mother and civilising force), but the presentation is different. In such ways Eastwood takes the traditional elements of the genre and presents them with a contemporary slant.

Similarly, if we compare Eastwood's character in *Unforgiven* to an earlier Western hero – for example, the Ringo Kid in *Stagecoach*

(Ford, USA, 1939) (see chapter 9) – we can see that, whilst the characters have features in common (as we would expect), there are significant differences.

The Ringo Kid is young; William Munny is old. The Ringo Kid is an outlaw but he has a clear moral code that we can identify with – he is seeking revenge for the murder of his father and brother. The audience is encouraged to sympathise with his murderous quest in many ways, not least because the Marshall, whose ostensible concern is to stop Ringo from killing the 'Plumber boys', seems more concerned with protecting him. In the final scenes of the film, when Ringo has succeeded in his quest and should be heading back to prison, the Marshall turns a blind eye and lets him escape. This condones his code of conduct, allowing the audience to applaud him for succeeding against impossible odds (as all good heroes should) and getting the girl.

In comparison to this, William Munny's past as an outlaw seems dark and murderous. He is referred to as killer of women and children. He is ashamed of his past, rejecting his former role with the often repeated phrase 'I ain't like that no more'. He got the girl, but she is long dead – the romantic happy ending is already in the past when the film opens. The Schofield Kid is enamoured of him, perceiving Will as a romantic, heroic figure and aspiring to be like him. As the narrative develops, he learns that the reality of murder is sickening and is finally able to reject the role of the Western hero, affirming after the murder of the second cowboy, 'I ain't like you Will'.

In spite of this much darker treatment, which appears to act as a critique of the idea of the Western hero, it is hard not to like the character of William Munny. There are many touches that strip his character of the expected heroic qualities and make him human and vulnerable. In the early scenes of the film he cannot shoot straight or mount his horse without falling off. On many occasions he talks of and expresses fear of death. When he gets beaten up by Little Bill, we see him crawl out of the saloon face down in the mud.

In these and other ways he is an unlikely hero and yet there is always the sense of another character, the ruthless killer of the past who could, and finally does, emerge at the end of the film. This character is transformed (with the help of a bottle of whisky and the magical art of cinema) into a man who can defeat impossible odds, who has the perfect instinctive aim of the true hero along with the ruthless determination to avenge his friend, which enables him to murder a room full of men in seconds. This ending, this transformation from inept and unlikely hero into the avenging angel that we expect of Clint Eastwood's star persona, presents us with many questions. It is worth considering why the change takes place? What motivates him to kill Little Bill? How is this different from the motivation to kill the two cowboys? Does this mean the audience responds differently to the different killings? Throughout the film Munny has made a reluctant return to his role as killer. Is the ending then a fall from grace or a rise to the occasion, a reclaiming of Munny's/Eastwood's true role as Western hero? How does this ending, which is essentially a return to the sort of behaviour the film has been criticising, affect us? Is it what we want/expect from a Western?

Some Things to Watch out for and Consider

- How does this film mythologise the West? Look at:
    - content/context of the written text at the beginning and end of the film;
    - the character of the Schofield Kid and his reactions to Will's past;
    - the character and role of English Bob;
    - the character and role of Beauchamp;
    - the use of names or titles – e.g. William Munny out of Missouri;
    - the ending of the film.
- How does this film de-mythologise the West? Look at:
    - the representation of the three 'heroes' and their collective flaws;
    - the scene in the gaol between Beauchamp, Little Bill and English Bob;
    - the killing of the first cowboy (what is the effect of the Kid's near-blindness, and how and to what effect has the film-maker drawn this scene out?);
    - the killing of the second cowboy and the different characters' reactions to it.
- In what ways does this film ask us to question our attitudes to violence, death and murder? Look at how the different characters react to, comment on or change their minds about these issues. Look at the motivation for the different acts of violence – is killing for money morally different from killing for revenge? Compare the violence of Little Bill with

that of the hero – does one seem more acceptable than the other? If so, why?
- In comparison to other Westerns you have seen, consider the representation of men, women, Native Americans, white people and black people.

Further Viewing

Stagecoach (Ford, USA, 1939)
The Searchers (Ford, USA, 1956)
A Fistful of Dollars (Leone, Italy / Germany / Spain, 1965)
For a Few Dollars More (Leone, Italy, 1964)
Once upon a Time in the West (Leone, Italy, 1968)
High Planes Drifter (Eastwood, USA, 1973)
The Outlaw Josey Wales (Eastwood, USA, 1976)
Pale Rider (Eastwood, USA, 1985)

39 THE PIANO
Campion, New Zealand, 1993

Awards

Academy Awards: Winner – Best Original Screenplay; Nomination – Best Director
Cannes – Winner: Golden Palm

Production Details

Production company/studio	Jan Chapman Productions / CiBy 2000
Producer	Jan Chapman
Director	Jane Campion
Cinematographer	Stewart Dryburgh
Editor	Veronika Jenet
Screenwriters	Jane Campion and Kate Pullinger
Music	Michael Nyman
Costume designer	Janet Patterson

Cast Includes

Holly Hunter	*Ada*
Harvey Keitel	*Baines*
Sam Neil	*Stewart*
Anna Paquin	*Flora*
Kerry Walker	*Aunt Morag*

FOCUS: Women Film-Makers and the Representation of Gender, Race and Nation

Since the Lumière Brothers' first screening at the Grand Café Paris in 1895, women have been involved in cinema. Witness Mme

Lumière feeding her baby in one of the first films ever screened. Her brief appearance (the film lasts for 20 seconds) in the archetypal role of mother could be described as one of the first female performances. It is in this role, as performers, that women have largely taken part in what is, and has been, a male-dominated industry. There have been exceptions (for example, Esfir Shub, Leni Riefenstal and Thelma Schoonmaker), but high-profile women film-makers are and have been rare. Jane Campion is one and *The Piano* made her a director of international significance. Her work is sharp, original and imaginative. The films should be viewed in their own right. However, given that she is one of the very few mainstream women film-makers currently working, we cannot avoid asking if there is anything uniquely female in her perspective.

The Piano, like Campion's other films, has a female protagonist. It presents us with the story of Ada, a nineteenth-century woman who has been voluntarily mute since she was 6. At the start of the film she is married off by her father to a stranger. To marry him she leaves her father's home in Scotland and travels to New Zealand. Thus it is the story of an outsider, a woman confined by the patriarchal conventions of her time who struggles against her fate in the rain and mud of colonial New Zealand.

In the opening image of the film the camera pans back and forth behind vertical dark lines surrounded by red light. Gradually we become aware that these bars are fingers. We cut to a close-up of Ada, eyes peering out from behind her fingers. Thus we are introduced to her as the central character of the film and to the first among many images of confinement that culminate with Ada's husband, Stewart, making a prisoner of her by boarding up the windows of the house and locking her in. Light spills through the cracks in the boards, enabling Ada and Flora to look out from their prison, echoing the opening image of the film. Shots of characters looking through things abound throughout the film, imparting a voyeuristic feel. We see Ada looking through doorways and windows, Stewart observing her through a camera viewfinder and characters at the theatre peeping through holes in the curtain. Flora and then finally Stewart observe Ada and Baines making love through the cracks in the boards of Baines's house.

All of these images contribute to the issues surrounding intimacy and invasions of intimacy that the film explores. These issues need to be understood in terms of the context of Ada's experience as a woman in a patriarchal society – a society in which the tradition is that men assume ownership and control of property, land and women (in short 'the means of production').

As part of its examination of a woman's life, *The Piano* carefully examines male roles as well as female ones. Male power and male inadequacy are explored principally through the contrasting characters of Stewart and Baines. To understand Ada we need to understand her relationships with these men and their perceptions of/feelings for her/women.

The characterisation of Stewart is particularly interesting. He represents Victorian Colonial values; he is concerned with the ownership of the land; he exploits the 'native' Maori population. In his role as Ada's husband he acts as her oppressor, committing acts of both emotional and physical violence against her, and yet Campion refrains from casting him as the villain of the piece. Instead, the film-maker invites us to sympathise with him. At different points in the film we see that he is nervous, baffled, impotent when faced with his strange new wife. A product of his society (and its belief in white male supremacy), he is conservative, traditional and deeply uncomfortable around women. Thus he seems genuinely incapable of treating Ada as an individual with possible desires and feelings of her own. To assert himself he must try and control her.

In contrast Baines – like Ada – is an outsider. He is a social outcast because he has cast off the values of his society and 'gone native', partly embracing the Maori culture. At least in contrast to the white Victorian values (embodied by Stewart) which act as Ada's oppressor, the Maori culture is represented positively. In a scene that might appear to represent the Maoris as stupid, we see them destroy the theatre performance, unable to comprehend that it is not real. It is significant, however, that what they react to with anger is a depiction of male violence against women that is deemed both acceptable and comic by the white audience. Similarly Baines rescues Ada from Stewart's violence against her. Is the film-maker suggesting that he is rescuing her from a culture, a set of social values and attitudes towards women as much as from an individual?

Whilst the film explicitly invites us to consider the issues surrounding representation of gender, race and nation and whilst the Maori culture is clearly associated with values that seem both more humane and freer than their white colonial counterparts, their representation remains controversial. Maori values are principally represented through Baines, who is presented to us as having embraced their culture. What are we to make of a white

New Zealand film-maker choosing a white American to represent black New Zealanders?

A less controversial but perhaps more fruitful area of analysis is the central character's muteness. This is important both psychologically – as a key to Ada's psyche and her responses to the culture in which she lives – and cinematically – as lack of speech provides opportunities for alternative means of communication. The film-maker relies heavily on carefully constructed *mise en scène* as a primary means of conveying Ada's relationship with the world, but perhaps her most important means of communication is her piano.

Aunt Morag describes Ada's playing as 'strange, like a mood that passes into you. To have a sound creep inside you is not at all pleasant.' Ada uses her playing as the primary means of expressing intense passionate feelings. As the film progresses, the audience learns to read her music and interpret the different states of feeling it expresses. Other characters' responses to her music are revealing. Stewart, like Aunt Morag, is uncomfortable/uncomprehending. Baines understands that asking her to play for him is asking something deeply intimate. Watching her play becomes a sexual act for him/both of them.

The final dream image of the film shows Ada's lifeless body floating above the piano – a dark ending suggesting that real liberation for the nineteenth-century woman can be found only in death. Is this really the end of Ada's story? Possibly, but the voice-over and preceding images suggest an alternative ending. We see Ada dressed symbolically in lighter colours in a new life with Baines, where she is learning to speak and with the aid of a metal finger is able to play again. Her mind's voice tells us: 'What a death! What a chance! What a surprise! My will has chosen life' – a controversial and ambiguous ending to an extraordinary film.

Some Things to Watch out for and Consider

- What do we know about Ada's relationship with her father?
- When she arrives in New Zealand, how is Ada's status (as property of her new husband) emphasised by the film-maker?
- Compare Stewart's initial reaction to Ada with that of Baines. What does it tell you about each man?
- Compare Stewart's actions and reactions to the piano (and Ada's playing) throughout the film with those of Baines.

- Hands and fingers, particularly Ada's, are an important motif in the film, witness the opening shot. Look at the different ways Ada speaks through her hands. What is the significance of Stewart's chopping off her finger? And Baines replacing it?
- Consider how the film-maker uses Ada's costume to indicate important aspects of her experience/character. You could compare:
  - the scene where she transforms her crinoline into a tent to the many scenes where we see her struggling through mud;
  - the wedding photo scene to the scene where Baines takes Ada and Flora back to the piano on the beach – both involve a removal of costume but indicate very different moods;
  - the two scenes where Stewart assaults Ada (look here also at the effects of lighting and changes in film speed).
- Consider also the Maoris' appropriation of Western costume. The women wear both male and female clothes. What do you think this conveys?
- Compare Stewart tightly buttoned up (why did the costume designer deliberately make his clothes a size too small?) with Baines in much looser more flamboyant style.
- Consider the importance of lighting. Compare the cold blue-white light that emphasises the whiteness of Flora and Ada's skin with the warm amber and rose colours used in certain sequences. What mood does the film-maker create through such use of different coloured light?
- Consider the importance of sound. Is the music in the film diegetic or non-diegetic or a mixture of the two? Can you identify recurring harmonies – do they indicate different things at different times? Why do you think Ada has chosen to be mute? What impact does this have on performance and use of sound? Why do you think she chooses to learn to speak at the end of the film?

Further Viewing

Two Friends (Campion, Australia, 1985)
Sweetie (Campion, Australia, 1989)
An Angel at my Table (Campion, Australia, 1990)

The Portrait of a Lady (Campion, NZ/UK/USA, 1996)
Holy Smoke (Campion, USA, 2000)
Blue Steel (Bigelow, USA, 1990)
Point Break (Bigelow, USA, 1991)
Strange Days (Bigelow, USA, 1995)

40 CHUNGKING EXPRESS
(Chongqing senlin)
Kar-wai, Hong Kong, 1994

Awards

Hong Kong Film Awards: Winner – Best Picture, Best Director and Best
Actor (Tony Leung Chiu Wai); Nomination – Best Actress (Faye
Wong), Best Art Direction (William Chang), Best Cinematography
(Christopher Doyle), Best Screenplay and Best Supporting Actress
(Valerie Chow).

Production Details

Production company/studio	Jet Tone Production Company
Producer	Chan Yi-kan
Director	Wong Kar-wai
Cinematographers	Christopher Doyle and Keung Lau-wai
Editors	William Chang, Hai Kit-wai, Kwing Chi-Leung
Screenwriter	Wong Kar-wai
Production designer	William Chang
Art director	Qiu Weiming

Cast Includes

Brigitte Lin	*The Woman in a Blonde Wig*
Takeshi Kaneshiro	*Cop 223*
Tony Leung Chiu-wai	*Cop 663*
Faye Wong	*Faye*
Valerie Chow	*The Air Hostess*
Chen Jinquan	*The Manager of 'The Midnight Express'*

FOCUS: International Art Cinema/Auteurism

'If my memory of her has an expiration date, let it be 10,000 years . . .' Thus *Chunking Express* announces itself as concerned with both the mundane (processed food expiry dates) and the numinous (time and memory). *Chungking Express* is a mixture of the shiningly real world of objects and the (childish) wonder of love young enough to ache but old enough to add a little world-weary style. It is fast, hip and very, very cool. Hardly surprising then that Quentin Tarantino's Rolling Thunder company acquired this for US release, and many critics applauded its postmodern approach and stylistics.

Wong Kar-wai was born in Shanghai, mainland China, in 1958. His family moved to Hong Kong in the early 1960s. In 1980 he graduated in Hong Kong as a graphic designer. He began a career in television production, graduating to 'AD' on a host of low-budget and low-quality series, while working on his own screenplays. Building on his production and writing experience Wong Kar-wai has scripted as well as directed his features. However, possibly in reaction to the tight restrictions of television, his cinema work has been characterised by a formal freedom based not least on the lack of any detailed screenplay.

In 1988 he directed his first film *As Tears Go By*. There are clear parallels in the subject matter and energetic visual style (as well as existential levels of violence) with Martin Scorsese's *Mean Streets*. However, like Scorsese's film, the milieu and visual world of the movie are unique (and uniquely Wong Kar-wai's).

The film was a huge hit in Taiwan and allowed Wong Kar-wai to collect together the young and smart actors of the 'new' Hong Kong cinema and make *Days of Being Wild* (1990) – a prime example of what David Bordwell has memorably dubbed 'avant-pop' cinema.

Wong Kar-wai is certainly a product of the (government-sponsored) production boom of the late 1980s and of the 'end of Empire' feeling of 1990s Hong Kong. Nonetheless he has his own visual signature (undoubtedly contributed to by the work of his cinematographer Christopher Doyle). He also has his iconographic actor Tony Leung Chiu-wai. His recurring themes are memory, rootlessness and the significance of random situations. He often makes use of repetition as a plot and visually arresting device. It is no exaggeration to see Wong as the Chinese Nicolas Roeg (who also enjoys playing with the icons and iconography of popular culture including Jagger, Bowie and Garfunkel). Of course Wong Kar-wai's films leave a rather sweeter aftertaste than the British master of the disjointed and diffracted.

Wong Kar-wai's style and choice of content could so easily slip into postmodern shallowness. But despite/because of its tangential approach, *Chungking Express* actually reveals insights into something (even if that something is rather shallow in itself). It is about the very meaninglessness of the 'postmodern'. It is about the end of history and it is about the end of hyper-capitalist Hong Kong, about to be handed back to be ruled from the 'Communist' mainland (Wong Kar-wai's next film – *2048* – deals with a future Hong Kong after 50 years of Communist rule).

Chungking Express is 'about' two love-struck cops and their obscure objects of desire. One female icon is a heroin dealer in deep trouble with her bosses after the cargo disappears, the other a seriously weird waitress who inadvertently gets hold of the keys to her admirer's apartment and reorders his life for him. *Chungking Express* is also 'about' moving pictures. It is impressionistic, constructed of splashes of motion, colour and sound.

The stories do not combine in any traditional sense. Indeed one follows the other but they do chime and rhyme with each other. The first story centres on Cop 223, who has broken up with his girlfriend of five years. He purchases a tin of pineapples with an expiry date of 1 May each day for a month. By the end of that time, he feels that he will either be rejoined with his love or that it too will have expired forever. The second story is of Cop 663 dealing with his break-up with his flight attendant girlfriend. He talks to his apartment furnishings until he meets a new girl at a fast food restaurant ('The Midnight Express').

The film's claim to postmodern status (even pre-eminence) has not been made by the director. He just called it a 'road movie', admitting it was made quickly from fragments of ideas while production of *Fallen Angels* was stalled. Nonetheless, possibly because of the production circumstances, there are clearly elements within the film that speak of the dreaded 'po-mo'. Most notably there is the use of insouciant bricollage in the structure, design – indeed in the diegesis – of the film. The sense of real/unreal and the anything-goes atmosphere is heightened in a Scorsesean manner by popular culture cross-referencing especially in the soundtrack. *Chungking Express* utilises Hong Kong versions of Western pop music: 'Dream Person' (a cover of

'Dreams' by the Cranberries) and 'Know Oneself and Each Other' (a cover of 'Know who You Are at Every Age' by the Cocteau Twins). The singer on these cover versions is Faye Wong. *Chungking Express* was Ms Wong's first foray into screen acting. Thus – in a postmodern coup – she is on the screen as 'Faye' whilst accompanying the action on the soundtrack. The musical driving force of the film is 'California Dreamin'' by the 1960s American band the Mamas and the Papas. The choice of song not only comments on and adds energy to the story; it also hints at the desirability and all-pervasiveness of American pop culture.

Chungking Express has been followed by *Happy Together* (1997) – lauded at Cannes – and *Fallen Angels* (1998). Wong Kar-wai's style has continued to develop and mature – as has his profile as darling of the critics – with the release of the masterful, achingly bitter-sweet *In the Mood for Love* (2000). The film reaches new heights in the juxtaposition of unbearable emotional restraint and sumptuous visual élan – all power to cinema as an international language.

Some Things to Think about and Consider

- Does Wong Kar-wai's style betray his TV background? Is it possible to see his 1990s work as a series of 90-minute soap operas?
- In what ways did Wong Kar-wai's visual style change when he moved away from action thrillers?
- 'For those of us not semiotically attuned, it is like looking at one of those 3-D pictures and seeing only two dimensions' (Fonoroff review in 1994). (How) could you convince Fonoroff of the other dimension to *Chungking Express*? A hint – David Bordwell finishes *Planet Hong Kong* (2000) thus: 'Deeply indebted to popular tradition, committed to a conception of light cinema, his confection nourishes all filmmakers who dream of movies that are at once experimental and irresistibly enjoyable' (p. 289).
- 'Experimental' and 'enjoyable' are all well and good – should 'key film texts' be 'light'?
- Are Hong Kong and Taiwanese films really contributing something new to the world of moving pictures?

Further Viewing

As Tears Go By (Wong Kar-wai, HK, 1988)
In the Mood for Love (Wong Kar-wai, HK, 2000)
The Killer (Woo, HK, 1989)
Face/Off (Woo, USA, 1997)
Performance (Roeg, UK, 1968)
The Man who Fell to Earth (Roeg, UK, 1976)
Bad Timing (Roeg, UK, 1979)
Mean Streets (Scorsese, USA, 1975)
Reservoir Dogs (Tarantino, USA, 1988)

Further Reading

D. Bordwell, *Planet Hong Kong* (London, 2000)
P. Fonoroff, *At the Hong Kong Movies* (New York, 1998)

41 BEAUTY AND THE BEAST

Trousdale and Wise, USA, 1991

Awards

Academy Awards: Winner – Best Music (Original Score) and Best Song, 'Beauty and the Beast'; Nomination – Best Picture

Production Details

Production company/studio	Walt Disney Productions / Silver Screen Partners
Producers	Howard Ashman, Don Hahn and Sarah McArthur
Directors	Gary Trousdale and Kirk Wise
Editor	John Carnochan
Screenwriters	Roger Allers (story), Linda Woolverton and Jeanne-Marie Leprince de Beaumont

Cast (Voices) Includes

Paige O'Hara	*Belle*
Robby Benson	*Beast*
Richard White	*Gaston*
Jerry Orbach	*Lumière*
David Ogden Stiers	*Cogsworth/Narrator*
Angela Lansbury	*Mrs Potts*

FOCUS: Hollywood Branding and Self-Reference; New Animation Techniques

Walt Disney Production's 31st animated feature *Beauty and the Beast* was a storming success musically, gathering Oscars for Best Original Music and Best Song, and producing a later smash-hit stage version. More notably, it was the first animated feature film ever to be nominated for the Best Picture Oscar – an acclaim that hailed the visual sumptuousness and grace of its animation work as much as its hilarious characterisations and array of memorable tunes. The breadth and height of popular and critical praise were a great boost to Disney, after a couple of decades of mixed success with films that simply did not live up to the visual splendour and virtuoso technique of earlier works that had been hailed as groundbreaking instant classics, such as *Snow White and the Seven Dwarfs* (1937). The sheer quality of the animated action and the richness and attention to detail of the frame-by-frame drawings had made *Snow White* a watershed product whose impact on audiences can be compared to that of the special effects in Kubrick's *2001: A Space Odyssey* (UK, 1968) three decades later.

Following *Snow White*, Walt Disney's aim was to stay at the pinnacle of achievement, and repeat its commercial success by making each release of a Disney animated feature film an event, part of the global experience of childhood. Before the accessibility offered by consumer video, even the screening of short clips on television showcases like *Disney Time* were special occasions, and Disney continue to limit video release to maximise interest and allow for cinema re-releases of its 'classics'. The benchmark pictorial quality of *Snow White* was soon held up by films like *Pinocchio* (1940) and *Bambi* (1942), and throughout the 1950s Disney pinned its success on a reputation for producing the definitive 'magic' of fairytale and childhood stories such as *Cinderella* (1950), *Peter Pan* (1953) and *Sleeping Beauty* (1959). The enormous appeal of the best Disney products was proved again with *The Jungle Book* (1967), although this time Disney seemed to have peaked. Through the 1970s and 1980s, as Disney became sidetracked and experimented more with mixing animation with live action, animation budgets were reduced, with a direct impact on picture quality and a downturn in audience enthusiasm. If the highly comic *Robin Hood* (1973) seemed weakened by the absence of the earlier colour-rich visual magic, *Basil the Great Mouse Detective* (1986) seemed completely unworthy of the Disney name.

The Little Mermaid (1989) had been an impressive recovery of form, with a simple and strong narrative line matched with very dramatic use of colour, but after another forgettable sequel, *The Rescuers Down Under* (1990), *Beauty and the Beast* was a conscious return to the safety of one of the great fairytale classics. It was also a great challenge for Disney, attempting a story that had already been tried at least once every decade since the earliest days of cinema, the most celebrated being Cocteau's stunningly atmospheric *Beauty and the Beast* (*La Belle et La Bête*, France, 1946). The Disney animation might be incomparable with Cocteau's black and white masterpiece, but it was a tour de force such as the company had not produced since *The Jungle Book*. Opening with the narrator's 'Once upon a time . . .' accompanied by picture-book images in a stained-glass style, the fairy storybook origins were exploited to maximum effect, even retaining some of the French tale's dark undertones, with an over-poweringly imposing castle design, judicious combination of threateningly dramatic music, and images layered with shadow. The Beast himself was made suitably scary at times, while his comic element was introduced early on and his charm allowed to develop. The fearful quality of the cavernous castle of the title sequence worked best in contrast with the song-filled, brightly sunlit 'Little Town' scene that introduces Belle, her father Maurice and her grossly vain and stupid suitor Gaston, which proved spectacularly that Disney was capable of soaring above past mediocrity and new competition from the likes of *An American Tail* (1986) from former Disney employee Don Bluth, who went on to make hits like *Thumbelina* (1994) for Warner Brothers. The scene was the first of several song-driven set pieces, so energetically skilful that they ensured the film's place as a great Disney classic. Intricately choreographed central action was also abundant with visual asides of humorous slapstick detail that could genuinely merit further viewings.

Disney had rediscovered a properly character-rich story, but enhanced further by animation that was once again amazing to see. The colours and luminosity, feeling of image depth, and simulation of live-action camera motion and lens effects used to depict characters and landscapes, candlelit rooms, scenes lit by quivering flames, moonlight and snowy reflection were simply without precedent. *Beauty and the Beast* also played out a homage and affectionate parody of the great era of Hollywood musicals and extravaganzas, with the candlestick Lumière based on Maurice Chevalier and his big number exploding into a full-blown Busby Berkeley pastiche. Angela Lansbury as the fussing Mrs Potts was a nod to Disney's own past, but overall the film was the nearest thing left to a proper Hollywood musical, complete with boisterous duets, street choruses and a classically feisty maiden as Belle. Audiences enjoyed a genre that they had no opportunity to experience with real actors in contemporary settings anymore. Most crucially of all, the work was a showcase for the interplay between traditional animation illustration skills and digital animation techniques, using computer programming to design the paths for motion that helped simulate the complex motion of three-dimensional camera moves, with curving 'crane' shots and circular motion around dancing characters. New levels of sophistication in visual choreography of action were being executed by applying digital modelling and motion manipulation to the graphic artists' visual creations. The elegance of motion that simulated ambitious camera crane shots added much to the spectacular image of the film, especially in scenes such as the title number's dance sequence. Computer-aided design seemed ready to revolutionise the process of sequencing, pushing out limits much further than the fluid-motion Steadicam had done for live action in the 1980s.

Beauty and the Beast helped rekindle interest in the achievements possible in mainstream animated cinema, and *The Lion King* (1994) was as impressive in terms of visuals, music and narrative line. At the same time, bland output like *Pocahontas* (1995) continued the impression that Disney pinned more on big-name voicing like Mel Gibson than on character and script.

Inevitably, computer-based animation has since made a great impact on big-screen 'cartoons'. The year 1995 also brought the first animation feature generated from start to finish on computers, *Toy Story*, from Disney subsidiary Pixar Animation Studios. *A Bug's Life* (1998) showed a visible picture quality improvement, which continued with *Toy Story 2* (1999). When SKG Dreamworks produced *Antz* (1998) from digital-only sourcing (except for the theatrical show-print), it was already clear that the computer had come of age. Whilst much visual work in these films is geared towards a kind of naturalism, simulating camera tracking, Steadicam and lens effects from live action cinema, it is interesting that a new enthusiasm for the more unrealistic stop-frame clay motion work of Aardman Animations also developed, culminating in the epic *Chicken Run* (2000). As authenticity of image manipulation improves continually and becomes a given, content may inevitably become the more vital battleground.

Some Things to Watch out for and Consider

- Identify key elements that you think made *Beauty and the Beast* succeed.
- What are the most memorable scenes for you – and what makes them so?
- Does the film remind you of specific Hollywood films you have seen?
- Are you aware of the animation skill while you watch the film? In any event, would that make a big difference to the film's impact?
- Is an understanding of live-action cinema necessary to appreciate the film?
- Would the film benefit from being improved visually? How?

Further Viewing

Beauty and the Beast (Stowe, USA, 1905)
Beauty and the Beast (Mathews, USA, 1913)
Beauty and the Beast (Newall, USA, 1922)
Beauty and the Beast (Cocteau, France, 1946)
Beauty and the Beast (Cahn, USA, 1962)
Beauty and the Beast (Marner, USA, 1987)
Snow White and the Seven Dwarfs (Hand, USA, 1937)
The Lion King (Allers and Minkoff, USA, 1994)
Thumbelina (Bluth and Goldman, USA, 1994)
The Swan Princess (Rich, USA, 1994)
Toy Story (Lasseter, USA, 1995)
A Bug's Life (Stanton and Lasseter, USA, 1998)
Antz (Darnell and Guterman, USA, 1998)
Toy Story 2 (Brannon and Lasseter, USA, 1999)
Chicken Run (Lord and Park, USA, 2000)

42 THE USUAL SUSPECTS

Singer, USA, 1995

Awards

Academy Awards: Winner – Best Supporting Actor (Kevin Spacey) and Best Screenplay Written Directly for the Screen

British Academy Awards: Winner – Best Film, Best Editing and Best Screenplay (Original)

Production Details

Production company/studio	Blue Parrot/Spelling International
Producers	Bryan Singer and Michael McDonnell
Director	Bryan Singer
Cinematographer	Newton Thomas Sigel
Editor	John Ottman
Screenwriter	Christopher McQuarrie
Music	John Ottman

Cast Includes

Stephen Baldwin	*Michael McManus*
Gabriel Byrne	*Dean Keaton*
Benicio Del Toro	*Fred Fenster*
Kevin Pollack	*Todd Hockney*
Kevin Spacey	*Verbal Kint*
Chazz Palminteri	*Dave Kujan*
Pete Postlethwaite	*Kobayashi*
Suzy Amis	*Edie Finneran*

FOCUS: Storytelling in the Movies and 'New Hollywood/Old Hollywood'

Before *The Usual Suspects* Singer had directed *Lion's Den* (1992) – a vehicle for Ethan Hawke – and *Public Access* (1993), neither notable for any particularly characteristic élan. Since *The Usual Suspects* Singer has been responsible for the disturbingly bland (considering the subject matter) *Apt Pupil* (1998) and the flashy but shallow *X-Men* (2000). Thus his œuvre does not cry out for auteur analysis. Yet, this one film has made a genuine impact on the public conscience – not least by the legendary character 'Keyser Soze'.

The film has to be seen with reference to *Casablanca* (see chapter 11) – the choice of title made that certain. As did the name of the film's production company (Blue Parrot). On a lesser scale than the earlier movie, *The Usual Suspects* has become a cult classic. It also forms bonds between strangers.

Like *Casablanca*, the strength of *The Usual Suspects* lies in its quality of performance and material. Of course the 'story' is utter nonsense – but the telling is too stylish to resist. The joy of the film is its ability to combine the best of modern Hollywood – action, pace, ostentatious shows of technique – with the virtues of old Hollywood – craftsmanship and tight structure along with the enduring atmospherics of *film noir* that have gripped audiences since the 1940s.

The film develops a sense of intrigue from the opening dockside conflagration. Verbal (Kevin Spacey), an eyewitness and participant, tells the story of events leading up to the final mayhem. Five New York villains – ex-cop Keaton (Byrne), con-man Kint (Spacey), sociopath McManus (Baldwin), droll Hockney (Pollack) and incomprehensible Fenster (Del Toro) – are rounded up by police in a manner that leads them to suspect a conspiracy. After release, they decide to conspire together to make some profit from their indisposition – but there is always the feeling that someone else is controlling events. All goes tolerably well until the influence of the legendary, seemingly omnipotent 'Keyser Soze' is felt.

The plot twists are always engaging. The storyline is regularly enlivened by the entry of strong (usually unpleasant) characters. The whole film takes off into areas of truth and illusion with the entry of Kobayashi, the all-too-real representative of the shadowy

Soze. So as not to make the film too talky (and presumably to attract the core audience of young men), Singer throws in plenty of explosions and gunplay too. The ending, in which the audience is finally drawn to the truth – thus allowing us the pleasure of two hours of intriguing puzzlement before enjoying the denouement from a position of omniscience – is a masterstroke of popular cinema.

The film is intricate, clever and ultimately fulfilling. The tale is told well – often by Verbal – it is gripping and it is fun – not least the cheating. Someone is playing games with the 'usual suspects', as the film-makers are playing games with us – for example, information is given and then withdrawn or contradicted. Both Gabriel Byrne's and Kevin Spacey's faces are shown as Keyser Soze; in the flashback sequence, Keyser Soze is played by a man with long hair that obscures his face; Bryan Singer played the part of Keyser Soze's hand lighting a cigarette; and composer and editor John Ottman played the close-up of Keyser's feet. Actor Gabriel Byrne, when asked at the Cannes film festival, 'Who is Keyser Soze?', replied, 'During shooting and until watching the film tonight, I thought I was!' Unlike Harrison Ford – revealed as a replicant many years after he made *Blade Runner* – Byrne saw the funny side of the situation.

The film covered its production budget of $6 million from the UK receipts alone. It took over $23 million in the USA (helped by a healthy batch of Oscar nominations). As befits a cult item, the video sales are consistently impressive.

Some Things to Watch out for and Consider

- *The Usual Suspects* as *Casablanca* manqué:
  - Compare and contrast the roles of Keaton and Ilsa Lund.
  - What characteristics unite and divide the two leading cops in the films?
  - In *Casablanca* who is Keyser Soze? In *The Usual Suspects* who is Ugarte?
  - Compare how flashbacks are used in both films – particularly with reference to point of view and how 'privileged' we are as spectators.
  - How does the final twist of *The Usual Suspects* echo/mirror the final scenes of *Casablanca*?

Further Viewing

Casablanca (Curtiz, USA, 1941)
Kiss me Deadly (Aldrich, USA, 1954)
Touch of Evil (Welles, USA, 1958)
Chinatown (Polanski, USA, 1974)
Reservoir Dogs (Tarantino, USA, 1991)
Pulp Fiction (Tarantino, USA, 1994)
L.A. Confidential (Hanson, USA, 1997)

43 WILLIAM SHAKESPEARE'S ROMEO + JULIET

Luhrmann, USA, 1996

Awards

Academy Awards: Nomination – Best Art Direction
Berlin: Winner – Best Actor (Leonardo DiCaprio)

Production Details

Production company/studio	Bazmark
Producer	Gabriella Martinelli
Director	Baz Luhrmann
Cinematographer	Donald McAlpine
Editor	Jill Bilcock
Screenwriters	Baz Luhrman and Craig Pearce (based on Shakespeare)
Production designer	Catherine Martin

Cast Includes

Leonardo DiCaprio	*Romeo*
Claire Danes	*Juliet*
John Leguizamo	*Tybalt*
Harold Perrineau	*Mercutio*
Miriam Margolyes	*The Nurse*

FOCUS: Auteur Theory and Audio-Visual Media/Film History

Baz Luhrmann's *William Shakespeare's Romeo + Juliet* is one of the outstanding films of the 1990s, although, judging from the opening half hour, the viewer would be forgiven for thinking otherwise. Right from the start, the director subjects our senses to the 'high concept' staccato assault and battery involving guns, music, graphics, explosions, rapid cuts, whirring helicopters and speeded-up action reminiscent of the *Keystone Kops*. All this cacophony dies, however, when we come to the balcony scene. Here, the 'star cross'd' lovers pledge their devotion in a shimmering swimming pool, and all of a sudden we realise there is a lyric impulse behind the crash and the flash, and that this obsession with the gorgeous and the immediate is part of a strategy to create a movie stylisation that can reflect and contain the equally stylised qualities in Shakespeare's verse. That said, Luhrmann is not particularly interested in 'bringing the Bard to the screen'. He is more occupied in hitching Shakespeare, like an outboard motor, to his own, dynamic form of modern (and postmodern) movie poetry.

That poetry is rooted in the language of television imagery and the perceptions it fosters. Every moment of the film assumes our eyes are goggle-box eyes, that long hours slumped on the sofa have accustomed us to the sheen of commercials and the energy of music videos. Moreover, it takes for granted that we have all bought into a dandified TV culture obsessed with physical style, where appearance is the sole barometer of the inner life and where to seem is automatically to be. In consequence, many of the apparently decorative elements here – costume, hair, lighting, the lush pin-up moments – are the main vessels of meaning, much more so than the immortal verse, which Luhrmann cuts and pastes according to his own movie needs, and which fulfils the role of the paparazzi at a film première: it is there to click shutters and make the whole event colourful, but it is not the true centre of attention.

The fall of hair on a face, the spangle of a sequin on a dress: ironically for a film so gripped by the up to date, this concentration on the sensual is closer to the language of the old silent films, where the face, body and clothes were the only means by which performers could communicate, and audiences receive, their meanings.

See Louise Brooks in *Pandora's Box* (Pabst, Germany, 1929) and notice how a simple curve of her neck can evoke a whole world of feeling. Back in those days, gesture was character, and Luhrmann's characters are also gestures, their outward form and physical rhetoric reflecting their inner worlds and conflicts. Watch Romeo and Juliet on what is effectively their honeymoon night; the camera caresses them, drinks in their qualities of skin and facial structure, as if the fates of these two lovers were so intertwined they were one and the same texture.

In imagery, too, the director gathers up textures and organises them into patterns. For example, notice how the lovers are consistently associated with water. We first gaze up at Juliet from the bottom of her bath, where she is dunking her head like a glassy-eyed mermaid; at the ball, a drugged-out Romeo sobers himself up in the same way and with the same expression. A few minutes later, when the duo first meet, they gaze at each other through the opposite sides of a fish tank, and the image develops in the balcony/swimming-pool scene until we reach the morning after the honeymoon, where the young woman sees her husband fall into the pool again, although this time the sight is a premonition of his, and her, death. By the time the tragedy has run its course and we have said farewell to the lovers in a liquid freeze frame, water has long been established as the image of the doom that has stalked the characters from the very beginning. They have lived fast, they have died young, and they have done it all in iambic pentameter.

This death/life opposition is vital in *William Shakespeare's Romeo + Juliet*. The two main characters are in the grip of what might be called the 'Rock and Roll Paradox', best summed up by Prince before he turned into a squiggle:

> Maybe I'll live life to the ultimate high
> Maybe I'll die just like heroes die.

In other words, how do we engage in the intensity of life and love, how do we get that transcendental buzz without social conventions crowding in and making it impossible to carry on? The brutal answer is, you cannot. Romeo and Juliet die, not because of a minor glitch in the postal system of Mantua/LA but because they find it impossible to reconcile their spangled vision of fulfilment with the inevitable compromises of the world; in the end, they burn themselves, and each other, out. The director is in love with the operatic aspects of this idea; he does not so much analyse it here as twirl a glitter ball in celebration.

Some Things to Watch out for and Consider

As you ogle this film, then, look critically at the glamour and glitz and assess to what extent the surfaces are pointing towards the depths. Scrutinise your own responses and think through the advantages and disadvantages of the approach. Whatever you decide, you will find it hard to deny that *William Shakespeare's Romeo + Juliet* is a whirlwind insight into the immediacy of being young. Luhrmann goes boldly where no Laurence Olivier or Kenneth Branagh has ever gone before, to a place where a Shakespeare film is not just a screen interpretation of the original, but the occupant of a parallel universe, a sexy, hyped-up poem in its own right.

- Think about the characters' surfaces. Ask yourself:
  - During the course of the film, how many different outfits does Romeo wear and what does each tell us about the kind of person he is at that moment?
  - What is the significance of the costumes he and the other characters wear at the ball?
  - How does Mercutio's appearance – his clothes, looks and actions – indicate the secrets of his character?
- Think about the meaning of images.
  - In terms of imagery, how are the numerous guns in this film explicitly connected to the duo's love and to their ultimate death?
  - How is the theme of 'my only love sprung from my only hate' expressed through imagery?
- How does music contribute to the meaning of the film?

Further Viewing

Pandora's Box (Pabst, Germany, 1929),
Henry V (Olivier/Beck, UK/USA, 1944)
Romeo and Juliet (Zefferelli, UK/Italy, 1968)
Strictly Ballroom (Luhrmann, Australia, 1992)

Much Ado About Nothing (Branagh, UK/USA, 1993)
Titus (Taymor, USA, 1999)

Further Reading

B. Luhrmann and C. Pearce, *William Shakespeare's Romeo + Juliet* (London, 1997)

D. Rosenthal, *Shakespeare on Screen* (London, 2000)

44 *TITANIC*
Cameron, USA, 1997

Awards

Academy Awards: Winner – Best Picture, Best Director, Best Art
   Direction, Best Cinematography, Best Sound, Best Sound Effects
   Editing, Best Score, Best Song, Best Costume Design, Best Film Editing
   and Best Visual Effects; Nomination – Best Actress (Kate Winslet) and
   Best Supporting Actress (Gloria Stuart)

Production Details

Production company/studio	Lightstorm / Fox / Paramount
Producers	James Cameron and Jon Landau
Director	James Cameron
Cinematographer	Russell Carpenter
Editors	Conrad Buff and James Cameron
Screenwriter	James Cameron
Music	James Horner
Costume designer	Deborah L. Scott

Cast Includes

Leonardo DiCaprio	*Jack Dawson*
Kate Winslet	*Rose DeWitt Bukater*
Frances Fisher	*Ruth DeWitt Bukater*
Bill Paxton	*Brock Lovett*
Kathy Bates	*Molly Brown*
Suzy Amis	*Lizzy Calvert*
Gloria Stuart	*Rose Calvert*
David Warner	*Spicer Lovejoy*
Danny Nucci	*Fabrizio De Rossi*
Billy Zane	*Cal Hockley*

FOCUS: Narrative Conventions and the New Hollywood Blockbuster

Titanic is probably most famous for its reputed budget in excess of $200 million, requiring it to gross $350 million to break even. In fact, the spiralling costs became part of the marketing campaign – with its 550 computer-generated shots, it was the most expensive film ever made – irrespective of content, a spectacle in itself. It broke all box-office records around the world to become the highest grossing film to date, taking in excess of $1 billion and equalling the record set by *Ben-Hur* (Wyler, USA, 1959) for winning the most Oscars. So wherein lies the secret of such success? An obvious and important answer would look at the promotion and distribution of the film, but for the moment let us look at the film itself.

It is a generally accepted fact by cinema-goers and critics alike that when we go to see a genre picture we know what to expect. With a film like *Titanic* we have more than expectations: we have foreknowledge. (There cannot have been many viewers who wondered whether the ship would sink or not, although anyone with a more detailed knowledge of the facts would have been in for a few surprises.)

So, if we know what is going to happen, why go and see it? The answer has to lie in the spectacular action sequences and special effects upon which the success of the New Hollywood blockbuster appears to be predicated (see *Star Wars*, chapter 28; *Raiders of the Lost Ark*, chapter 31; *Jurassic Park*, chapter 36; *The Matrix*, chapter 49). Cinema is a voyeuristic art form – what better subject than the most famous sinking in history? But spectacle alone is not enough. We want a story. As D. W. Griffith himself realised (see chapter 1), we want the spectacle to be personalised.

The first hour or so of the film is devoted to this end – first by presenting the story as an extended flashback (the personal account of a survivor) and then, through her, introducing us to various characters whose fate and reactions we follow as the film progresses. In the first few scenes of the flashback Cameron sets out the themes he is going to explore, primarily through the *mise en scène*.

Our first glimpses of the young Rose (Winslet) are a detail shot of her gloved hand filmed from above as she emerges from a car obscured by the brim of an enormous hat. Notice how the choice

Titanic. Courtesy of Pictorial Press

of shot emphasises these details of her costume, telling us she belongs to a privileged class (suggesting she is an object/trophy?). This is reinforced by the voice-over: 'To me it was a slave ship taking me back to America in chains. Outwardly I was everything a well-brought-up girl should be. Inside I was screaming.'

From these images of wealth and privilege we cut to Jack (DiCaprio), who is represented as poor but free and daring. Thus he wins his passage on *SS Titanic* and presents us with the embodiment of youth, energy, optimism and joy in his helter-skelter race to board the ship: the opposite to the measured progress of Rose and her party. These kinds of oppositions continue throughout the film (with Rose changing sides), and Cameron uses the structure of the ship to highlight and reflect the structure of the social classes. Thus, when Jack first sees Rose on the 1st class deck, she is above him both literally and symbolically. The effect is enhanced by the use of (sun)light glancing off her hair to create a halo, an angelic image. Ironically, it is Jack (the Christ figure who sacrifices himself) who will redeem Rose.

If Rose presents us with the image of an angel in the heaven that is 1st class, then the opposite image is the vast engine room, which, with its semi-naked sweating workers and pits of fire, is like a vision of hell. In their position at the bottom of both the social scale and the ship, these workers are significantly the first to die. Through the juxtaposition of such images Cameron makes his position on the class system very clear. This is an American film where the hero is the Wisconsin farm boy without airs and graces and where we are encouraged to sympathise with everyone – except the rich.

The rich are represented primarily through the characters of Cal (Rose's fiancé) and Rose's mother. Both are very negative character portraits. When Cal first gives Rose the Heart of the Ocean pendant, he describes its royal lineage and claims royal status for himself: 'We are Royalty, Rose.' Thus, although he is American, we are encouraged to associate him and his super-rich fellow passengers with the corrupt elitism of European Aristocracy rather than the egalitarianism of America. Cal is presented as quintessentially selfish, possessive and heartless, in direct contrast to Jack. Similarly, Rose's mother is presented as a mercenary – perfectly capable of sacrificing her daughter's happiness to gain a fortune. The only rich character who is exempt from such negative qualities is Molly Brown (Kathy Bates). She is despised by her fellow 1st-class passengers for having new money as opposed to an aristocratic pedigree. She is shown to have a warm heart through her desire to help Jack and her plea to row the lifeboat back at the end of the film to save those freezing to death in the water. Her good qualities seem directly in proportion to her lack of 'pedigree'. Similarly Rose's good qualities develop as she learns to leave the corrupt world of her mother and fiancé behind.

The narrative structure of *Titanic* is complicated (and made unwieldy) by the use of the extended flashback and the fact that a number of different stories are being told. Is this film a love story or a disaster movie? As a combination of the two is it successful?

The use of the extended flashback means we have a story within a story and we can view the structure of the narrative in a number of different ways. Given that the 'New Hollywood blockbusters' are often accused of dispensing with the virtues of the classic Hollywood narrative (see *Stagecoach*, chapter 9), a comparison to classic narrative conventions is interesting. Is this film structured round a series of loosely linked action-packed sequences in the episodic style of New Hollywood or does it conform more faithfully to classic narrative conventions? Does the classic Hollywood pattern of equilibrium, crisis, new equilibrium and closure apply to *Titanic*?

We could say, for example, that the initial equilibrium is the excavation of the *Titanic* in search of the 'Heart of the Ocean'. The crisis is the empty safe. This causes Rose to be brought on board to tell her story. Her story reveals what happened to the missing pendant. Resolution and closure come when she throws it into the ocean.

Alternatively, if we are viewing the film as a disaster movie, we could say that the initial state of equilibrium is the state on board before the ship hits the iceberg. The iceberg is the crisis dramatically disrupting the previous calm. The crisis is resolved by the sinking of the ship. If we view the film as a love story, the crisis comes much earlier with Rose's suicide attempt, which causes her to meet Jack and begin to break with Cal.

Whichever way we view it, the narrative does appear to have much in common with the classic Hollywood pattern. Events are clearly linked by cause and effect and motivation is clear. In spite of the central cause – the hitting of the iceberg – the narrative is clearly character led. All loose ends are tied up at the end – hence closure.

Some Things to Watch out for and Consider

- To what extent do you think *Titanic* emulates the classic Hollywood narrative whilst grafting on contemporary special effects? Which aspects of the film do you like most? Why?
- The collision with the iceberg could be described as the central cause of the film, precipitating the dramatic spectacle of the sinking of the ship. This comes quite late in the narrative, however. What do you think is the reason for this? What other chains of cause and effect can you identify? You could consider:
  - the balance of power between the sexes;
  - the balance of power between the rich and the poor;
  - Cal's treatment of Rose in the early scenes of the film;
  - the ambitions of those involved in the design and running of the ship;
  - the role of the journalist;
  - Rose and Jack falling in love;
  - Cal's jealousy.
- *Titanic* appears to present us with a hybrid of different genres. At times we are clearly watching a disaster movie, at

others it seems more like a thriller. The term for this blending of genre characteristics is 'bricolage'. Given that genre operates on audience knowledge and expectations of the conventions of a particular genre, how effective do you find it? What different genre characteristics can you identify in the film?

- Consider how Cameron paces the film from the point of impact with the iceberg. What devices does he use to build tension and engage our sympathy with the characters' plight? You could consider:
  - the different storylines involving Jack, Rose and Cal;
  - the presentation of other characters singled out by the narrative preparing for, or meeting with, their deaths;
  - the juxtaposition of images of stillness with the graphic scenes of disaster;
  - the juxtaposition of sound and image, particularly the contrasting effect of orchestral music with scenes of chaos and disorder.
- The representation of some of the characters has been discussed briefly above. Certain messages and values about wealth, class and nation are created through the presentation of the characters. What of Jack, the hero? What qualities of character do we associate with him? How are these created? Look at his actions and dialogue, costume and changes in costume, as well as what the camera does – where is Jack in the frame? What messages and values about America are presented through his characterisation?
- Compare and contrast the critical and audience response to *Titanic*. Contemporary critics of the film were less than kind – for example: 'As Cameron sails his lonely craft toward greatness, he should realise he needs to bring a passenger with him. Preferably someone who can write' (Kenneth Turan, *Los Angeles Times*).
  - How far do you agree with this kind of comment?
  - What do the viewing figures suggest about audience response to the critics?
  - What factors do you think outweighed critical opinion for the audience?
- Why did Titanic sweep the board at the Academy Awards so totally in 1997?

Further Viewing

Titanic (Negulesco, USA, 1953)
A Night to Remember (Baker, UK, 1958)
The Terminator (Cameron, USA, 1982)
The Abyss (Cameron, USA, 1989)

Further Reading

J. Collins, H. Radner and A. Preacher Collins (eds.), *Film Theory Goes to the Movies* (New York, 1993)
R. Maltby, *Hollywood Cinema* (Oxford, 1995)

45 THE IDIOTS
(Idioterne)
Von Trier, Denmark, 1998

Awards

Cannes: Nomination – Golden Palm
European Film Awards: Nomination – European Film Award and Best Screenwriter
London Film Festival: Winner – FIPRESCI Award ('For its attempt to rethink film language and social rules from scratch and willingness to accept the limitations of both its method and cultural assumptions.')

Production Details

Production company/studio	Zentropa (plus 16 co-partners)
Producer	Vibeke Windeløv
Director	Lars von Trier (uncredited)
Cinematographers	Casper Holm, Jesper Jargil, Kristoffer Nyholm and Lars von Trier
Editor	Molly Marlene Stensgård
Screenwriter	Lars von Trier

Cast Includes

Bodil Jørgensen	*Karen*
Jens Albinus	*Stoffer*
Anne Louise Hassing	*Susanne*
Troels Lyby	*Henrik*
Nikolaj Lie Kaas	*Jeppe*
Henrik Prip	*Ped*
Luis Mesonero	*Miguel*
Louise Mieritz	*Josephine*
Knud Romer Jorgensen	*Axel*
Trine Michelsen	*Nana*
Anne-Grethe Bjarup Riis	*Katrine*

Paprika Steen	*The High Class Lady*
Erik Wedersøe	*Svend, Stoffer's Uncle*
Michael Moritzen	*The Man from Municipality*
Anders Hove	*Josephine's Father*

FOCUS: Movements in Art Cinema (New Waves)

The Idiots is the most well-known and artistically successful product of a brave – if possibly foolhardy – group of Danish film-makers who formed *Dogme '95 (Dogma 95)*. Some of their rhetoric brings to mind a fundamentalist sect. The movement began with a manifesto – a 'vow of chastity' no less – which certainly makes identifying characteristics easy:

> *I swear to submit to the following set of rules drawn up and confirmed by DOGMA 95:*
>
> 1. Shooting must be done on location. Props and sets must not be brought in (if a particular prop is necessary for the story, a location must be chosen where this prop is to be found).
> 2. The sound must never be produced apart from the images or vice versa. (Music must not be used unless it occurs where the scene is being shot.)
> 3. The camera must be hand-held. Any movement or immobility attainable in the hand is permitted. (The film must not take place where the camera is standing; shooting must take place where the film takes place.)
> 4. The film must be in colour. Special lighting is not acceptable. (If there is too little light for exposure, the scene must be cut or a single lamp be attached to the camera.)
> 5. Optical work and filters are forbidden.
> 6. The film must not contain superficial action. (Murders, weapons, etc. must not occur.)
> 7. Temporal and geographical alienation are forbidden. (That is to say that the film takes place here and now.)
> 8. Genre movies are not acceptable.
> 9. The film format must be Academy 35 mm.
> 10. The director must not be credited.

Furthermore I swear as a director to refrain from personal taste! I am no longer an artist. I swear to refrain from creating a 'work', as I regard the instant as more important than the whole. My supreme goal is to force the truth out of my characters and settings. I swear to do so by all the means available and at the cost of any good taste and any aesthetic considerations.

Thus I make my VOW OF CHASTITY.

Copenhagen, Monday 13 March 1995
On behalf of DOGMA 95

Dogme '95 was founded by four Danish film-makers: Lars von Trier, Thomas Vinterberg, Soren Kragh-Jacobson and Kristian Levring. It is interesting that so aggressive a statement of intent should emerge from Denmark. Vinterberg has stated publicly that it is the result of Denmark being 'a small country'. Thus energy comes not only from the usual reaction to Hollywood but also from the reaction to bigger neighbours like Germany. As with earlier movements, there is also a technological imperative. As they put it on their official web site (www.dogme95.com): 'Today a technological storm is raging, the result of which will be the ultimate democratisation of the cinema. For the first time, anyone can make movies. But the more accessible the media becomes, the more important the avant-garde.'

The *Dogme* group clearly positioned themselves as a new 'new wave', with references to '1960' on their web site. The web site declaims – perhaps only half seriously – in language that echoes the manifestos issued by Dziga Vertov's group in the 1920s:

DOGMA 95 has the expressed goal of countering 'certain tendencies' in the cinema today.
DOGMA 95 is a rescue action!
. . . To DOGMA 95 the movie is not illusion!

Von Trier had already achieved a minor international hit with *Europa* (Denmark, 1991) and some commercial success and notoriety with *Breaking the Waves* (Denmark, 1996), which had mixed controversial subject matter (disability, impotence, casual sex and displaced voyeurism) with a taste for jarring cinematography. *Breaking the Waves* now seems like '*Dogme*-lite' or a preliminary sketch for the full-blown work – *The Idiots*.

The *Dogme* manifesto declares special effects, costumes and elaborate camera perspectives obsolete for a purpose. The artistic aim was to achieve the highest possible degree of immediacy in the film-making process. *The Idiots* achieves the *Dogme* aim and in the process throws down a challenge to film-making in its second century.

Von Trier's film is a study in embarrassment and a disturbing attack on concepts of normality and civilisation. A group of young(ish) middle-class people, disenchanted with the facile nature of the society they live in, retreat to a country house, where they play at being 'spasses' (physically and mentally retarded). The 'encounter group' material does wear after a while, but the strength of the film is in the group's confrontations with the straight world. Much of the action is very uncomfortable to watch. Nonetheless, some sequences, particularly the visits to the swimming pool and a scene where a group of Hell's Angels forget their machismo to help Jeppe go to the toilet, are very moving. When two damaged characters, Jeppe and Christina, emerge from the spassing 'gang bang' to achieve tenderness and an adult relationship for the first time in their lives, Von Trier achieves a kind of humanist dignity rarely seen on screen.

On the other hand, Von Trier has never lost his reputation for shocking for its own sake. In the case of *The Idiots*, apart from the profoundly controversial subject matter, we are confronted with clearly genuine penetrative sexual intercourse on screen. In addition, like much of Jean-Luc Godard's work, *The Idiots* can be seen as embarrassingly 'badly made' (shots go out of focus, 'characters' are caught looking at the camera, and so on).

The refreshing witty atmosphere that surrounds *Dogme* has allowed spurious rows to rage on its web site and rumours to circulate of an application to film in 'dogme style' by Steven Spielberg. The 'vow of chastity' is still attracting film-makers and encouraging new talents to seize the opportunities available for lower-budget, higher-content work.

The founding brotherhood continues to produce entertaining and interesting work. In a move echoing Visconti's move from realism to opera, Von Trier had already completed his musical *Dancer in the Dark* (France, 2000) – admittedly in his own idiosyncratic style. The initial tranche of Dogma was completed when the fourth founder, Levring, completed *The King is Alive* (Denmark/France, 2000). The film – shot on digital video – follows a group of disparate characters stranded in the deserts of Namibia. In true '*dogme*-style', characters are given time to develop and express complexity (not least through rehearsing Shakespeare's King Lear). The typical claustrophobic atmosphere is produced by tight hand-held camera and restricting some of the action to the broken down bus. Levring commented on *Dogme '95* in October 2000: 'I am not sure it will carry on. Someone is bound to come up with a new idea and a new way of doing things' – to which we must give a loud cheer, for thus cinema adapts, develops and survives.

Some Things to Watch out for and Consider

- Criticism of *The Idiots* – and indeed all of the *Dogme* films – has focused on two issues:
  - the lack of technical polish;
  - the embarrassing and/or controversial subject matter.

  How could you justify the style and content of these films? Would you bother?
- European film-makers seem much more prone than their American colleagues to forming groups, taking 'positions' or even writing manifestos. Why is this? In what ways does it aid/restrict the development of artistic (or commercial) success?

Further Viewing

The Man with the Movie Camera (Vertov, Soviet Union, 1929)
Breathless (Godard, France, 1959)
Celebration (*Festen*) (Vinterberg, Denmark, 1998)
Julian Donkey Boy (Korine, USA, 2000)

Further Reading

R. Kelly, *The Name of this Book is Dogma '95* (London, 2000)

46 FACE/OFF
Woo, USA, 1997

Production Details

Production company/studio	Douglas / Reuther
Producer	Douglas Pernut
Director	John Woo
Cinematographer	Oliver Wood
Editors	Christian Wagner and Steven Kemper
Screenwriter	John Woo

Cast Includes

John Travolta	*Sean Archer*
Nicholas Cage	*Castor Pollux*
Joan Allen	*Eve Archer*
Alessandro Nivola	*Troy Pollux*
Dominique Swain	*Jamie Archer*

FOCUS: International Style

Face/Off is at one level just another glossy big-budget American action movie in the tradition of films like *The Rock* (Bay, USA, 1996) and *Con Air* (West, USA, 1997), but it stands as an introduction to one of the most influential stylists of the 1990s – John Woo. It also indicates the growing impact of the sensibility and style of the Hong Kong film industry on Hollywood. Just as the Hollywood of the 1930s drew on the personnel and techniques of German expressionism, at the end of the twentieth century it drew on the personnel and techniques of Hong Kong. The reception of Woo's films opened the doors of Hollywood for Hong Kong directors and stars such as Chow Yun-fat, Michelle Yeoh, Jackie Chan, Tsui Hark, Sammo Hung, Ronnie Yu, Ringo Lam and Yuen Wo-ping.

Born in 1946, Woo came to prominence with a sequence of thrillers set among the Hong Kong triads: *A Better Tomorrow* (1986), *A Better Tomorrow II* (1987), *The Killer* (1989), *Once a Thief* (1991), *Bullet in the Head* (1990) and *Hard Boiled* (1992). These turned Woo into a cult figure in the West. Moving to Hollywood, he directed *Hard Target* (1992) and *Broken Arrow* (1996). *Face/Off* was his third Hollywood production, and, of his American films, the one that best illustrates Woo's characteristic themes and style.

Face/Off is the story of Sean Archer (John Travolta), an FBI agent embittered by the death of his 5-year-old son at the hands of a terrorist, Castor Pollox (Nicolas Cage). As the film opens, Pollux plants a bomb in Los Angeles but is wounded and lapses into a coma. In an attempt to discover the whereabouts of the bomb, Archer has Castor's face grafted in an effort to trick his brother, Troy, into revealing the whereabouts of the bomb. The trauma of having his face removed wakens Castor. Enraged, he has Archer's face grafted on, before killing everyone that knows what has happened. Now the roles are reversed: Pollux can call on the resources of the Police and FBI; Archer has to turn to Pollux's motley crew of terrorists.

While *Face/Off* demonstrates some of Woo's characteristic thematic concerns and their transformation in a Hollywood context, it is his mastery of violent action that gave him his reputation in the West. If Hollywood pursues realism in the portrayal of violence, Hong Kong pursues a hyper-realism: rather than recording acts of violence, the Hong Kong film-maker constructs a profoundly cinematic spectacle using all the resources that film provides. Woo is a master of the resulting style, which shoots a scene in small chunks from different angles (segment shooting) and then builds up the scene in the editing suite (constructive editing), so that the scene exists only on film; the actors never play it through.

Woo's techniques are demonstrated early in the film in a gunfight that leads to the capture of the Pollux brothers. The sequence begins as the private jet that the terrorists were using to escape crashes into the side of a hangar; it ends 4 minutes and 36 seconds later as Archer looks down at Pollux's body. At first viewing, the sequence is an exhilarating, hyper-kinetic roller-coaster; it is only with repeated viewings that it is possible to see how this effect is achieved. The sequence is built up from 176 separate shots – an average duration of 1.6 seconds. Woo is not simply cutting for effect. Each of these shots is a carefully worked-out building block for the sequence as a whole. How carefully worked out does not really become obvious until one works through it frame by frame. Each shot is calibrated for maximum effect and each shot contributes to telling the story.

It is Woo's mastery of timing and tempo that makes the editing so effective. The sequence has the rhythmic architecture of a three-act play. The first breathless act culminates in the capture of Troy Pollux, the second in Castor Pollux's encounter with Archer; the third is their conversation and the subsequent wounding of Pollux. This interlude prepares the way for a rapid acceleration in the tempo of the action. Within this architecture the sequence mixes slow, accelerated and normal speed action – slow motion captures the details of the action, while acceleration marks out the leading characters from those around them.

Face/Off is late-1990s popular entertainment, but it also tells us about the subtle shifts in film as audiences and producers adapt to the globalization of film.

Some Things to Watch out for and Consider

- Is 'international' cinema necessarily action driven? And/or high concept?
- Must popular cinema become increasingly kinetic?
- Will demographic change affect the content of mainstream product?
- Is the vast body count in Woo's work:
  - acceptable?
  - cathartic?
  - desensitising?
- Compare your answers to the same questions with reference to:
  - Martin Scorsese
  - Alfred Hitchcock
  - John Ford.
- Wong Kar-wai began with action movies (with *As Tears Go By* (Hong Kong, 1988)); Ang Lee has essayed a martial arts movie (*Crouching Tiger, Hidden Dragon* (USA, 2000)) after art-house success. John Woo keeps on making them. What strengths in film-making technique and visual power are developed and exercised in this relatively undervalued genre?

Further Viewing

The Killer (Woo, HK,1989)
Hard Boiled (Woo, HK, 1992)
Broken Arrow (Woo, USA, 1996)
MI2 (Woo, USA, 1998)
The Rock (Bay, USA, 1996)
Con Air (West, USA, 1997)
Crouching Tiger, Hidden Dragon (Lee, USA, 2000)
Chungking Express (Wong Kar-wai, HK, 1994)
In the Mood for Love (Wong Kar-wai, HK, 2000)

Further Reading

D. Bordwell, *Planet Hong Kong* (London, 2000)
S. Neale (ed.), *Contemporary Hollywood Cinema (London, 1998)*

47 THE BLAIR WITCH PROJECT

Myrick and Sánchez, USA, 1998

Production Details

Production company/studio	Haxan Entertainment (Marketing: Clein + Walker) – Artisan
Producers	Gregg Hale and Michael Monello
Directors	Daniel Myrick and Eduardo Sánchez
Cinematographer	Neal Fredericks
Editors	Daniel Myrick and Eduardo Sánchez
Screenwriters	Daniel Myrick and Eduardo Sánchez

Cast Includes

Heather Donahue	*Heather Donahue*
Joshua Leonard	*Joshua 'Josh' Leonard*
Michael C. Williams	*Michael 'Mike' Williams (as Michael Williams)*

FOCUS: Marketing

Tagline: In October of 1994, three student film-makers disappeared in the woods near Burkittesville, Maryland, while shooting a documentary. One year later, their footage was found.

It cost less than $100 000 to make. Artisan Entertainment picked it up at the Sundance Festival for a million. It made $29 million in its first weekend in the USA. It has produced a furore in the entertainment press as 'the most profitable film of all time' (*Screen International*, 1 Oct. 1999).

The Blair Witch Project is not that good (or bad) a film. The teen horror is not an original genre. Failing to reveal the villain is not an original ploy. It is clever to make a virtue out of bad production values by producing a spoof 'documentary made by students', but the fact remains that it has all the faults of a documentary made by students. There is no development. Much of the action is incoherent. The material is not strong enough to carry the full-length status of the film – although it must have seemed like a very neat idea at the time. Added to which: the acting is derisory, the script is muddled and the story is a rather lukewarm reheating of the old 'let's go into the woods scenario', even with a 'let's all split up' dénouement.

It was a brave move to make a film in this genre that eschews special effects to produce audience response, but horror films do still have to be scary. Much is made of its clever and knowing stance, and the references to *Deliverance* (Boorman, USA, 1972) are funny. The central problem with the film is the difficulty in achieving some level of emotional engagement with the protagonists. These are not the shallow but basically sympathetic teenagers that inhabit the *Scream* franchise. Even the final 'impassioned plea' from awesomely irritating 'Heather Donahue' (played by Heather Donahue!) does little to endear the viewer.

Actually the real 'hero' of this saga – as in the character who moves the action along and engineers a satisfying closure – is Amir Malin, the head of Artisan (*The Blair Witch Project*'s distribution company). As a feature in *Screen International* put it: 'it was Artisan's specialised care that built *The Blair Witch* project into such a phenomenon.' A national word of mouth for the film was built via a web site: blairwitch.com (using 16 hours of footage not in the finished film). This site created a whole virtual milieu around the film. If you click on 'film-makers', you get information not on the directors – Daniel Myrick and Eduardo Sánchez – but on the fictional characters in the film. You can watch video of the police investigation or explore the documentary evidence on the Blair witch if you so wish. As of 1 October 1988 the site had received over 50 million hits. Artisan financed a mock-documentary (of a mock-documentary!) *The Curse of the Blair Witch*. The spoof got repeated showings on the sci-fi channel.

For all its pretensions (i.e. marketing), as grass-roots independent film-making *The Blair Witch Project* received a very carefully placed platform release. The film was promoted to 15–24 year olds, but the follow-up promotions looked for an older audience. Only then was the film ready for a much wider distribution pattern on the back of a phenomenal wave of audience interest. At the same time the film opened in France with 111 000 admissions.

A good performance but not remarkable. The French distributor has since admitted to a mistake. It should have hit more screens but in September not August. The hype needed to build. Artisan was then taking a much more proactive approach in other territories. This included recommending platform release and making its web material available to foreign partners.

The UK platform release took place on the weekend of 22 October 1988. The film took over £600 000 and achieved a huge per screen average (showing a major advantage of 90-minute films – more showings per day, particularly if you can add one in at midnight). On the following (Halloween) weekend, *The Blair Witch Project* was distributed to 450 cinemas in the British Isles. By then it had taken $141 million in the USA plus $15 million internationally.

The hype continued through the film's phenomenal autumn – rumours about the production spread. Stories about how hysteria was engendered amongst the cast were carefully planted by the film-makers. Even the *Sight and Sound* reviewer bought the sensationalism wholesale and reacted in the predictably pompous manner. *The Blair Witch Project* became a 'must-see' movie well beyond its ostensibly young-ish hip-ish target audience. As a media event it was up there with *The Phantom Menace* (Lucas, USA, 1999) and for a tiny fraction of the cost. Here is the real importance of *The Blair Witch Project* – intelligence *can* outsell bombast.

Some Things to Watch out for and Consider

The sequel to *The Blair Witch Project* received a worldwide release at Halloween 2000. It was launched with a huge WWW festival. The original film's directors did not direct. The low-budget atmospherics were replaced by special-effects bombast. The audience turned against it.

Of course, Hollywood – even when presented with something fresh and new – can very quickly package a property into anonymity. But first-time film-makers take note: no matter what, the audience wins in the end.

Further Viewing

Nosferatu (Murnau, Germany, 1922)
Don't Look Now (Roeg, UK/Italy, 1973)
The Exorcist (Friedkin, USA, 1973)
Scream (Craven, USA, 1996)

48 ALL ABOUT MY MOTHER

(Todo sobre mi madre)

Almodóvar, Spain, 1999

Awards

Academy Awards: Winner – Best Foreign Language Film
Cannes: Winner – Best Director and Prize of the Ecumenical Jury; Nomination – Golden Palm
European Film Awards 1999: Winner – Audience Award, Best Director, Best Actress (Cecilia Roth) and Best Film

Production Details

Production company/studio	El Deseo SA (Spain), FR 2 (France) and Renn Productions (France)
Producers	Agustín Almodóvar and Michel Ruben
Director	Pedro Almodóvar
Cinematographer	Affonso Beato
Editor	José Salcedo
Screenwriter	Pedro Almodóvar
Production designer	Antxón Gómez

Cast Includes

Cecilia Roth	*Manuela*
Marisa Paredes	*Huma Rojo*
Candela Péña	*Nina*
Antonia San Juan	*Agrado*
Penélope Cruz	*Sister Rosa*
Rosa María Sardà	*Rosa's Mother*

Fernando Fernán Gómez   *Rosa's Father*
Toni Cantó   *Lola*
Eloy Azorín   *Esteban*

FOCUS: The Auteur and International Art Cinema

In *All about my Mother*, a woman (a single mother) working in Madrid sees her only son die on his 17th birthday as he runs to seek an actress's autograph. She makes an effort to reconcile herself to the disaster and to bring together some of the disparate and unfinished business of her life. She returns to her home town of Barcelona, at least in part to seek out the boy's father, a transvestite named Lola who does not know he has a child. So far we are in the realms of soap opera at its most melodramatic. However, Almodóvar exhibits his usual mixture of flamboyance and humanity to develop a story of complexity and power.

Almodóvar's films are very personal (he writes as well as directs his movies). His flamboyance and moral relativism are so surprising as a product of Spanish cultural life under the regime of General Franco that a purist auteur/biographical position seems (almost) reasonable.

The young Almodóvar was not artistically or temperamentally suited to provincial life in Franco's Spain. He gravitated to Madrid in 1968. Almodóvar could not afford film school and in any event the film-making schools were closed in the early 1970s by Franco's government.

Almodóvar found a job in the Spanish phone company and saved his salary to buy a Super 8 camera. From 1972 to 1978 he devoted himself to making short films with the help of his friends. The premières of those early films developed into events and were famous in the milieu of the Spanish counter-culture that developed as Francoism faded. Almodóvar became the central figure of 'La Movida' – a brash popular cultural movement based in Madrid. Elements of the counter-culture have become the subject – and indeed stars – of his films.

His first feature film, *Pepi, Luci, Bom and the Other Girls* (*Pepi, Luci, Bom y otras chicas del montón*, 1980), was shot on 16 mm film and blown up to 35 mm for public release. The film was a breath of fresh air, not only in Spain – where Carlos Saura (e.g. with *Cria*

Cuervos, 1976) had shown film could still tell truths but in a rather understated way – but across Europe. Almodóvar's early films, including the existentially shocking *Matador* (1986), made him the darling of the 'art-house' cinema and exhibited the flowering of his authorial style. Almodóvar's themes – dangerous then and still liable to cause offence – are personal idiosyncrasy and the revealing of the sexual chaos that lies beneath 'normal' life. His style was and remains theatrical, yet firmly cinematic in its sheer visual energy and the ability to change pace apparently at will. However silly the plots and characterisation might become, all could be forgiven for his so ostentatiously exhibited belief that basically love and a little common humanity can conquer all. He is not immoral, he simply refuses to take moral stances against *anything*. Not to be *against* anything is either brave or foolish – especially in a Spain still emerging from the shadow of the strongly held differences that had led to a civil war. Almodóvar quickly proved himself to be a wise and brave fool.

In 1987 he and his brother Agustín Almodóvar established their own production company, El Deseo, and were responsible for the release of a worldwide hit with *Women on the Verge of a Nervous Breakdown* (*Mujeres al borde de un ataque de nervios*, 1988). Until *All about my Mother* the film remained his best. It is arguable that for a decade Almodóvar veered into self-parody and lapses of even his (questionable) taste with *Tie Me Up! Tie Me Down!* (*Átame!*, 1990) and *High Heels* (*Tacones lejanos*, 1991), as well as *Kika* (1993), which treats sexual assault as a subject of farce.

The auteur of excess returned to form with *The Flower of my Secret* (*La flor de mi secreto*, 1996) and *Live Flesh* (*Carne trémula*, 1997), where the material is stronger and able to take the weight of Almodóvar's flamboyance.

Having launched into his usual emotional roller-coaster in *All about my Mother*, Almodóvar sets the travails of his protagonists in his usual counter/subcultural milieu – for example, the mother (Manuela) seeks out her friend Agrado, who, like her ex-lover, is a transvestite. It is also typical of the director's writing style that small personal stories interweave into baroque patterns of coincidence and mutual illumination. Through Agrado, Manuela meets Rosa, a young nun bound for El Salvador, and becomes personal assistant to Huma Rojo, the stage actress her son admired. She helps Huma manage Nina, co-star and Huma's lover. Manuela also takes it upon herself to look after Rosa during a difficult pregnancy.

The film contains echoes of Gorky, Brecht and Beckett as well as Lorca. Its filmic points of reference are *All about Eve* (Mankiewicz, USA, 1950) and *A Streetcar Named Desire* (Kazan, USA, 1951). Mothers (and fathers) as well as 'the actors' live out the pain as well as the pleasures of love and friendship. Although much of the material is painful, the film itself is a celebration of the strength of women and of feminine traits – shown by women and some men. However histrionic Almodóvar's style may be, *All about my Mother* is a celebration of real life, the theatre and cinema itself.

As the final (train) images of the film show, life is a journey – and no less worthwhile for that.

Some Things to Watch out for and Consider

- How is it possible that Pedro Almodóvar – a product of Francoist Spain – could come to make such splendidly colourful and sexually complex films?

- *All about my Mother* seems to be a perfect candidate for newer approaches to thinking about film. In the twentieth century, theoretical positions – from structuralism to post-structuralism – tried desperately to keep up with the audience and spectator. Any contemporary discussion of such issues is liable to focus on questions of identity and has to take note of the work and influence of Michel Foucault. Foucault challenged the 'common-sense' view that individuals have a single self-contained identity or character. Watching Almodóvar's films, particularly *All about my Mother*, is liable to raise these issues too.

- Almodóvar's exploration – even celebration – of multilayered identity may lead the viewer to the ideas of Judith Butler. Butler prefers to see the possibility for a person to form and choose his or her own individual identity. For Butler – and surely for Almodóvar – gender is a performance. This idea of identity as free-floating performance is one of the key ideas in 'queer theory', increasingly influential within film studies.

- The mass media are the primary means for images – alternative or otherwise – to be disseminated. It is worthwhile considering how an artist like Almodóvar illuminates and contributes to the war of images that rages around us (if it does).

Further Viewing

Women on the Verge of a Nervous Breakdown (Almodóvar, Spain, 1987)
All about Eve (Mankiewicz, USA, 1950)
A Streetcar Named Desire (Kazan, USA, 1951)
Chungking Express (Wong Kar-wai, HK, 1994)

Further Reading

J. Butler, *Gender Trouble* (1990)
P. J. Smith, *Desire Unlimited: The Cinema of Pedro Almodóvar* (1994)

49 *THE MATRIX*
Wachowski Brothers, USA, 1999

Awards

Academy Awards: Winner – Best Editing, Sound Effects Editing, Visual Effects and Best Sound

British Academy Awards: Winner – Best Achievement in Special Visual Effects and Best Sound

Blockbuster Entertainment Awards: Winner – Favourite Actor (Action/Science Fiction) (Keanu Reeves) and Favourite Supporting Actor (Action/Science-Fiction) (Laurence Fishburne)

Grammy Awards: Nomination – Best Soundtrack Album

MTV Movie Awards: Winner – Best Movie, Best Male Performance (Keanu Reeves) and Best Fight

Production Details

Production company/studio	Silver Pictures, Village Roadshow/Warner Brothers
Producer	Joel Silver
Directors	Andy Wachowski and Larry Wachowski
Cinematographer	Bill Pope
Editor	Zach Staenberg
Screenwriters	Andy Wachowski and Larry Wachowski
Production designer	Owen Paterson
Music	Tim Commerford
Art director	Hugh Bateup
Special effects	George Borshukov
R&D/technical supervisor	Bullet Time, Steve Courtley
Special effects supervisor	Zareh Nalbandian
Producer	Animal Logic

Cast Includes

Keanu Reeves	*Thomas A. Anderson/Neo*
Laurence Fishburne	*Morpheus*

Carrie-Anne Moss	*Trinity*
Hugo Weaving	*Agent Smith*
Gloria Foster	*Oracle*
Joe Pantoliano	*Cypher/Mr Reagan*
Andy Wachowski	*Window Cleaner* (*uncredited*)
Larry Wachowski	*Window Cleaner* (*uncredited*)

FOCUS: New Technology/New Cinema

The Matrix was launched via a massive 'teaser' campaign featuring taglines such as: 'Believe the unbelievable' and 'Reality is a thing of the past', which recalled the epic blockbusters of an earlier age. The sense of intrigue and conspiracy was fuelled via the prosaic: 'What is the Matrix?' and the rather racier: 'Unfortunately, no one can be told what the Matrix is. You have to see it for yourself.' And 'The future will not be user friendly.'

As the film was released, Warner Brothers felt confident to announce that 'In 1999, the Matrix has you,' as well as, 'On March 31st, the fight for the future begins.'

Thus *The Matrix* was launched with a mixture of mock 'Discovery Channel' hokum and lines that could have been uttered by Bill (or Ted) in a previous Keanu Reeves fantasy flick. Nobody could claim that they had not been warned about the intellectual content of *The Matrix*. Few could have realised how spectacular the visuals would be.

The Wachowski Brothers (Andy and Larry Wachowski) are from Chicago. They began as comic book writers. The kinetic energy – especially within the frame – (visual) strength and (narrative) weakness of their films come directly from their early graphic training. Together they wrote the breathtakingly silly screenplay for *Assassins* (1995) before directing *Bound* in 1996. Their directorial debut was a very stylish (lesbian) *film noir* starring Jennifer Tilly and Gina Gershon. The edgily sexual new *noir* atmosphere plus the anti-authority (and achingly sexy) central characters would all be driving forces in their sci-fi hit, as would be the high energy Bill Pope photography and Zach Staenberg editing.

In the near future, a computer hacker Thomas Anderson (code-named Neo – played by Keanu Reeves) discovers that all life on Earth may be nothing more than an elaborate façade created by a malevolent cyber-intelligence. Why? Because 'our' life essence is being 'farmed' to fuel the Matrix's campaign of domination in the real world (whatever that might be). Neo joins like-minded Rebel warriors Morpheus (Laurence Fishburne) and Trinity (Carrie-Ann Moss) in their struggle to overthrow the Matrix. Morpheus introduces Neo to the real world. In reality, it is 200 years later, and the world has been laid waste and taken over by advanced artificial intelligence machines. Neo is greeted as 'The One' who will lead the humans to overthrow the machines and reclaim the Earth.

Teetering as it does on the edge of portentousness, *The Matrix* is a good deal of fun. *The Matrix* is also one of the most successful Hollywood blockbusters of recent years. It is notable for its distinctive visual style and also for its ideological reading of late capitalism. While the former has been widely noted, the deeper resonance of its story has been less analysed.

Visually, *The Matrix* combines elements of the Hong Kong action film with digital technology. The debt to Hong Kong cinema is personified in the presence of Yuen Wo-ping as action choreographer. Yuen is a distinguished director in his own right: his *Snake in the Eagle's Shadow* (Hong Kong, 1978) and *Drunken Master* (Hong Kong, 1978) turned Jackie Chan from a Bruce Lee clone to a rising star. On the screen *The Matrix* draws freely from Hong Kong in its kung fu, in its use of 'wire work' to allow the actors to perform leaps and tumbles smoothly, and in its choreographed gunplay. The sequence where Neo and Agent Smith find themselves each with an empty gun pointed at the other's head is pure John Woo. In genre terms *The Matrix* resembles what are sometimes known as 'manga in motion': live action renderings of Japanese comic books or *anime* – for instance, Yuen Kwai and David Lai's *Saviour of the Soul* (Hong Kong, 1991).

While the Wachowskis draw heavily on Hong Kong expertise and films, they bring a Hollywood budget and Silicon Valley technology to the process. This allowed them to present action in what they term 'bullet time' – which shows movement in ultra slow motion while the camera appears to move relative to the object. For instance, we see Neo avoiding bullets as the cameras move around him. This process is made possible by a combination of computer-generated effects and the technique pioneered by Eadweard Muybridge in the 1870s of using a series of still cameras to record objects in motion. If this is all that can be said about *The Matrix*, we would be faced with an action film that draws freely on technology and the techniques of Hong Kong cinema to produce a visually inventive entertainment, but the film has intellectual ambitions that go beyond those usual in the genre.

Early in the film Neo is visited in his room by a friend intent on buying some illicit software. He goes to retrieve the software and hide the money in a hollowed-out book; as he does so we glimpse the book's title: *Simulcra and Simulation*. This is a sly reference to a book by the French social theorist of the postmodern, Jean Baudrillard. Influenced by Marshall McLuhan, Baudrillard is notorious for his contention that, in a society dominated by electronic media, our notion of reality is transformed. What the media present to us is no longer a representation of an existing reality but a simulation that lacks a referent in the real world – that is, it is 'hyper-real' – more real than reality. Running through the film is the need – enunciated by Morpheus – for Neo to understand what is real and what is not real. In the final sequence of the film, Neo's ability to stop the bullets of the agents comes from the fact that he understands that they are not real. If there is explicit reference to Baudrillard, one can also detect the ideas of another social theorist at work – Karl Marx. Marx argued that all economic value comes from the labour of the workers. *The Matrix* portrays a society where workers no longer even sell labour; they are reduced to human batteries being fed and maintained in a state of utter passivity in exchange for their energy. They are maintained in this state through the power of the matrix. For Marx, one of the key elements in the dominance of the capitalist class was the fact that it controls the creation and dissemination of ideas and representations. In this reading of the film, the role of Morpheus and his companions is to restore the workers to consciousness. The resistance is what Lenin would recognise as a vanguard revolutionary party. Is the Matrix an allegory of a world dominated by media? Is it a call for the workers of the world to cast off their chains and seize the levers of power? It might be, but the problem is that they/we are too busy watching *The Matrix* on their/our DVD players.

From a budget of $63 million, the film has taken $203.6 million (non-USA) and $171.383 million (USA) at the theatrical box office alone. The value of sales in DVDs, videos, games and sunglasses can only be dreamed of. *The Matrix* is a fan thing. On the Internet Movie Database its 'User Rating' is 8.5/10 (from 44 418 votes), to give it a rating of 39th most popular film *ever*. It is hardly surprising that *Matrix 2* (2002) and *Matrix 3* (2003), directed by the brothers and with (largely) the same cast, are to follow.

Some Things to Watch for and Consider

- What would you recommend for further viewing on this film?
- Which would you suggest for further reading: Baudrillard and Bordieu, or DC comics? Both? Neither? What else?

50 EYES WIDE SHUT

Kubrick, USA, 1999

Awards

French Syndicate of Cinema Critics: Winner – Best Foreign Film
Venice Film Festival: Filmcritica Award for Stanley Kubrick

Production Details

Production company/studio	Warner Brothers
Producers	Stanley Kubrick, Brian W. Cook and Jan Harlan
Director	Stanley Kubrick
Cinematographer	Larry Smith
Editor	Nigel Galt
Screenwriters:	Frederic Raphael and Stanley Kubrick (from Arthur Schnitzler's novel *Traumnovelle*)

Cast Includes

Tom Cruise	*Dr Bill Harford*
Nicole Kidman	*Alice Harford*
Sidney Pollack	*Dr Victor Ziegler*
Sky Dumont	*Sandor Svavost*
Todd Field	*Nick Nightingale*
Marie Richardson	*Marion*
Vanessa Shaw	*Domino*
Rade Serbedgia	*Milich*

FOCUS: Auteurship; Stardom; *mise en scène*

A most apt celebration for cinema's *fin de siècle* was the long-awaited release of the final work by Stanley Kubrick. *Eyes Wide*

Shut was Kubrick's enigmatic adaptation of Schnitzler's *Traumnovelle*, which he had dreamed of making for over 30 years. Most of Kubrick's films could be cited as key texts, under an array of headings, including genre, *mise en scène* and innovation. *Eyes Wide Shut* is best fêted here as an embodiment of one of cinema's greatest auteur's most coveted qualities: his uniqueness. Legendary for his perfectionism (obvious from every image in his films), he regretted not finding more subjects to tackle, and the gap between each film widened from *2001: A Space Odyssey* (1968) onwards. Some projects eluded him to the end, in particular his desire to film an epic on the life of Napoleon Bonaparte, but he exerted an unequalled control over his creations, from conception to casting, publicity and distribution. Kubrick enjoyed unprecedented creative freedom, afforded him by Warner Brothers, who funded his last five films, seeming genuinely proud of their relationship and helping Stanley to realise his vision. For his part, Kubrick made them money, genuinely hoping to reach the widest audience.

Kubrick's choice of Tom Cruise and Nicole Kidman as the stable, beautiful couple whose marriage is pushed to the precipice by a single exchange of dangerous honesty was his casting masterstroke. Going for two of Hollywood's most bankable names was a classic Kubrick move, combining precious commercial appeal with the mischievous challenge of subverting audience expectations of known stars, just as he had done by casting Ryan O'Neal as *Barry Lyndon* (1975). This time Cruise and Kidman's real-life marriage added an extra element of pure fascination to Kubrick's tale of sexual jealousy, which concerns itself with the frighteningly precarious nature of the most intimate male–female relationship, and the heartbreaking conflict between truth, honesty and deepest love. Tom and Nicole served Kubrick's interest in the confusion between reality and dream perfectly. And the First Couple served up some more quintessential Kubrick for the father figure they admitted to being in awe of: acting performances that seem to go far beyond scripting, strangely mannered yet volatile; truly surprising as they become fully complicit in the destruction of their image, past and imagined. The shattered Cruise persona has a hand in the dramatic impact of Bill Harford's shaken discomfort, which constantly jolts him into silent fear. Alice's exploding burst of hilarity, pursued by bitterness and apprehension during 'that fucking laughing fit', holds complexity of feeling that is quite beyond words and simply has to be seen. The emotionally heightened nature of these performances, breaching limits of naturalism, fit a long-standing Kubrick trademark. His cinema is filled with such arias, duets and ensembles that are the direct result of his quest to capture that 'something' from beyond the plain imperatives of plot and human logic.

Kubrick's mythical 'recluse' image was inevitably stoked by journalists who could not get interviews. Certainly he did not care to explain his work or question others' interpretations, but did equate cinema with another often non-verbal art form – music.

His orchestration of framed action, camera movement and music intensified with every film as a formal ideal. Enthused by the creative possibilities of new technology, he stretched the Steadicam's capabilities in *The Shining* (1980), creating a profoundly disturbing dichotomy between its free-glide and those locked reverse zooms and fearful symmetry that he chose frequently as a cradle for his characters' precarious struggle for existence. *Eyes Wide Shut* shows his unique aural-kinetic poetry taken to its greatest heights. The ceremonial preparations for the secret masked orgy that Bill discovers and attends (while smarting from Alice's confession of her adulterous sexual fantasy) is like a breathtaking distillation of so many of Kubrick's qualities and fascinations: stark narrative tension leading us towards Harford's gratification or discovery; mesmerising cinematographic motion; gracefully intricate *mise en scène* unfolding within a simple revolving structure – a knife-edge fight for our senses between natural loveliness and dark grotesquerie; the impossible beauty of the female form locked in an organised circle; music speaking the cold malevolence of control, but still subject to passages of organic struggle for escape towards an emotional outpouring of lament and humanised yearning; everyone wearing masks – a motif recurring across *The Killing* (1956), *A Clockwork Orange* (1971) and others. Kubrick recognised its pliable dramatic power, and its ability to snare those who cannot sense meaning beyond simplistic metaphorical definition.

Predictably, critics were confounded by finding no terms of reference with which to compare *Eyes Wide Shut* (including Kubrick's earlier work). The critical response was hamstrung by bemoaning the film's failure to live up to (the critics' own) expectations. His films could *always* be relied upon to do that. Genre, as with *The Shining* (1980) and *Full Metal Jacket* (1987), could be his narrative seed, but was never a dramaturgical formula: horror film with little darkness and claustrophobia, but where vast space and light offered no respite from supernatural terrors; Vietnam War movie uninterested in epic sweep, plunged instead inside a microcosm of militaristic social control then thrown out with a handful of infantrymen to observe their ensuing baptism by fire of first kill and loss. Escaping genre, *Eyes Wide Shut* continued Kubrick's shift away from cinema fettered by realism. Providing a staggering wealth of 'authentic' detail in its art decor, the overall effect is unreal, dreamlike; feeling stripped down and primal in both image composition and plot construction – cinema as an out-of-body experience. Its pristine travelling images create a hallucinatory journey, but moments like Kubrick's bold visual cuts on silence and reversing screen direction make it a frequently disturbing one. Classically, Kubrick's rule breaking shapes the film's most quietly disconcerting exchanges between characters in conflict. A paradoxical quality in his visual approach always matched his resistance to neat endings. Dreams and reality, and surviving an experience of their dangerous blurring, are one of the film's most overt themes, but it is impossible to judge that this is somehow more central than the meditations on sexual desire, love, fidelity, abuse, truth and imagination.

It is easy to sense that Kubrick's films might be an uneasy or unsatisfying experience for some viewers – *Eyes Wide Shut* most of all. Several things may get in the way, including, inevitably, expectations of star vehicle conventions, Hollywood dramatic closure, or preference for clearer delineation of the tragic and comic. In this respect, earlier films such as *Paths of Glory* (1959) and *Dr Strangelove* (1963) are more conventional, 'easier' narratives: human tragedy and clear black comedy. *Eyes Wide Shut* is virtually devoid of comedy at plot level, but is cinematically mischievous, sprinkled with references to Kubrick's previous films, and it ends on a note (word) that can be taken as iconoclastic or touchingly optimistic. There is none of the shock that could make one shy away from moments in *The Shining*, yet it is marked by an understated sense of profound horror at several points. The scene where Ziegler tells Harford 'the truth' about the orgy and the prostitute reported dead is one – a masterpiece of cinematically shaped psychological drama that explains everything – or nothing . . .

Most crucially, *Eyes Wide Shut* is a film that invites projection of the viewer's emotions into its unique and hyper-real dream/nightmare – an extraordinarily unusual quality in a big-budget, studio film. Possibly the richest exposition of Kubrick's concern with love, evil and human fragility, *Eyes Wide Shut* is certainly the ideal embodiment of another of his most personal qualities – an acceptance of mystery.

Some Things to Watch out for and Consider

- What are the most memorable images/scenes in the film after first viewing? Can you find other scenes that seem just as important in terms of conveying the themes that are part of the story?
- Look at the use of colour in each scene. What do you notice? Are there any patterns here?
- What do you feel is the significance of Bill's visit to Marion, the bereaved woman?
- Can you think of 'gaps' in the plot that other directors would have filled?
- What does this suggest about Kubrick as a film-maker? Or cinema generally?
- What do the individual star personas of Cruise and Kidman (and their combination) bring to *Eyes Wide Shut*? (Have the events in Tom and Nicole's personal life *since* the film affected your reading of the film?)
- Is Alice as important a character as Bill? Why/why not?
- What did you think of Alice's last few lines (and final word), which end *Eyes Wide Shut*?

Further Viewing

Killer's Kiss (Kubrick, USA, 1955)
The Killing (Kubrick, USA, 1956)
Paths of Glory (Kubrick, USA, 1957)
Spartacus (Kubrick, USA, 1960)
Lolita (Kubrick, USA, 1962)
Dr Strangelove (Kubrick, USA, 1964)
2001: A Space Odyssey (Kubrick, USA, 1968)
A Clockwork Orange (Kubrick, USA, 1971)
Barry Lyndon (Kubrick, USA, 1975)
The Shining (Kubrick, USA, 1980)
Full Metal Jacket (Kubrick, USA, 1987)
Far and Away (Howard, USA, 1992)

INDEX